Going Moder[illegible] [illegible]itish

Art, Architecture and [illegible] in Devon c. 1910-1960

Edited by Sam Smiles

intellect™

EXETER, ENGLAND

First Published in 1998 by
Intellect Books
School of Art and Design, Earl Richards Road North, Exeter EX2 6AS

Cover Design: Sam Robinson
Layout Design: Emma Parkin
Production: Robin Beecroft
Julie Strudwick
Sarah Vick

A catalogue record for this book is available from the British Library

ISBN 1-871516-95-1

Front cover illustration: Matthew Dawson Burgh Island Hotel (1929-34)
Photographer: Tim Grevatt

Presented as the catalogue of 1998 exhibitions at the Royal Albert Memorial Museum, Exeter and Plymouth City Museum and Art Gallery.

Printed and bound in Great Britain by Cromwell Press, Wiltshire

Contents

Acknowledgements

Refuge or Regeneration:
Devon's Twentieth Century Identity 1
Sam Smiles

Architecture in Devon 1910 - 1958 15
Jeremy Gould

Dartington - A Modern Adventure 43
David Jeremiah

The Ceramic Heritage of Devon 79
Doug Fitch

Illustrations 93

Selected Biographies 147

Index 153

ACKNOWLEDGEMENTS

The authors would like to thank the owners of many of the buildings and works of art mentioned in this book for allowing access and sharing their time and knowledge. In particular, thanks are due to the following who helped with information and references and answered many questions:

Robert Alcock of Exeter University; Maureen Atrill of Plymouth City Museum & Art Gallery; Geoff Bates of Holford Associates Architects; Peter Child of Devon County Council; Robin Clutterbuck of Buckfast Abbey; Mr. & Mrs. John Cole; A. Colombini of Charles E. Ware Architects; Esmé Cooper; Marianne De Trey; Devon County Record Office at Exeter and Plymouth; Vernon Duker; Professor Alec Eden; Exeter City Council; Peter Harrild; Gareth Hughes on Plymouth and many other references for Devon and elsewhere; Ceri Johnson of The National Trust; Lewis & Hickey Architects; Sam Lloyd on W. Curtis Green; Ray Lomas of Torbay Hospital; Kendall McDonald; Hugh Meller of The National Trust; Chris Pancheri of Torbay Borough Council; Fred Payne on Torbay Hospital; Mr. & Mrs. Paul Petrides; Plymouth City Council Planning Department; Mr. & Mrs. Richard Pool; Tony Porter of Burgh Island; Leslie Retallick of Torre Abbey Art Gallery; The Royal Albert Memorial Museum; Royal Institute of British Architects Drawings Collection; John Schofield; Leonard Stocks; Graham Thorne on Plymouth; Torquay Museum; Paul Vincent; Diana Ward on Fred Harrild; Peter Wickham on Gerald Saunders; Hilary Williams of High Cross House (Dartington); Michael Willis of Lucas Roberts & Brown Architects; John R.A. Wilson on Torquay and Fred Harrild.

As this book was first published in conjunction with the 'Going Modern and Being British' exhibition at the Royal Albert Memorial Museum, Exeter in 1998, we would like to record our grateful thanks to Kevin Jones and Fay Squire who organised the exhibition.

We also wish to acknowledge the fine work of David Garner, David Griffiths, Jonathan Thompson and Sarah Vick, for help with the illustrations, and to Emma Parkin for the book design.

EXETER CITY COUNCIL

INVESTOR IN PEOPLE

Refuge or Regeneration: Devon's Twentieth Century Identity

Sam Smiles

This exhibition is intended to examine some aspects of art, architecture and design in Devon in the first half of the twentieth century. In doing so its primary purpose is to fill in a historical gap, to present a chronicle of what was achieved here, by visitors and residents alike, and to allow an assessment of that achievement to be made for the first time. But at another level the exhibition cannot avoid raising very particular difficulties concerning modernism and modernity in twentieth-century Britain. To put it at its simplest, modernity and the rural seem to be antithetical concepts, for modernity as lived experience is characteristically associated with metropolitan culture rather than life in the country. For much the same reasons modernism, which is to say creative practice which self-consciously articulates a modern sensibility, has come to be associated especially with artistic developments originating in large urban centres.[1]

In what ways, then, can Devon be aligned with modernism and modernity? How can it make any sense to talk of the modern in such a rural environment and in such a socially conservative context? What have modernity and modernism to do with unspoiled country, traditional rural life and seaside leisure 200 miles or more from London? Yet if it seems bizarre or paradoxical even to begin such an enquiry it is worth making the effort, for in doing so another Devon begins to emerge from behind the timeless idyll of the tourist industry, a Devon whose response to twentieth century developments is surprisingly varied and complex.

For the purposes of this exhibition such an enquiry is framed with reference to an article published in 1932 by the artist and designer Paul Nash,

> Whether it is possible to 'go modern' and still 'be British' is a question vexing quite a few people today...The battle lines have been drawn up: internationalism versus an indigenous culture; renovation versus conservatism; the industrial versus the pastoral; the functional versus the futile.[2]

In his essay Nash drew attention to a widely-perceived debate between two sorts of British identity, the historic heritage and the progressive present, and questioned whether it was possible to find any accommodation between the two.[3] The importance of Nash's example, as with many of his contemporary artists and critics, is that he sets up a binary opposition in which the rural becomes the pole of conservatism, stasis and indigenous culture while the urban, namely London, aligns itself to modernity, internationalism and change.[4] To represent Britain c.1910-1950 in these terms has the merit of offering a clear distinction between two sorts of cultural life and it was a distinction that many who lived through that era might have agreed with, but the polarities are, of course, too neat to withstand historical scrutiny. Modernism, the characteristic vanguard art of this era, was not a monolithic practice which only addressed international and progressive issues within an urban setting. Similarly, modernity, which is to say the advent of technological, economic and social change, was not restricted to the cities even if its impact was greatest there. For the bulk of the population modernity was not simply to be found in the art galleries, architecture and street life of a great metropolis but was experienced instead as a slow alteration in day to day living: cheap railway travel, the coming of motor traffic, the building of airports; widespread mains gas and electrification; mass entertainment, especially radio and cinema; easier communications, telegraphy and the telephone; the construction of houses, hotels, hospitals, schools and offices in modern materials and to modern plans; the availability of consumer items in modern designs; new domestic technologies for cooking, heating, lighting and cleaning; changes in educational practice, in industrial and agricultural organisation; increasing mechanisation of the work-place. Was this diffusion of modernity far-reaching enough to allow modernism, albeit in an attenuated form, to flourish in places which were so removed from metropolitan experience? And, if so, might this attenuated modernism be seen as focusing precisely on Nash's conundrum, going modern without ceasing to respect the British context? Notwithstanding our response to these enquiries, the fundamental question remains whether modernism makes sense if it is not full-blooded, cosmopolitan and urban-centred; whether any accommodation between modernity and tradition risks compromising modernism to the point where its distinction from other cultural orientations simply collapses.

Devon provides an excellent case-study for such issues, to see what 'going modern' may have meant in a county which was regularly portrayed as quintessentially and traditionally English,[5] to ascertain whether it was possible to go modern in the heart of the country. This is not to make a particular claim for Devon, to suggest that it has somehow been denied its proper status within any account of British art, architecture or design. In terms of this region's contribution to British modernism Cornwall's significance is more legitimate and better known, and rightly so, with the art colonies at Newlyn and St Ives. For Devon the case is different. With a very few exceptions, artists of historical importance associated with the county did not spend any length of time resident here. Nor is it possible to isolate and identify a regional architecture or design aesthetic which might positively distinguish modernism in Devon from elsewhere.

What the exhibition intends to demonstrate is more modest and more elusive, namely what 'modern' meant away from a metropolitan centre. Although the county cannot be presented as instrumental in the development of modernism it was nevertheless bound up in the steady transformation of art, architecture and design in our century. From the 1910s to the 1950s a variety of nationally significant artists worked here, some of them for protracted periods.[6] More surprising, perhaps, is the extent to which modern architecture made its presence felt between the wars.[7] Similarly, the rebuilding of Plymouth and Exeter provides two well-documented instances of rational town planning as it was understood and promulgated in the 1940s and 50s.[8] Finally, the Dartington experiment provides a unique example of progressive thinking in the widest modern context, an attempt to unify the arts and industry with education and rural regeneration.

Devon's reception of modernism is most easily demonstrated by the advent of artists to the county, using its landscape as a source of subject matter for painting (Figs. 1-8). The best example of this activity centres around the farm of Applehayes at Clayhidon in the Blackdown Hills. Applehayes was owned by Harold Bertram Harrison, who had studied at the Slade from 1896-8 as a mature student after working in Argentina. Although considerably older than his fellow students he became friends with Spencer Gore and Henry Tonks and after he bought Applehayes in 1909 Harrison invited Slade students and other artists to paint in Devon. Stanley Spencer, Mark Gertler and William Roberts all visited his property as students in 1911 but Applehayes is particularly associated with three members of the Camden Town group: Robert Bevan, Charles Ginner and Frederick Spencer Gore.[9] Applehayes was no ordinary farm but a well-provided and extensive rural estate which Harrison had equipped with specially-built studios for artists. The work produced there records the Devon landscape in ways which owe a considerable debt to French Impressionist and post-Impressionist art. Gore's earliest work at Applehayes is deliberately subservient to actual appearances, painted out of doors and strongly influenced by Camille Pissarro; on later visits his style is more considered, using preliminary drawings and sketches to construct a landscape in flat decorative blocks of colour akin to Gauguin's procedure. Bevan had met Renoir and Gauguin and his use of a heavy bounding outline indicates his familiarity with Gauguin's cloisonné style as well as the work of Van Gogh. Ginner was attempting to combine Cézanne's constructional use of colour with Van Gogh's heavy impasto, using a thickly painted, densely coloured surface to build up a landscape. Two other members of the Camden Town group also worked in Devon. Lucien Pissarro worked around Dartmouth in March 1913, convalescing after suffering from lung congestion, and returned to the area early in 1921 and again from March to September 1922.[10] Walter Sickert was in Chagford in the summer of 1915, also convalescing, and there produced a number of studies of the locality. Rushford Mill, on the river Teign, is close to the town and represents the one Chagford composition Sickert brought to completion as an exhibited picture, using a thickly-painted patchwork of high-toned pigment to articulate the composition as a flat mosaic of colour.

As a group these paintings offer a particularly interesting insight into Devon's relationship to modernity. Attractive though they undoubtedly are, they do not make an important contribution to any overall assessment of these five painters' technical achievements and historical status. It is not at Applehayes, Dartmouth or Chagford that their best and most significant work was produced and perhaps this has something to do with the inescapably traditional nature of the subject-matter they chose to explore in Devon. One could almost represent their work here as the last gasp of a nineteenth century landscape sensibility, making sketching tours and painting the rural landscape of Devon in much the same way as their eighteenth and nineteenth century predecessors had done.[11] That the formal means of representing that landscape had altered to accommodate developments in French painting of the 1870s and 1880s does not disguise the fact that the image of Devon was still fundamentally a picturesque landscape, a place of sunlight, recreation and tranquillity seemingly immured from the realities of industrialisation, urban life and social developments (Figs. 103-4).

Most of the artists who followed the Camden Town group made equally incidental use of Devon, spending a few weeks in the county either recuperating from illness or on short painting expeditions or commissions (Figs. 4, 10).[12] For all these painters' commitment to a contemporary style, in Devon it was predominantly landscape that they exploited and their subject matter struggles to escape the picturesque clichés of maritime life and the natural scene. It appears that such fleeting encounters with Devon could provide little inspiration beyond an image that seems removed from twentieth-century experience and unmarked by characteristically modern features.

This general impression of Devon was fostered by its representation in literature, dominated by nature and wild country and peopled by a colourful English peasantry. Arthur Conan Doyle's *Hound of the Baskervilles* (1902) may have exaggerated Dartmoor's wilderness but it created an association that remained embedded in popular perceptions. Similarly, Eden Phillpotts' *Dartmoor Cycle* of eighteen novels, written between the 1890s and the 1920s, maintained Dartmoor's romance in ways analagous to Thomas Hardy's evocations of the Dorset landscape. Phillpotts' interest in vernacular life and the Devon dialect was often vitiated by sentiment and his novels today are little known, but in the 1910s and 1920s his impact was considerable. When his play *The Farmer's Wife* opened in London in 1924 it was a popular success and ran for three years in the West End, further promulgating his vision of rural Devon to a metropolitan audience. A more provocative rendering of Devon life was provided with the publication of Stephen Reynolds' *A Poor Man's House*, describing his life with a fisherman's family in Sidmouth. Reynolds' book was a popular and literary success and a highly necessary corrective to those ubiquitous Edwardian stereotypes of simple-minded and ignorant Devon folk. As Reynolds himself put it,

> I am often asked why I have forsaken the society of educated people, and have made my home among 'rough uneducated' people, in a poor man's house. The briefest answer is, that it is good to live among those who, on the whole, are one's superiors...It is true that one becomes much coarser. One acquires a habit of talking with scandalous freedom about vital matters which among the unscientific educated are kept hid in the dark - and go fusty there...For all my elaborate education and painfully gained stock of knowledge, I find myself silenced time after time by the direct wisdom of these so-called ignorant people. They have preserved better, between knowledge and experience, that balance which makes for wisdom...To live with the poor is to feel oneself in contact with a greater continuity of tradition and to share in a greater stability of life.[13]

Yet for all Reynolds' integrity his decision to live among fishermen could not help but confirm Devon as a repository of traditional values. A fishing community in Sidmouth does indeed offer a vision of wisdom and experience, continuity and stability quite distinct from the intellectual ferment of the metropolis or the unionised work-forces and new technologies of progressive industry. In both Phillpotts and Reynolds' writings Devon's working communities, rural and maritime alike, are depicted as though their lives are bounded by the turning of the seasons and the traditions of their almost telluric way of life. Specifically modern working-class experience, whether it was the heavy engineering of the Plymouth ship-yards or the struggles for recognition undertaken by the Exeter Trades Council, was something that seems to have been beyond literary recognition.[14]

It was perhaps Henry Williamson, above all, who codified the idea of Devon as a place in tune with natural cycles and the rhythm of the seasons, isolated from the more urgent rhythm of urban and industrial Britain. He moved to north Devon in

1921 and remained there for the next fourteen years, finally finding literary and financial success with the publication of *Tarka the Otter* in 1927, which won him the Hawthornden Prize. *Salar the Salmon* (1935) cemented his reputation as a nature writer and likewise confirmed Devon's reputation as an unspoiled natural environment. Like Reynolds and Phillpotts, Williamson attempted to capture the folk-wisdom of Devon in dialect and to saturate himself in the traditions, thoughts and feelings of the community among which he lived. Whether his nature-writing hindered his more serious ambitions as a novelist is debatable, but in the context of this exhibition it is as a nature-writer that his rendition of Devon is significant, for Devon allowed him to engage with values which seemed to be threatened elsewhere. Williamson's credo can perhaps be summed up in his description of playing with his children,

> ...I had got back, for a while, to the land of enchantment, of unself-consciousness, to the world of otters, deer, salmon, water, moonshine...the only world in which perhaps there was consistency, form, integrity.[15]

Williamson's almost mystical identification with a pre-industrial and at times atavistic England is thus a return to innocence, to the integrity of a natural life. But this return makes sense only because these values can no longer be taken for granted, and his writings are complicated by his use of Devon as an antidote to the industrialised horror of modern warfare he had witnessed in the trenches. Equally and fatally, his deliberate removal from the modern world, his attempts to secure 'integrity' in nature and the organic rural community led him into political naiveté. The 1930s saw his political sympathies swerve towards adulation of Adolf Hitler and the extreme nationalism of Sir Oswald Mosley's British Union of Fascists.

Looking back on his early days in Devon, Williamson published *The Children of Shallowford* in 1939 and in 1945 *Tales of a Devon Village* and *Life in a Devon Village*, commemorating the passing away of that organic community which he had enjoyed in the 1920s as a refuge after the first world war. It is noteworthy in this connection that the two best-known literary monuments to social nostalgia written in this period were also produced in Devon. Flora Thompson moved to Dartmouth in 1928, where her husband had been made the town's postmaster, and stayed there and at Brixham until her death. *Lark Rise* (1939), *Over to Candleford* (1941) and *Candleford Green* (1943) chronicle the lost world of rural life on the Oxfordshire/Northamptonshire border as she remembered it from her own youth in the 1880s and 1890s. When the trilogy was reissued in 1945 as *Lark Rise to Candleford* H.J. Massingham's introduction was emphatic about the book's value as 'an index to social change, of great complexity and heavy with revolutionary meaning.' Thompson had written 'a tragic epic...at just the right time - namely, when the triumphs of industrial progress are beginning to be seen for what they are.'[16] At exactly the same time, Evelyn Waugh was chronicling the end of another social world, Catholic and aristocratic England, in *Brideshead Revisited*, written at the Easton Court Hotel near Chagford in 1944 and published in the following year.[17]

If Devon is the matrix of nostalgia it is not fortuitous. As the twentieth century has shown, the countryside can be used as a foil to a harsh, cold, modern world of social anomie, ugliness and continual renewal. Arthur Wragg's engraving in his book *Jesus Wept* (Fig.9) exemplifies that contrast.[18] Bright sunshine falls on a GWR poster advertising Glorious Devon, an invitation to the young woman and child looking up at it to escape their present reality. The city-scape is thronged with people and traffic; a bank, a pawn-broker's and a second-hand furniture shop dominate the street and hunched shadowy figures underneath the bridge become ciphers of deprivation. The picture's inscription 'There is a green hill - far away' seems to insist on the absolute division between the here and now of urban living and the real or illusory promise of something better in the country.[19]

Devon, it seems, was the pre-eminent county for that sort of contrast and John Betjeman's introduction to the *Devon: Shell Guide* (1936) encapsulated this feeling in one plaintive sentence,

> Despite the main roads, the electric-light poles, the tin signs and the tourists, there are still parts of inland Devon which remind me that England was once a beautiful country.[20]

As mass tourism developed in the early years of the century it was this idea of Devon as an untouched reminder of what England had once been which was promoted. Even the most cursory glance through the tourist guides of the 1920s and 1930s confirms the strengthening of this stereotype; the terms in which the attractions of the county are represented do not differ in any significant respect from William Howitt and Francis Heath's enthusiastic descriptions of Devon in the nineteenth century, but what they describe has now become an increasingly endangered vision.[21]

The country idyll was of course always a myth and Devon was exposed to twentieth century culture no matter what the tourist industry and the cult of nostalgia might suggest. Devon was not simply hedgerows and country lanes, pastoral agriculture and small fishing communities. The Royal Navy's dockyards at Devonport had long given Plymouth an industrial base in ship-building, engineering and allied occupations and the city was densely populated with over 220,000 inhabitants in 1939. The road junction at Plymouth's St. Andrew's Cross had the highest traffic density outside

London in the south of England.[22] But, as Betjeman noted, the biggest observable cultural alteration to the county as a whole was tourism itself whose workings threatened to disturb Devon's tranquillity and to mar its beauty.

At the turn of the century Devon had been a relatively select tourist destination, with mass tourism still in its infancy. In the Edwardian era much was to change. Torquay may have managed to preserve its essentially Victorian image of gentility but other resorts were changing fast, with caravan sites, holiday camps and amusements springing up to accommodate the diversified tourism of the inter-war years. The most sophisticated and wealthy visitors made use of new hotels in modern or art deco 'moderne' styles, like that on Burgh Island (Cover illustration) which Agatha Christie used as the setting for *And then there were None* and *Evil under the Sun.*[23] But other classes of tourist could now afford to travel to Devon too. Torbay's identity as the English Riviera, with the social cachet that implied, was threatened by these new vacationers who arrived in increasing numbers. Distinguishing Torquay's appeal from the more cosmopolitan and populist attractions of Brighton and Blackpool a local newspaper declared,

> Torquay's peculiar charm for the holiday-maker is that it provides as few other seaside towns do, a restful place for the jaded toiler in busy manufacturing towns, a place where he can bask in the sun by the seaside or recline in the shady nooks around the coastline, enjoy a morning dip, go bathing or fishing and vary his programme by excursions inland by charabanc or motor. What he does not want, and what he will protest against, are itinerant minstrels, donkey boys, swings and roundabouts, so-called carnivals or fetes, or gymkanas, or whatever fancy names the promotors choose to give them .[24]

Notwithstanding the feelings of Torquay residents, more popular entertainments and new tourist accommodation were important elements within the local economy. Modernity in the form of mass leisure activity would make its presence felt, especially along the south Devon coast (Fig. 105).

Improved holiday entitlement and increasingly good road and rail access opened Devon up to mass tourism from London, the Midlands and even quite distant northern cities. The GWR ran two trains every weekday from Paddington, 'The Limited' to Plymouth and 'The Torbay Limited' to Torquay. The Southern Railway embarked passengers at Waterloo for Exeter. The LMS dovetailed its network with the GWR at Bristol and ran a special train, 'The Devonian', every weekday from Leeds and Bradford to Torquay and Paignton. Then, as now, all major roads and railway lines to the west country converged on Exeter, the hub of tourism in Devon.[25] The impact of tourism on the county's infrastructure was considerable. Construction of the Exeter bypass in 1938, for example, was prompted by concerns over heavy traffic congestion, with Bank Holiday traffic taking three hours to travel the two miles through the city.[26]

Devon, then, was caught up in modernity in quite complex ways. Its economy and infrastructure were altering to accommodate new forms of leisure at the same time as its public image presented the county as a respite from modernity, an unchanged rural idyll of organic communities, folk wisdom and natural pleasures. To a very large extent that is the fate of any tourist destination but in the circumstances of inter-war Britain this paradoxical situation has a particular resonance. As Nash's essay clearly states, the problem of tradition versus change was vexing quite a few people if only because the whole debate seemed to circle around the identity of Britain itself, what kind of country it was or might become. Faced with unchecked alteration and development, demolition and renewal, many were vociferous in their protests at the ruin of Britain. One of the chief agitators for legislation to control the despoliation of the countryside was Clough Williams-Ellis. His impassioned introduction to *The Face of the Land* (1930) invoked Georgian England, Austen, Trollope and Hardy, Canaletto, Gainsborough, Constable, Turner, Cotman and others besides to witness 'the hectic Saturnalia of ugliness in which we are squandering our inheritance'. Standing on the edge of a Sussex common one November afternoon he encountered the modern landscape,

> I stood on a sixty-foot reinforced concrete motorway along which hooted and thundered an immense and largely unnecessary traffic at an extravagant speed between uncompromising pallisades of steel and concrete. Beyond the dirty drab of the concrete kerbs, heaps of broken asphalt littered the weed-grown waste, from which rose gigantic black telegraph posts on the one hand and electric power pylons of latticed steel upon the other, so forcing horsemen and walkers alike relentlessly on to the unyielding surface of the oil-stained road. A few yards from the Commons's end stood a shed of corrugated iron that a score of eye-splitting signs in crude enamels proclaimed to be a garage.[27]

Four years earlier, as part of the same demand for an end to untrammelled development, Patrick Abercrombie recommended setting up a National League for the Preservation of Rural England and declared

> ...we are apt to forget that the greatest historical monument that we possess, the most essential thing which *is* England, is the Countryside, the Market town, the Village, the Hedgerow Trees, the Lanes, the Copses, the Streams and the Farmsteads.[28]

The establishment of the Council for the Preservation of Rural England in 1926 translated Abercrombie's ideals into action and Devon and Cornwall were among the first counties to be surveyed under its auspices, the CPRE report on Devon by W. Harding Thompson being published in 1932.[29] In the context of these debates it's easy to see why Devon was seen as particularly worth preserving. Despite the advent of mass tourism, motoring, and other indices of a modern culture, it had yet to suffer the indiscriminate development seen in the home counties and the hinterlands of the great industrial cities of the midlands and the north. As the quintessential representation of England, its preservation said something about national identity too. At bottom was the perception that without progress the economy would stagnate, but that unqualified progress might destroy what being British meant. As the CPRE report noted, with reference to new building materials in Devon, modernisation had to be reconciled with tradition if the country as a whole was not to be ruined.[30]

Along with recommendations about sensitive architecture, the CPRE report was chiefly concerned to limit ribbon development along major roads and commercial despoliation of the countryside. Seen from the inhabitants' point of view, however, Devon urgently needed to modernise and to foster economic growth. Rural Devon was seriously deficient in many of the amenities of modern living. The National Farm Survey of 1941-3 revealed that under 30% of Devon farm holdings had a piped water supply and less than 15% had an electricity supply.[31] Devon may not have suffered from the full impact of the agricultural depression of the 1920s but there was nevertheless a definite migration from the predominantly agricultural communities in the inland areas of the county to the towns and resorts on the coasts where a better standard of living might be enjoyed, working in tourism or the service industries. The south east of Devon, in particular, from Sidmouth to Torquay, saw the introduction of amenities which brought it into line with the rest of urbanised England, while the older and more traditional small villages and farm settlements declined still further. This social isolation was commented upon in a survey of the region produced in 1947,

> The "foreigner" from a northern city who comes in summer to taste, perhaps superficially, of the pleasant, unhurried life of Devon and Cornwall, may condemn its people for being stupid and backward, even while secretly he considers the peaceful, picturesque, isolated village as an ideal spot in which to end his days. But let him retire into that village permanently; let him live there for years, winter and summer, with little means of leaving it, and with no contact with urban life - and in time he will begin to understand from within himself that strange mentality of people in remote rural parts.[32]

It is in this context that the Dartington experiment is so important. Ending years of economic decline and restoring aspects of the rural economy to financial health could only be achieved by the most progressive means. Capital injection alone was not enough; the whole basis of what constitutes a viable social community needed to be rethought. At Dartington, a blue-print for a new society was being elaborated through experimentation in education, agriculture, the creative arts, architecture and light industry. As Christopher Hussey described Dorothy and Leonard Elmhirst's programme,

> Underlying the whole conception is the assumption that modern conditions have revolutionised life, and the aim that, while desirable features of the old order should be incorporated in the new - such as the arts and rural crafts, old buildings, and country scenery - the general intellectual outlook should be untrammelled by tradition.[33]

In Nash's terms Dartington was hesitant about 'going modern,' maintaining ties with the arts and crafts movement of the turn of the century and never quite fulfilling its potential as an artistic community, a British Bauhaus uniting all the arts and crafts with architecture and progressive education in a truly radical enterprise. Equally, 'being British' can only partly describe such a cosmopolitan institution, founded with an American fortune, inspired by an Indian poet and social reformer, Rabindranath Tagore, and whose architecture, arts and educational programmes were dominated by American and European talent. In effect, the Dartington experiment can be seen as answering Nash's question by widening understandings of what 'modern' and 'British' might mean. The regeneration of the cultural life of the local community would fuse aspects of past and present, British and international, economic and spiritual to produce a complex new order. Mark Tobey, Cecil Collins and Bernard Leach worked in the same environment as the choreographers Rudolf Laban and Kurt Jooss, the theatre director Michael Chekhov and many other visitors and residents whose presence at Dartington virtually comprises the creative and intellectual who's who of the period.[34] For all its uniqueness, Dartington's investment in modern architecture and design, together with its patronage of the contemporary fine and performing arts, represents a significant outstation of the modern in Devon and was recognised as such at the time.[35]

While it isn't easy to draw conclusions from Devon's place in twentieth century British culture, what does seem to emerge is a better understanding of how the county was caught between its representations and its reality. In that respect it is worth invoking Raymond Williams' insights into the country and the city,

> ...the common image of the country is now an image of the past,

> and the common image of the city an image of the future. That leaves, if we isolate them, an undefined present. The pull of the idea of the country is towards old ways, human ways, natural ways. The pull of the idea of the city is towards progress, modernization, development. In what is then a tension, a present experienced as tension, we use the contrast of country and city to ratify an unresolved division and conflict of impulses, which it might be better to face in its own terms.[36]

For Williams this tension reflects the predicament of modern societies aspiring to recover a sense of mutuality, sharing and connection which their present circumstances deny them. With Devon, the tourist industry and the writings of Reynolds, Williamson and Phillpotts promoted the idea of an alternative 'organic' way of life to the 'mechanical,' abstracted, commercialised and consumer-led ideals of modern England. Similarly, the Dartington experiment and the attempts at humane city planning for the rebuilding of Exeter and Plymouth can all be seen as attempts to reconcile the imperatives of progress and modernity with sensitivities to social needs and local usage. Whether such developments really did face that conflict of impulses in its own terms, as Williams recommends, or whether they were hesitant or conservative responses to the advent of modernity is a moot point. Seen from a revisionist point of view, however, the most resolutely modernist architecture built in Devon should not necessarily be promoted over more hesitant stylistic experiments. For if architecture, too, is judged by its response to place and to tradition the best modern architecture in Devon may ultimately be that which combines technical sophistication with local appropriateness.[37]

Perhaps the chief value of examining Devon and modernism is the light it throws on Nash's dilemma, for it exaggerates the antithesis of 'modern' and 'British' by revealing what the stakes were and maybe still are. Terms like British, English or tradition are typically invoked as naming words, as though we could point to specific features which they represent. In reality they operate rhetorically working at an abstract level of connotation to suggest a state of being which might oppose the instability, change and state of becoming that has always been the hallmark of modernity. Modernity promises an advance into the future, a place which doesn't yet exist and therefore can't be known; England and its cognate terms stand for history and for location, a place known and often revered. To work in the gap between these two extremes has been this century's particular challenge.

1 This is not to deny, of course, that modern art can address landscape nor that artistic colonies existed in rural and coastal villages, both of which phenomena are important ingredients of European modernism. But in both of these cases the debates that animated the production of that art, the art market that supported it and the audience for it were all metropolitan.

2 Paul Nash 'Going Modern and Being British', *The Weekend Review*, 12 March, 1932, pp. 322-3. Nash developed this argument in his writings on design: 'We are faced to-day with much the same task as that

which the [Adam] Brothers undertook in the early part of the eighteenth century. We are invaded by very strong foreign influences, we possess certain solid traditions. Once more we find ourselves becoming conscious of a renaissance abroad, and are curious and rather embarrassed by the event; at once anxious to participate and afraid to commit ourselves, wishing to be modern, but uncertain whether that can be consistent with being British'. Paul Nash *Room and Book*, New York 1932, p.7.

3 In his own art Nash provided a partial answer to the question by adopting landscape and prehistoric features which were recognisably British yet treating them within the terms suggested by a modern and 'international' art practice.

4 Seen from a conservative point of view this new urban culture may have lacked authenticity. As Arthur Bryant declared in a 1933 BBC radio talk, '...the most important thing about our English civilization is that it grew in the country and has only comparatively recently moved to the town.' Arthur Bryant *The National Character* (1934), cited in Virginia Button 'The Aesthetics of Decline - English Neo-Romanticism c.1935-1956,' unpublished PhD dissertation, Courtauld Institute of Art, 1991, p.36.

5 'What do they know of England who do not Devon know? It is English to the core in its fine little towns, its quaint seaports, and its hundreds of lovely villages. Nowhere is the face of our Motherland more like herself ... If we would see England faithfully set before us, easily, quickly, comfortably, let us come to Devon and run through its villages, and in and out of its ancient ports, up and down its little hills, and climb to the majestic heights of Dartmoor...everywhere we shall feel ourselves at home among these people whose heroes made us largely what we are.' Arthur Mee *Devon*, London 1949, p.1.

6 Some of the more well-known include Jack Yeats, Walter Sickert, Lucien Pissarro, Spencer Gore, Robert Bevan, Charles Ginner, Winifred Knights, Edward Wadsworth, Edward Burra, Cecil Collins, Mark Tobey, David Jones, John Skeaping, Henry Lamb, Michael Ayrton, David Bomberg, John Piper and Stanley Spencer.

7 If the identifying signature of a modern house of this period is defined as the possession of a flat roof, then Devon saw the construction of more modern houses than any other county in the U.K. except London and Surrey. See Jeremy Gould 'Gazetteer of Modern Houses in the United Kingdom and the Republic of Ireland,' *The Modern House Revisited - Twentieth Century Architecture 2, The Journal of the Twentieth Century Society*, no.2, 1996, pp. 112-126.

8 The Luftwaffe obliterated most of Plymouth's city centre in March and April 1941 and Exeter's in May 1942. Plymouth's strategic importance as the key to the western approaches and one of the centres of naval operations had made it especially vulnerable. Exeter was caught up in the reprisal bombings known as the Baedeker raids, after the German tourist guide of that name used to select targets. German radio announced on 4 May, 1942: 'We have chosen as targets the most beautiful places in England. Exeter was a jewel. We have destroyed it'.

9 No work by Gertler, Spencer or Roberts has been located but surviving letters would place their respective excursions to Devon in July (Gertler), August (Spencer) and September 1911 (Roberts). Gore began working at Applehayes in 1909 and returned in 1910 and 1913. Ginner painted there in 1912, 1913 and 1914. Bevan painted at Applehayes in 1912, 1913 and 1915, returned to Clayhidon from 1916-19, renting a cottage three miles from Applehayes itself, and lived and worked in the area from 1922 until his death in 1925. See Rosalind Billingham *Artists at Applehayes - Camden Town Painters at a West Country Farm, 1909-1924*, Herbert Art Gallery & Museum, Coventry, 1986.

10 On Pissarro's first two visits he stayed at The Mill, Blackpool Vale, to the west of the town but the early season made painting difficult. On his third visit, staying at Channel View, Dartmouth, he enjoyed excellent weather and finished 21 paintings. See W.S. Meadmore *Lucien Pissarro*, London 1962, pp.138, 173, 180-1.

11 See Sam Smiles and Michael Pidgley *The Perfection of England - Artist Visitors to Devon c. 1750-1870*, Royal Albert Memorial Museum, Exeter, 1995.

12 Apart from those working at Dartington, these include Winifred Knights, Edward Wadsworth, Edward Burra, David Jones, John Skeaping, John Nash, Henry Lamb, Stanley Spencer, David Bomberg, Barbara Hepworth, John Piper, Claude Rogers, Tom Monnington, Hans Feibusch and Michael Ayrton.

13 Stephen Reynolds *A Poor Man's House* (1908), London 1928, pp. 315-7.

14 For information on Devon industry in the 1930s and 40s see John Murray *Devon and Cornwall. A Preliminary Survey*, Survey Committee of the University College of the the South West, Exeter, 1947, pp.173-247; for trades unionism in Exeter see Andrew Kirkby *In the Cause of Liberty - Exeter Trades Council, 1890-1990*, Exeter 1990.

15 Henry Williamson *The Children of Shallowford*, London 1939, p. 156.

16 H.J. Massingham 'Introduction' to Flora Thompson *Lark Rise to Candleford* (1945), republished Harmondsworth 1980, pp. 14-15.
17 The hotel was run by Carolyn Postlethwaite Cobb, an American divorcée, and her lover Norman Webb. It catered specifically to the needs of writers and enjoyed a faintly Bohemian reputation. Waugh stayed there several times in the 1930s to work without distraction.
18 Arthur Wragg *Jesus Wept. A commentary in black and white on ourselves and the world today*, London n.d. [1935], np.
19 As befits a Christian Socialist, Wragg's title comes from a hymn, the green hill being Golgotha, and so he posits a spiritual rather than an earthly alternative to modern city life, but it is telling that Devon is represented in the place of salvation.
20 John Betjeman *Devon: Shell Guide*, London 1936, p.9.
21 William Howitt *The Rural Life of England*, London 1838; Francis Heath *The Fern Paradise*, London 1875.
22 J. Paton Watson and Patrick Abercrombie *A Plan for Plymouth*, Plymouth 1943, pp. 49-51. This figure is derived from the 1938 Ministry of Transport census.
23 Agatha Christie was born in Torquay and lived in the area for much of her life. There is a special display devoted to her local connections at the Torre Abbey Museum in Torquay.
24 *Torquay Times*, 6 July 1923, quoted in Nigel Morgan 'The Social Tone of Torquay in the 1920s,' in Todd Gray (ed.) *Devon Documents*, Exeter 1996, p. 130.
25 For a good example of the promotion of tourism see *The "Come to Devon" Guide*, Exeter, 1935.
26 Thomas Sharp *Exeter Phoenix - A Plan for Rebuilding*, London 1946, pp. 65-68.
27 Clough Williams-Ellis *The Face of the Land*, The Year Book of the Design and Industries Association, London 1930, p. 13.
28 John Sheail *Rural Conservation in Inter-war Britain*, Oxford 1981, p. 63.
29 Devon was the third CPRE survey to be published, behind Cornwall and the Thames Valley.
30 'It would be unwise to hinder any new developments in architectural form, which naturally changes to meet the needs of modern requirements and in accordance with the new materials that modify methods of construction...Modern design does not necessarily mean a complete break with tradition; indeed it is more akin to the best work of the seventeenth and eighteenth centuries, when builders satisfied the requirements of structure in a straightforward manner, with due regard for scale and proportion'.W. Harding Thompson *Devon. A Survey of its Coast, Moors, and Rivers with some Suggestions for their Preservation*, London 1932, p.168. Significantly, however, the only named and approved modern architecture in this report is Lutyens' work at Beer, Mortehoe and Castle Drogo and Lady Astor's Housing Trust at Mount Gould, Plymouth.
31 John Sheail *Rural Conservation in Inter-War Britain*, Oxford 1981, pp. 25-6.
32 John Murray et al. *Devon and Cornwall. A Preliminary Survey*, Survey Committee of the University College of the South West, Exeter, 1947, p.63.
33 Christopher Hussey 'High Cross Hill, Dartington, Devon', *Country Life*, February 11, 1933, pp. 144-149.
34 Seen negatively, however, the Dartington experiment and the Elmhirsts' patronage would support Virginia Button's argument that the English cultural élite seemed unable to accept the existence and validity of an industrial, urban-based and implicitly proletarian culture and that it resisted the political implications of modernist art practices. See Virginia Button 'The Aesthetics of Decline - English Neo-Romanticism c.1935-1956,' unpublished PhD dissertation, Courtauld Institute of Art, 1991.
35 John Betjeman intended to include a panegyric on Dartington in his *Shell Guide* to Devon; see Betjeman's letter to W.B. Curry, dated 9 January 1936, in Candida Lycett Green (ed.) *John Betjeman Letters Volume One:1926 to 1951*, London 1994, p. 156. This proposal was not in fact carried out but the gazetteer entry on Dartington is still very positive: '...a unique scheme for combining rural life with industrial, which, though sounding Utopian, is made possible. Connected with the estates are a sawmill with a handsome factory on the Plymouth-Totnes road; large farms, one on the English, the other on the Danish system; a co-educational school to which modern authors and intellectuals send their sons; and a firm of builders who actually improve the landscape with their homes (vide the Staverton Estate at Churston)...' See John Betjeman *Devon: Shell Guide*, London 1936, p. 27. Sean O'Casey, Ben Nicholson and Barbara Hepworth were among those who educated their children there, O'Casey actually moving to Totnes in 1938 to be close to Dartington and living in Devon for the rest of his life.
36 Raymond Williams *The Country and the City*, St Albans 1975, pp. 356-7.
37 For an opposed view see Kenneth Frampton 'Towards a Critical Regionalism: Six Points for an Architecture of Resistance' in Hal Foster (ed.) *Postmodern Culture*, London 1985, pp.16-30.

Architecture in Devon 1910 - 1958

Jeremy Gould

INTRODUCTION

Devon is known for its wild moorland, green valleys, rugged coastline and quaint thatched villages. It is not an obvious county in which to study the history of modern architecture. But, because of these powerful rural images, its apparent remoteness and its relative ease of access (particularly from London), over the past two centuries it has consistently attracted visitors and new residents who have brought with them or demanded a new architecture which has been quietly integrated with the old. Thus Devon has examples of buildings by most leading Victorian architects many of which were experimental or produced early in careers, and demand for the new continues well into the twentieth century. This new architecture is difficult to classify; it does not fit easily into the conventional parameters of modernism[1] but has its origins in the vernacular architecture of the county, contemporary British architectural fashion centred on London, Continental modernism and Scandinavian revivalism. This essay analyses these influences and places the new architecture of Devon in its British and European context.

The modern in architecture was primarily a new attitude to the use of space and light coupled with the notion that the analysis of function would result in new forms. With that came the use of new building materials - steel and concrete for structures and glass, lightweight metals and synthetic materials for finishes, although traditional materials were often used when budgets allowed or experience prevailed. Applied ornament became more abstract and stylised and, although there were brief periods of purism, architecture in Britain remained decorated until the 1950s. Architectural education changed too. The traditional education of the architect as articled pupil gradually gave way to full time university courses, led by Liverpool University[2] and the Architectural Association in London. Thus architectural attitudes tended to be polarised between those architects who had trained before, and probably fought in, the Great War and those who graduated after it. Another important change was the speed of communication of new ideas. The printed photograph, mainly in black-and-white, radically changed the appearance of architectural publications[3] which thrived throughout the period. Architectural theories and the latest buildings from the Continent and elsewhere simultaneously became the common currency of architects in London and Devon.

EDWARDIAN ARCHITECTURE

Typical of the new buildings of Devon is the rebuilding of the Abbey at Buckfast (1883-1937, Fig. 11). The monks were from France via Ireland with novices recruited from Swabia, and their architect, Frederick Walters, was an academic specialist in church architecture from London.[1] The Abbey Church took its plan form from the uncovered medieval foundations but the visible architecture was based on Fountains and Kirkstall with a tall, Gothic Benedictine tower. The interior reflected the Cistercian origins of the original building and of the new monks but its sparely decorated, clean-cut stonework is curiously modern too, relying mainly on light and space for architectural effect. The structure was traditional but at the later west end Walters used steel roof trusses, illustrating the change from Victorian historicism to twentieth century pragmatism.

The Victorians never entirely substituted the Gothic for the Classical manner, but the Institute of Chartered Accountants (1888-93) in the City of London by John Belcher and Beresford Pite set a trend for the Baroque Revival which, in its reworking of the English Renaissance (the architecture of Wren, Hawksmoor and Vanbrugh), successfully caught the mood of nationalism at Victoria's Jubilee and the confidence of the Edwardians. The first example in Devon was the Royal Naval College at Dartmouth (1899-05) by Aston Webb, its inspiration coming distantly from Wren's Chelsea Hospital but with a suggestion of Shaw's Bryanston in its striped chimneys and its dominant siting above the valley.

Other examples followed such as the Museum & Art Gallery in Plymouth (1907) by Thornely & Rooke with its grand order of columns and the Town Hall at Torquay (built 1906-07 and 1911-13, Fig. 12) by Thomas Davison. The competitions for the City Halls for Belfast and Colchester[2] firmly established the Baroque as the accepted style for the type. Torquay Town Hall was also a competition (1905) and, like Belfast and Colchester, the winner was a London architect. The composition is almost symmetrical with a central entrance and pediment and clock tower based on Wren's St. Stephen Walbrook. The façades are composed with a repeated Renaissance window, and the corner to Union Street is turned with a domed, rusticated drum (the entrance to the Library)[3], a favourite Edwardian device borrowed from the Beaux Arts. Inside, the grand stair is Italian inlaid marble, the Council chambers oak panelled with *scagliola* columns - the expression of civic pride and propriety. The drum motif appeared again in the original unexecuted design for the Torquay Pavilion (1906)[4], the concert hall and café, a ponderous Baroque exercise in stone by Watson & Watson of Torquay. The scheme was redesigned (1908-11, Fig. 13) by the Borough Surveyor, Major Harvey A. Garrett[5] , who simplified the plan, turned the drums into open, cast iron framed pavilions with light copper roofs and clad the steel framed building in shiny white Doulton faience. To this he added florid plaster ceilings and Queen Anne windows with figurative stained glass. The effect is suitably frivolous, like a Victorian pier or Colonial palace, but it demonstrates how near to Art Nouveau Baroque could become when it lost its pomposity. In a way, it is Devon's first consciously modern building.

Edwin Lutyens would have preferred to design Castle Drogo (1910-30, Fig. 15) as a classical house

> a delicious lovely house with plenty of good large rooms in it[6]

but his client, Julius Drewe, demanded a castle on a vast scale which suited his romantic ambitions as the supposed heir to 'Drogo de Teigne'. The sources and development of Lutyens' design have been well recorded[7]. Clearly Norman Shaw's Flete (1878-83) near Plymouth was familiar and Lutyens had just completed the repair of Lindisfarne Castle which closely resembles the first sketches for Drogo with its battered stone walls and angular geometries. His Red House, Godalming (1899), also on a steep site, had very similar bay windows (except that they are brick and timber) and the plain Tudor mullioned and transomed window remained Lutyens' favourite type, although when translated into granite it became severe and monumental. In their consistency, the elevations at Drogo are abstract and scaleless. For example, the main door seems too small and the spandrel above is apparently detached and unsupported; the south bay window is flanked with angled crenellations which, in perspective, appear as fins separate from the wall surface. Inside too there are surreal juxtapositions of scale and materials. The wall surfaces are unadorned granite or, where decorated, the decoration appears as *appliqué*. In the dining room the mahogany panelling seems to support a frieze of granite and the 'Wrenaissance' plaster ceiling is deliberately over-scaled as are the shallow granite arches of the hall. By contrast, the structure of the main stair is merely suggested in flat courses of stone and there is a calculated confusion of inside and outside space in the relationship of the drawing room window into the stair well and the large east window. Thus

Lutyens is playing architectural games with scale, materials and space and in this he translates Edwardian ambition into ideas which are essentially modern.

THE ARTS AND CRAFTS

All Saints Clergy House in Harwell Street, Plymouth and the lodge at Flete (both 1887) by J.D. Sedding introduced the Arts and Crafts movement to Devon but it was Edward Prior's The Barn at Exmouth (1896-97),[1] the first 'butterfly' plan in England, which confirmed the Arts and Crafts as the style for domestic architecture in the county for the next thirty years. With William Lethaby, who was born in Barnstaple and had been Shaw's assistant at Flete, Prior was one of the founders of the Art Workers Guild which included Sedding, C.F.A. Voysey, Leonard Stokes and William Morris in its early membership. The Barn is made of beach pebbles with sandstone dressings and (originally) thatched with speargrass. Prior's passion for local, natural materials

> the velvet thatch, the warm soft tile, the silver splashed lead, the hoary roughness of stone...how charmingly these lie in the lap of the countryside[2]

and their production by honest craftsmen seemed particularly suited to Devon with its strong tradition of vernacular architecture. Of course, this was an outsider's interpretation and it is significant that Arts and Crafts architecture in Devon was mostly designed by outside, urban architects for a wealthy, middle class clientele who saw the county as a place for holidays or retirement and its population as charming rural peasants. There was always a slightly patronising relationship between the Arts and Crafts and the true vernacular. Ernest Gimson designed Coxon, Budleigh Salterton (1910) in thatch and cob, Penlee at Lydford (1908-11) by Halsey Ricardo (who had visited The Barn) is a version of a Devon longhouse and Voysey himself designed the cottage hospital at Halwill (1899) with characteristic tapering chimneys and big gables.[3] Most influential on later houses was Lutyens' picturesque group of cottages at Milton Abbot (1909) with their tiled swept eaves and carefully composed box windows.

After the Great War, the influence of the Arts and Crafts Movement slowly declined but Lutyens' influence remained paramount, through his published work and through his many former pupils. Especially important in Devon were Fred Harrild and Oswald P. Milne. Harrild was articled to Lutyens from 1908-11 and would have seen the beginning of Drogo and Milton Abbot which probably brought him to Devon. He established his office in Totnes in 1920 and continued there until 1932.[4] His work was almost all domestic, for the middle classes,[5] and divides into two types - the first, a fairly conventional interpretation of the Arts and Crafts based on Voysey and Lutyens and the second, a freer, informal style based on the Devon vernacular. Both exhibit a love of architectural detail inherited from Lutyens - plain boarded doors, iron latches and hinges, inglenook fireplaces and open loggias. Of the first type, Casa di Sole (1925-28, Fig. 16) at East Portlemouth and Little Tor (1932, Fig. 17) at Torquay are typical examples. Both are rendered with tall chimneys and steep, tiled roofs and romantically sited on hillsides, the former with Italianate arched windows and painted jalousies,[6] and Little Tor approached across a bridge through the ruins of a previous building. Livermead, Torquay (1925-26) and two houses at Holne, Tumbly (1926) and Pixie's Hill (1928, Fig. 14), are examples of his vernacular style with informal plans, rough stone walls and thatched roofs which seem to parody the vernacular, based on Arcadian imagery rather than academic study of the real thing. There are other houses in Devon which show similar tendencies.[7] Most important are Cock Rock (1925-26) at Croyde and Higher Trayne (1941) near Ilfracombe by Oliver Hill. Hill was also an admirer of Lutyens, yet he could produce almost convincing designs in any style from Georgian to streamlined modern and in an Arts and Crafts manner, similar to Harrild, in which he was at his most comfortable and inventive.[8] Cock Rock (Fig. 18) was a thin, wandering plan of two storeys with a heavy thatched roof, leaded lights, painted brick and stone walls, elm boarding and massive chimneys. The result is appropriately theatrical,[9] like a contemporary film set. Higher Trayne was the conversion of a small farmhouse and barn. Hill applied vernacular features, thatch roof and crow-stepped gables, referring to Scotland rather than Devon,[10] but the new, V-shaped windows to the music room (barn) are not copies but are designed to integrate inside and outside spaces. Against this elevation he designed a delicate garden with reflecting ponds and luscious planting giving an effect of painterly prettiness.

The integration of house and garden was fundamental to the Arts and Crafts.[11] Mostly, these gardens were in the style first made popular by Gertrude Jekyll and then Vita Sackville-West, consisting of informal borders carefully selected for colour and texture. Harrild's garden at Glen Gorse (1930-34, Fig. 19)[12] in Torquay is of a different order. Its inspiration comes from Lutyens again, from the Mughal Garden of the Viceroy's House, New Delhi designed from 1917-29. The garden is designed as a series of experiences, first revealed through a tiered sequence of free-standing stone circles and then via a terrace to a broad, formal canal with curved ends and formally aligned round and rectangular stepping stones, like a miniaturised version of Delhi. The buildings are both sham castle and Tuscan Renaissance remembered from study tours to Tivoli and complete with cypress trees. From Cyril Farey's visionary perspectives, here was Italy and Imperial India in Devon, about as far removed from the origins of the Arts and Crafts as it was possible to be. It is an extraordinary vision. In contrast, Coleton Fishacre (1924-26) and its garden at Kingswear by Oswald Milne for Rupert d'Oyly Carte is a tamer, English affair. Milne worked for Lutyens from 1902-05, somewhat earlier than Harrild, and had established his practice in London before the War specialising in houses. Like Hill, he was able to work in any style[13] but usually it was a simple version of the Arts and Crafts or a stripped neo-Georgian. Coleton Fishacre is composed along the contour of a hill with a cranked plan and is in stone with small 'cottage' windows, dormers and a big, swept slate roof (Fig. 20). Its interior, however, has clear, unornamented volumes, plain coved cornices and restrained decorative fireplaces and skirtings. The effect is almost modern and became more so when the client replaced the traditional furnishings with furniture designed by Milne and carpets by Marion Dorn.[14] His other style is well represented by Fourways (c.1927) at Budleigh Salterton[15] which is symmetrical with Georgian sash windows, sliding jalousies and eaves line broken with semi-dormers. The towns and especially the resorts of north and south Devon have many such houses[16] since the style could be adapted by architects and speculative builders alike to any size or scale, detached or semi-detached or, even, divided into separate apartments.

Probably through Rupert d'Oyly Carte, it was to Milne that Leonard Elmhirst turned for the first school buildings and houses on the Dartington Estate that he had bought in 1925. Elmhirst and Dartington rightly have a reputation for their progressive ideas and exceptional vision, but in their choice of architects, they were suprisingly conservative, always commissioning firms with established reputations for the required building type. The Aller Park Junior School (1929-31, Fig. 74) was designed by Delano & Aldrich of New York who had designed the student building at Cornell University, built in memory of Dorothy Elmhirst's first husband. The result is Ivy League Tudor which, although of the highest quality, stylistically belongs to an earlier age. Milne's work - Foxhole Senior School (1931-32, Fig.79) in his neo-Georgian mode, and Barton Farm Cottages and houses at Orchard Park, Staple (both 1931) with colourwashed walls and tiled roofs - neither captures the inventive spirit of the Arts and Crafts nor of Dartington. Milne was replaced at Dartington by Louis de Soissons, principally because of his ability to produce cheap housing. De Soissons was Canadian, had trained at the Ecole des Beaux Arts in Paris and had also worked briefly for Lutyens. At the age of 30 he was appointed as chief architect and planner to the embryonic Welwyn Garden City[17] where he was an immediate success. His brand of miniaturised Arts and Crafts-cum-Georgian red brick house appealed to English tastes and pockets. At Dartington (Huxhams Cross and Broom Park, Week (both 1932, Fig.75) the type is translated into concrete block walls with asbestos roofs but the careful grouping around outside spaces proved that, however modest the architecture, the sum was greater than the parts. At his St. James' Priory Estate (from 1933, Figs. 21, 77) in Exeter,[18] the houses are more like Welwyn, picturesquely grouped around closes, neatly but not showily detailed with garden walls, gates and tidy planting. The Arts and Crafts had grown up, it had become rational and economical but these were not sufficient recommendations to sustain it. It had run out of ideas. There is one other building which demonstrates this. It is the Drum Inn (1933-35) at Cockington designed by Lutyens himself near the end of his career, the only part of the ambitious development plan for the village to be realised.[19] It is thatched, 'C'-shaped enclosing a courtyard and flanked by two great, brick chimney stacks. Although its bulk is cleverly concealed against the hillside, the building assumes a form inappropriate to its function (a small hotel) and at odds with the scale of the village cottages. It appears that even Lutyens was unable to sustain the wit of his early houses and that his architectural energies were by now concentrated elsewhere.

Dartington was responsible for other inspired commissions. The first, important to the Arts and Crafts, was the appointment of William Weir to the repair of the derelict medieval buildings (1926-38). Weir had worked for Leonard Stokes and was Philip Webb's assistant and a lifelong committee member of William Morris's Society for the Protection of Ancient Buildings.[20] The work is the first major example in Devon of the Society's philosophy of careful 'honest' repair, where new work was not copyist and was deliberately differentiated from the old which was carefully consolidated *in situ.* It is in sharp contrast to the academic reconstruction of Buckfast or the radical re-styling of Belcher & Joass at Tapeley or Tapper at Bicton. Weir's philosophy is exemplified in the design of the new roof to the Great Hall (1927-32). The new oak hammer beam trusses (oak from the Estate, of course) are of Weir's design suggested only by the 'shadow' of the original profile on the gable wall and they are finished without pseudo-medieval mouldings or 'antiqued' staining (Figs. 23, 94). They sit on a concrete edge beam, which ties the old stone walls together, with an asphalt parapet gutter. The pragmatic resolution of an aesthetic and constructional problem allows the modern and the old to exist comfortably together.

THE MODERN MOVEMENT

The Great War resulted, at least, in a belief in the power of technology and it is here that the Modern Movement begins in England, specifically with the many de-mobbed Royal Engineers who were unemployed in a depressed economy. Lloyd George's call to 'build homes fit for heroes to live in' resulted in the patenting of many new building methods based on steel and concrete[1] intended to produce cheap buildings quickly. Most of them failed through their impracticability or excessive cost but their legacy was the idea of the integration of structure and architecture and the pared, engineers' aesthetic that many of them displayed. For example, the Thurlestone Hotel (1922) was extended by William Grose[2] with a concrete frame and concrete blocks made from beach sand producing a large, unadorned, symmetrical flat roofed building with no particular aesthetic precedent. Petter and Nissen[3] produced houses for Bampton Urban District Council (1926, Fig. 22) in a system adapted from the eponymous army hut with curved corrugated iron roofs, prefabricated concrete slab walls and Crittall's metal-framed windows. The result is totally original, an example of form following function and structure.

The first consciously modern house in Devon was William Walter Wood's Oversound House (1930, Fig. 24) at Down Thomas near Plymouth. It is cubic, white rendered and flat roofed with symmetrical façades and corner metal windows. Oversound House was

> ...built in concrete for South Devon is lacking in good brick clay. The rectangularity of the treatment contrasted well with the landscape [and] looked to the sea, which called for white. I think it is safe to say that all of my houses were evoked by local materials, conditions, traditions etc. I tried hard to evade doing what was merely fashionable.[4]

Wood had taught at the Royal School of Engineering at Cairo and was head of the Department of Architecture at Plymouth Central School of Arts & Crafts. He had first-hand knowledge of Parisian architecture and architects[5] - Le Corbusier, Raymond Fischer and Robert Mallet-Stevens, whose houses in the Rue Mallet-Stevens in Paris (1927) were particularly influential with their compositions of flat planes, corner windows and cubic massing. The house may have shocked those critics only used to contemporary Arts and Crafts houses[6] but it was well received by the architectural *cognoscenti* and was exhibited at the Salon d'Automne in Paris in 1931. Other houses followed.[7] White Walls (1931) at Torquay was a more developed composition on a steeper hillside with a semi-circular bay window composed against a long façade perforated with regular windows, very similar to those in Paris. These houses introduced new ideas from the Continent but it was Dartington and Leonard Elmhirst, with their second inspired commission, who introduced buildings actually designed by a foreign architect. The first was High Cross House (1931) for the new headmaster, W. B. Curry, by the architect William Lescaze. Lescaze had trained in Zurich, had worked in Paris but had established his practice with George Howe in Philadelphia where he had built the Oak Lane County Day School and where Curry was headmaster. This, and all of Lescaze's American work,[8] was firmly in the mould of Continental modernism, thus the appointment from Dartington was both safe and revolutionary for it gave Devon, and England, the first important group of buildings and the first school in this style. High Cross (Fig. 27) is composed with a long, rectangular blue-painted block against the road with the living rooms as cubic blocks, painted white, stacked against it. The study cube has a curved corner with a long ribbon window cutting through it, defying structural logic, and the main block is cut away at the corner and supported on thin steel posts.[9] The composition of the house is caught somewhere between the floating forms of contemporary houses by Le Corbusier and those of many Continental architects, like Mallet-Stevens, which were firmly rooted to the ground. Walter Gropius, who first visited Dartington in 1933, was unimpressed by the plan form and Lutyens, who visited in August 1933, found the house

> the most miserable house I ever saw - all talk and no house - looked about £2,000, but it actually cost £8,000. You cannot live without reflected light...You go blind without window bars whereon the mindless eye may rest...[10]

Yet, despite these criticisms, Elmhirst and Curry persevered and, from this date, Dartington rejected the Arts and Crafts and adopted and adapted modernism which seemed to be in harmony with their educational aspirations. Of the first of three boarding houses (1933, 1934 and 1935,) for Aller Park Junior School, the *Architectural Review* stated

> This functional severity at first shocks those who think that houses in the country should suffer like moths from 'mimecry', so disguising themselves as natural outcrops that you should have to stumble on them before you see them.[11]

The boarding house was

> modern in spirit, and its form is meant to express the independence of rigid tradition, the fearlessness of new ideas [and the] frankness, cleanness and openness [of] a community...[12]

The boarding houses are the clearest of Lescaze's's designs, a simple corridor plan with the upper floor of bedrooms appearing to float above the landscape amongst the trees, a relationship with nature that the Arts and Crafts could never have attempted (Fig. 28). Lescaze also designed the Central Offices (1935) which were steel framed, the gymnasium for Milne's Foxhole (1934) and one other major house, for Kurt Jooss (1935).[13] In all these he was assisted by Robert Hening who emerges as the real architectural hero of Dartington. He arrived as Milne's assistant and remained as resident architect to Weir, Lescaze and, later, to Anthony Chitty and seems to have been successful with all of them. It was his suggestion to introduce cavity walls at High Cross[14] (and used in all the buildings thereafter) and it was his responsibility to persuade reluctant builders that such buildings were possible at all. Dartington had one brief flirtation with Walter Gropius, now a refugee based in London,[15] who converted the medieval barn into a theatre (1933-38), again with Hening assisting) and designed an unexecuted amphitheatre (1935, Fig. 86) for the tilting yard.

Surprisingly, the buildings of Lescaze and Wood had no immediate influence on the architecture of Devon. Change was slow and other influences - from the exhibitions in Paris, Stuttgart and Stockholm[16] to the, by now, numerous examples of modern architecture in England and elsewhere promoted by the architectural press - were needed. The first examples by local architects are small houses. Gerald Saunders produced Shrinkhills (1934, Fig. 25) at Tiverton, Bill Tozer designed High & Over (1934-35) at Dartmouth for a friend as a wedding present, R.M. Challice designed Vitacop (1935) at Exeter for a builder and Melville Aubin designed Sunpark (1935, Fig. 26) at Brixham, based on a Daily Mail house, for a developer as the first house of a never completed estate.[17] W.F.R. Ham designed the houses and flats below Taddyforde Court, Exeter (from 1933), the first example of flats in the modern style in the county. These houses are all white rendered with standard 'horizontal' Crittall metal windows and flat roofs, owing more to Crittall's village at Silver End, Essex and to the type of decoration which flowed from the Art Deco Exhibition, than to theories promoted by Le Corbusier or Gropius.[18] The style suited the seaside and Devon has examples at Bigbury, Teignmouth, Putsborough and, notably, at Torquay. There were attempts by speculative builders to build estates of houses but these foundered no doubt because of public suspicion of the unfamiliar.[19] The most ambitious of these was at Churston Ferrers (from 1935) developed by Staverton Builders, the building firm of Dartington, with William Lescaze as architect, Henry Wright[20] as planner and Beatrix Farrand as landscape architect. The plan dispersed the houses around closes with open spaces and footpaths on the 'Radburn' principle (Figs. 31, 78) and focused on Elberry Cove where a streamlined hotel was planned.[21] Staverton produced a lavish brochure for the scheme which was at once educational, technical and a long apologia for the architecture and planning.

> ...looking at one of the little groups into which these houses are placed, you will see, at last, that there is a beauty about this architecture which is like no other - a beauty owing nothing to sentiment and everything to its expression of the social ideals of this age...the houses are, in fact, precisely 'right'. They sink into the setting. They do not insist upon admiration as unrelated works of art. They quickly become - as they are intended to be - part of the landscape.[22]

The style was well suited to other new seaside building types. The lido, Tinside Pool (1928-35), at Plymouth was designed by J. Wibberley, the City Engineer, Architect and Planner, who drew upon Art Deco sources and that almost-modern style promoted by the Empire Exhibition of 1924.[23] The buildings are clad in limestone tiles and are decorated with stained glass panels depicting seaside activities. Increasingly, Devon was being promoted for holidays, especially for the middle classes from the conurbations who travelled by train or by motor car on the improved trunk roads.[24] Thus the seaside hotel becomes an important new type. The Thurlestone Hotel has already been mentioned but the Saunton Sands Hotel (1937) by Alwyn Underdown is a more committed modern statement set as one huge, white block, like an ocean liner above the cliffs, symmetrical with a pattern of projecting balconies. The hotel at Burgh Island, Bigbury (1929, Fig. 30) was built as a holiday house to the design of Matthew Dawson of London by Archibald Nettlefold, the industrialist, to entertain his London theatrical friends. The house was a rational, concrete framed block but its plainness was alleviated by a semi-circular bay to which Nettlefold added machicolations.[25] In the early 'thirties it became an hotel and a Palm Court and a new wing were added. The architect appears to be one Brakespeare of Plymouth who introduced a lavish extravagance of Art Deco decoration, light fittings, mirrors and, in the Palm Court, a coloured glass dome and fountain. The Queen's Hotel (c.1937, Fig. 29), facing the harbour at Torquay, probably by A.J. Seal of Bournemouth,[26] had curved, white balconies and a fine, decorated interior. It is not far removed from contemporary examples in Miami or Shanghai and demonstrates how international this type of architecture had become by the late 'thirties.

Torquay too provides another example of the local authority adopting modernism for new building types. The Borough Engineer and Architect, P.W. Ladmore, like his Edwardian predecessor, was responsible for a series of rational, modern structures[27] the best of which are the municipal electricity showroom, Electric House (1935), and the Public Library (1935-38) which are the more surprising as they are extensions to the back of Davison's Town Hall. Both are faced in Portland stone and are carefully detailed. The Library is almost symmetrical about its monumental entrance block but Electric House is composed with horizontal lines against a tower formed by the office entrance (Fig. 32). Electric House was exceptional for its interior which was a studied exercise in 'thirties detailing with curved fibrous plaster ceilings, specially made light fittings, walls panelled in Indian silver greywood, birds eye maple and Australian walnut, black and green Vitrolite glass and radiator grilles in anodised Birmabright metal.[28] The Library was more sober but the Borough employed Oscar Faber[29] as engineer and his arched concrete rib structure is exposed within the reading rooms. The otherwise plain interior has the same power as the examples of early Continental modernism it resembles. Opposite Electric House is Castle Circus House (1935, Fig. 33), a speculative office building, designed by Stewart Lloyd Thomson.[30]

Its façade too is clad in stone but it is of thin sheets of travertine marble separated by bands of windows with the structure expressed only as regular, thin mullions. The upper floor is recessed so that the roof plane forms a floating cornice. The effect is of lightness, quite unlike Ladmore's work, and the building is a true pioneer, looking forward to office buildings of the 'sixties when this pattern became quite standard.

Every town in Devon had a cinema, the first probably the Paignton Picture House of 1914 in a Baroque-cum-Art Nouveau manner. In the thirties their design was dominated by the major film distributors and their architects who produced designs special to each location but with standardised materials and details. They were intended to seduce, they were exotic, deliberately unlike anything the public was used to and, of course, they were immensely popular. The best examples are the massive Odeon (1937, Fig. 34) in Exeter designed by Roger Bullivant of the Birmingham office of Harry Weedon with its entrance flanked by pylons of brick decorated with stone 'pilasters' and the Astor (1931) at Barnstaple by W.H. Watkins of Bristol for British Gaumont, an extraordinarily eclectic concoction with a roof of green glazed tiles.[31] On a smaller scale, is the Tivoli (1932) at Tiverton by Gerald Saunders,[32] a sweet, symmetrical modern façade at the end of its street with two porthole windows, an early and pleasing use of this motif.

Towards the end of the'thirties, modern architects began to use traditional materials. This was due in part to the practical difficulties experienced in using concrete or white render in the English (or Devonian) climate but also due to the influence of artists like Paul Nash and architects like Le Corbusier who now advocated a less doctrinaire and more plural attitude to materials, colours and textures. Thus architects 'rediscovered' brick, stone and timber as suitable materials for new architecture. In Devon there was one outstanding example of a modern house - the Cedar House (c.1937, Fig. 35) at Bigbury by the London architect, Felix Goldsmith, which was flat-roofed, metal-windowed and horizontal in emphasis, like earlier houses, but was timber-framed and clad in wide, natural cedar boarding. The new airport building at Exeter Municipal Airport (1937, Fig. 36) was clad in brick and stone with a regular, lightweight steel framed structure. It was designed by Robert Hening and Anthony Chitty[33] and the client was the Straight Corporation, founded by Whitney Straight, Dorothy Elmhirst's son.[34] Like Hening's contemporary cottages at Dartington,[35] it is a gentle, understated architecture and with it modern architecture seems to have come of age.

LARGE BUILDINGS AND EXETER UNIVERSITY

Most of the modern movement buildings in Devon were small. Commissions for larger buildings from more conservative clients who regarded the modern as risky went to older, established architects. The Public Library (1925) at Exeter was designed by Sydney Greenslade who had won the competition for the National Library of Wales at Aberystwyth in 1909 with a severe, neo-Classical design. Exeter Library is brick with symmetrical façades of Classical origin but the heavy cornice assumes an almost cubist manner showing that Greenslade was aware, at least, of contemporary brick architecture in Germany (Fig. 40). Torbay Hospital (1925-28) is plain, neo-Georgian, also of brick with sash windows and a mansard roof of Cornish slate. It was designed by Charles Holden of the London firm of Adams Holden & Pearson who had completed the Bristol Royal Infirmary in 1911[1] and who were then designing the first of their pioneering Underground stations for London Transport. The plan encloses a central courtyard which is axial to the sea view and is raised above the entrance to give privacy to the wards. The ends of the ward wings are open loggias, similar to those at Bristol, a careful modern insertion into the traditional design (Fig. 38). At one side is a separate Chapel (1925-30) of unornamented Beer stone with a plain interior and barrel vaulted timber roof (Fig. 39). The design is understated, neither modern nor revivalist. This period of English architecture is exemplified by Brian O'Rorke's design for Ashcombe Tower (1933-35) near Dawlish, the country house for Major Ralph Rayner, the Member of Parliament for Totnes. O'Rorke was young, this was his first house and he was just completing the designs for the luxury cruise ship, RMS Orion. The exterior, which incorporated an older tower, is traditional, pitch-roofed and rendered but with random stone quoins around the windows (Fig. 37). The interior, and notably the design of the main living rooms, is emphatically modern but in a grand manner with specially designed furniture by O'Rorke and carpets and fabrics by Marion Dorn. It is one of the finest modern interiors of the decade.[2]

The appointment of E. Vincent Harris to design the University College of Exeter seems to have been on the recommendation of Sydney Greenslade. Harris grew up in Kingsbridge and had worked in Exeter and for London County Council. The first University plan is in their joint names.[3] This showed an axial arrangement of neo-Classical buildings around courtyards based on Oxbridge colleges or, even, the Royal Naval Hospital at Plymouth and there are references to Aston Webb's Dartmouth College. The adopted plan (1931), however, created an axis from the distant Cathedral to the highest point of the site where Harris placed an isolated lookout tower and about the axis he dispersed the buildings, more or less following the contours of the hill. The first buildings constructed were the Washington Singer Laboratories (1931), Mardon Hall (1933), Roborough Reading Room (1938-40) and the Hatherly Laboratories (1948-52, Fig. 41). Mardon Hall is the most conservative, strict neo-Georgian with stone urns on the parapets. The other buildings are more interesting.

Harris's primary architectural source is Lutyens - that is, Lutyens in his early country house phase - and Harris skillfully takes motifs like the bay window of Deanery Garden (1899-02), the windows from The Salutation (1911) or Great Maytham (1907-09)[4] or the stone trimmed arch from the Thiepval Memorial (1927-32) and collages them to compose the repeated bays of much larger buildings. In this transfer, he simplifies the details so that the compositions are a play between solid (brick) and void (window), always unified under steeply pitched Lutyens-esque tiled roofs. The façades are kept flat and sharp-edged, modulation being introduced through added porches at Washington Singer or huge bay windows at Roborough, giving the buildings a massive scale, like Lutyens at Drogo. The interiors are very plain with exposed concrete columns and ceilings and utilitarian joinery. The best of his buildings at Exeter is the Chapel (1956) built as a memorial to his mother. It is placed across the main axis, blocking the view from the hill to the Cathedral, which may have been an act of protest against William Holford, who superseded Harris as University planner, and whose Queen's Building (1956-58) destroyed the axial space. Thus the nave is at right angles to the axis and only the outside pulpit acknowledges the view. The nave is a tall, simple space of white painted brick, lit with four stone mullioned Deanery Garden windows, a tiled floor and W. T. Monnington's ethereal painted ceiling (Fig. 42). It is a beautifully judged balance between function, form and space.

THE MODERN CHURCH

The Victorian preference of the Gothic style for churches lasted well into the twentieth century as demonstrated by Edward Maufe's competition winning Guildford Cathedral (1932). From the mid 'thirties both the established church and Rome commissioned churches which sought a new style more suited to the age.[1] These churches served the expanding suburbs - in Devon of Plymouth, Exeter and Torbay - or replaced buildings destroyed in the War. Principal among church architects were Louis de Soissons of Welwyn and N. F. Cachemaille Day, who worked briefly in de Soissons' office,but established his own office in London in 1936. Cachemaille Day's St. Paul, Paignton (1937), is red brick Gothic with an impressive tower and Tudor mullioned windows held between brick piers modelled on Albi Cathedral, a favourite reference. It is typically eclectic, searching for a new style. St. Martin, Barton (1938-61) in Torquay is more daring - loosely based on a Romanesque model with massive white walls and stout arcaded windows. The nave is one space incorporating the chancel. The altar rail and pulpit are smooth modern but the baldacchino is Byzantine with red columns and flat reliefs of gilded angels. The inspiration for St. Luke's, Milber (1933-63) is also Romanesque but the plan, supposedly revealed in a dream to the incumbent W. Keble Martin, is unique.[2] It is a Roman cross on which is superimposed a St. Andrews cross giving it three naves, all of which were intended to be barrel vaulted. All these churches bring the celebrant and the congregation close together and anticipate the Liturgical Movement of the 'fifties and 'sixties.

After the War, Frederick Etchells, the translator of Le Corbusier, rebuilt St. Andrew's (1946-56), the parish church of Plymouth. Following the philosophy of Weir at Dartington Hall, he reconstructed the nave and aisle vaults in thin concrete resting on concrete beams and re-ordered the chancel to give a clear, open space paved with Delabole slate. Louis de Soissons' two Plymouth churches, George Street Baptist Church (1956) and the Unitarian Church (1955), next to it, both reflect his admiration for the architecture of Nantucket. The elegant portico and copper spire of the Unitarians (Fig. 43) is a more literal transposition but the Baptist church is a subtle composition around a small courtyard with a shallow vaulted arcade surrounded by buildings with delicate details and light, overhanging eaves and verges, suggesting classical porticos. Its scale, however, is more suburban than urban. St. Sidwell (1957) at Exeter by Lucas Roberts & Brown is a more muscular affair in brick with exposed concrete portals in the nave and originally designed to have a tall, glazed bell tower over the main entrance (Fig. 50).[3] The most developed church of this period is the extraordinary Ascension, Crown Hill (1956-58) in Plymouth by Robert Potter and Richard Hare of Salisbury, based on the plan of Ninian Comper's St. Philip, Cosham.[4] The exterior has a conventional form faced in local limestone with a pitched roof gabled over the transepts. The interior, however, reveals a folded concrete vault painted deep red supported on slim, precast concrete octagonal columns (Fig. 49). The gallery is cut away so that light enters around it and on to the font. The central altar has a light domed baldacchino and the east window behind is reduced to small mysterious hexagonal openings filled with dense stained glass. The glass is by Geoffrey Clarke and the baldacchino decoration by Robert Medley; Hans Feibusch provided murals to St. Sidwell and George Street Baptist Church (Fig. 44) and John Piper the Astor window at St. Andrew.[5] By the end of the 'fifties, the Church emerges as a major patron of modern architecture and significant modern artists.

THE PLANS FOR PLYMOUTH AND EXETER

Architectural writing of the late 'thirties and early 'forties on town planning is a constant diatribe against the conditions in existing cities and towns.

> A hundred years of change has finally destroyed its unity…motor traffic has wrecked the calm rhythm of its streets: commerce has invaded its squares and terraces: wear and tear and the remorseless march of time have played havoc with its fabric.[1]

> The centre of the city is a jungle of commercial blocks, neo-classic or pseudo-modern, through which the congested traffic creeps in a dense haze of petrol fumes; in the 'undeveloped' quarters the slums linger on, while around the town spreads unending suburbia, the result of everyone trying to escape the unpleasantness of the modern town...[2]

Such thinking was encouraged by the publication of Le Corbusier's *Ville Radieuse* and his plan for Paris (1925) which, provocatively, had proposed the demolition of the area north of Notre Dame.[3] The spread of suburbia in the 'thirties was also attacked by the Council for the Preservation of Rural England and writings in the *Architectural Review*[4] and it was under these influences that younger architects proposed ideal solutions to the problems of city planning. These show a remarkable consistency. The cities are low density with strictly zoned activities - civic centre, shopping, schools, recreation and housing - distributed amongst lawns and trees. The endpapers of Tubbs' *Living in Cities* contrast the old and new city - the old showing mixed uses, traffic congestion, pollution and spreading suburbia and the new with zoned separated uses, a bypass, new buildings set in parkland (with 'dignified surroundings' to the Gothic cathedral) and shops and offices together along a 'boulevard'. Fry's 'Borough Unit' in *Fine Building* shows the railway station with shopping linked to the town hall precinct behind which are schools, a museum and housing and beyond which, through a park, are cinemas and eventually open parkland, sports fields and a motorway. The diagram is very similar to the built plan of Welwyn Garden City, except that at Welwyn the planning of the civic spaces is strictly axial. Two problems stood in way of realising such ideals - the fact that the pattern of the old city could not be adapted to the new and that private ownership of land made large-scale redevelopment impossible. The destruction caused by the War (Fig. 106) and the compulsory purchase of city centre land authorised by the 1944 Town & Country Planning Act solved both problems and it was in a mood of optimism and adventure that plans were made for rebuilding.

The plan for Plymouth by Patrick Abercrombie and J. Paton Watson, the City Engineer and Surveyor, was published in 1943 and adopted in 1944.[5] It was truly radical. It proposed the complete removal of the old city centre except for St. Andrew's church and the formation of a grand axis, Armada Way (Fig. 56), from the railway station in the north to the war memorial[6] on the Hoe to the south. Across the axis a grid of streets formed the main shopping and office area and this was enclosed by a double road which diverted through-traffic. Within the ring, activities were graded from the north with Government offices, then shopping, the civic centre, law courts, banks to hotels in the south. A grander east-west road (Royal Parade) separated the commercial from the civic areas. The plan was in the Beaux Arts manner with circles (roundabouts) marking the cross-axes and linking to existing roads on the periphery. There is, at least, a superficial resemblance to Lutyens' plan for New Delhi[7] and to Welwyn in the relationship of the shopping areas to the axis and railway station. On the architecture, Abercrombie was clear:

> If we are to recapture the wonderful continuity of the street scene obtained by Nash and Wood the Younger, as in Old Regent Street and Bath, but in the modern idiom, then it is essential that the new streets shall be designed as a whole. We recommend that a design in outline for the whole architectural treatment in the reconstruction area should be prepared.[8]

The perspective drawings to the Plan by J.D.M. Harvey gave a seductive image far beyond Abercrombie's descriptions (Figs. 47, 48). The new Guildhall is shown to be neo-classical, the theatres stripped modern but the pylons which Abercrombie required to identify the ends of the axis are shown as strong, tapering towers in the manner of the architect, Thomas S. Tait. Tait had been coordinating architect to the 1938 Glasgow Exhibition and its axial plan and circular gardens were Harvey's source for Plymouth.[9] Tait's first Plymouth building was Dingles' Bakery and Store (1946-50, Fig. 45) in Beaumont Street, out of the central area. It is a long block on a podium clad in precast concrete panels with a square, brick bookend tower with characteristic porthole windows enclosing the lifts and stair.[10] The first new building in the city centre was Messrs. Joseph's NAAFI (1948-50, Fig. 46) in the 'hotel zone' where Armada Way meets Notte Street. It is also brick and a fascinating amalgam of motifs. The elevations are based on Norwich City Hall of 1932-38 which was based on Scandinavian examples[11] and this explains the curious columns flanking the window to the tower on Notte Street. The tower is based on the architecture of the Dutch architect, W.M. Dudok, whose style was made popular in England in the 'thirties by Sir John Burnet, Tait & Lorne.[12] The new buildings of the centre are all clad in Portland stone, in response to Abercrombie's recommendations. The City appointed William Crabtree[13] as coordinating architect and Tait to the coordinating architects' panel which had to approve all new buildings. The first street to be constructed was Royal Parade with Tait's Dingles Department Store (1949-51) and Tait and Alec French's Pearl Assurance (1950-51) flanking Armada Way and then W.J. Reed's Co-Operative Wholesale Society (1950-51), Tait and French's Royal Insurance (1950) and Donald Hamilton, Wakeford & Partners' Norwich Union (1950-52) turning the corner into Old Town Street (Figs. 52, 53, 54). Together they form the grandest ensemble of early 'fifties buildings in the country.[14] Their architecture is derived from Tait and his influence on the committee was considerable. He treats the buildings as sculptural masses with a residual Beaux Arts base and cornice (this usually a recessed eaves) and corners expressed as battered pylons.[15] Pearl Assurance most closely follows this model, but at Dingles, Tait accentuated the horizontal lines of the side wings introducing sculpted stone panels between the windows and stepping the blocks against the tower rather in the manner of Mendelsohn.[16] The plan forms of the Co-op and Norwich Union keep to the street lines thereby forming curved façades and in this they resemble Crabtree's Peter Jones. The Co-op has windows of glass bricks divided by widely spaced columns but the Norwich Union pulls its columns away from the façade under a thin concrete cornice like the 1937 Museum of Modern Art in Paris and here the neo-classical influence is most obvious.[17]

The east end of Royal Parade was closed with the National Provincial Bank (1955), a *tour de force* designed by B.C. Sherren, the bank's own architect. To the road he placed a grand portico of stone-clad columns forming a porch faced in blue mosaic (Fig. 55). The main mass of the building is perforated with small, square windows, the roof is curved copper topped with a lantern and the sides and back are partly clad in rough stone, referring to the architecture of the Barbican behind. There are two other outstanding buildings. The City Architect, H.J.W. Stirling[18], reconstructed the Victorian Guildhall (1951-59) and produced what must be the finest post-Festival of Britain interior in the country which is only hinted at in the wavy canopy that he cut into the main elevation and in the new copper roof to the tower. He embellished the interior with sculpture by David Weeks (the Labours of Hercules), glass by F.H. Coventry and the finest hardwoods and marbles for the details (Fig. 51). The Pannier Market (1956-59, Figs. 57, 59) by Walls & Pearn of Plymouth is in vigorous, rough concrete, a series of huge shell vaults in the 'fifties tradition established by Stockwell Bus Garage and the Brynmawr Rubber Factory.[19] It too has sculpture by David Weeks (Fig. 107) and it marks the end of a tradition when public architecture and public art were considered together.

The plan for Exeter by Thomas Sharp[20] was published in 1946. It is a curious compromise, uncertain in the debate of issues and reluctant to propose radical solutions even though large areas of the High Street and beyond had been destroyed. More or less his proposals followed the layout of the old streets - the only new proposal being that of opening views of the Cathedral, notably from the east down a new shopping precinct (Princesshay). Otherwise, he proposed the clearance of areas of 'outworn' buildings around the City wall so that the medieval area stood isolated from the suburbs across a linear park, the character or purpose of which was never made clear. This was then bisected by a ring road with a clover-leaf intersection at Exe Bridge on the west. It all seems uncannily like Tubbs' *Living in Cities*. That it lacked the singular idea of Plymouth made it easier for the City authorities subsequently to erode it.

On the architecture, Sharp is clear that imitations are not acceptable and

> ...the general principle can be stated in the axiom that new buildings should be in the common idiom of their own day...In a time of confused contradictory and changing 'styles' there is nothing so dangerous as style itself: and the buildings which will best stand the test of time in this city will be those which show no stylistic tricks at all but which depend for their effect on being clean well-proportioned and honest.[21]

The perspective drawings by A.C. Webb which accompanied the plan were non-committal (Fig. 64). When the real architecture arrived it was in brick, taking its inspiration partly from the destroyed Georgian buildings, partly from Welwyn and from Greenslade's Library and the neo-Georgian Telephone Exchange (1934) in Castle Street which survived the blitz. However, it would be wrong to describe the new architecture of the High Street merely as neo-Georgian; its patterns of brick trimmed with stone are both subtle and inventive and often beautifully detailed. Most 'correct' is Lloyds Bank (1950-53, Fig. 61) by E. Victor Beer of Charles E. Ware of Exeter which is neo-Roman with a fine banking hall in cream marble and square Corinthian columns. Lucas Roberts & Brown designed the flanking Commercial Union (1950-52, Fig. 58) and Pearl Assurance (1950-52) which, like their Martins Bank, Bedford Street (1948-52), most closely followed the Georgian model. However, their Westminster Bank (1950-55), on the corner of Castle Street, has the first floor windows framed out and the upper floor windows as small squares within a mass of brickwork, a composition which has parallels in contemporary work by Maxwell Fry and Ralph Tubbs.[22] There are many variations on this theme in the High Street and Sidwell Street and the first buildings of Princesshay (1954) by Percy Burnett of London have long bands of windows above thin concrete canopies.[23] Marks & Spencer (1950-51) by Lewis & Hickey and Boots (from 1956) by C. St.C. Oakes are similar symmetrical compositions with taller centre pieces, the former with concrete Egyptian columns and the latter with an early curtain wall of glass and panels. Opposite, 8-12 High Street (1952) by L.H. Fewster of London reverses the composition with the alleyway to Princesshay flanked by twin blocks faced with chevron curtain walling. Most dynamic of all is Alec French's Mendelsohnian sweeping canopy (1952) at the corner of High Street and Bedford Street which matches Lucas Roberts & Brown's shops (1949, Fig. 60) on the other side of St. Stephen's Church and Colsons (from 1950, now Dingles) by Beech & Curnow Cooke of Exeter, all detailed in Bath stone and pale brick.[24] This contrasts with Barclays Bank (1953) by W. Curtis Green, Son & Lloyd, a studied essay in civic proportions with the office wings on High Street and Bedford Street enclosing the great drum banking hall and circular grand stair.[25]

These buildings are contemporary with Vincent Harris at the University and it was Harris's former assistant, Donald McMorran, who was appointed to design the new headquarters for the County Council (1955-64, Fig. 62) at St. Leonard's, Exeter.[26] These too are brick modern-Georgian, but laid out as a campus enclosing or suggesting courtyards. The details, especially the clock tower and the sumptuous interiors of the council chamber and committee rooms, look to Scandinavian neo-classicism of the early part of the century and, in particular, to Östberg's Town Hall in Stockholm.[27] McMorran sensed that the modern movement had been a too narrow interpretation and was looking for alternative sources and materials just as Anthony Chitty had done in the 'thirties. Sir William Holford was appointed to Exeter University as architect and planner in 1955 to replace Harris. He too looked to Scandinavia but to Denmark for a more human, less monumental architecture than that of Harris or McMorran. His Queen's Building (1956-58, Fig. 63) seems more suited to the increasingly liberal times and to an institution that had gained its independence and was receiving students who did not remember the War. The building is a series of linked blocks around courtyards dominated by a taller slab parallel to Harris' axis with a grid of small windows in the side elevation and a tall, four-storey window on the gable. The entrances are through the courtyards and alongside a sinuous brick screen wall which is based on the Assembly Hall[28] at Aarhus; the choice of materials is catholic - stone, brick, tiles, lead, copper and timber. It is at once daring and fresh without the formality or reserve of the High Street buildings; it looks forward to a new age.

CONCLUSION

Devon has an exceptional range of early twentieth century architecture. The depth of the influence of Lutyens and his sometime assistants will surprise many critics, Dartington is the unique example of a modern movement school in Britain and there were more modern movement houses in Devon than in any county except Surrey. In a rural county, the urban centres of 1950s Plymouth, Exeter and its University are outstanding amongst contemporary architecture. The interiors of Castle Drogo, Coleton Fishacre, Ashcombe Tower, Plymouth Guildhall and County Hall are nationally important. There are many twentieth century gardens and churches which would reward further detailed study and the architecture of the 1950s has yet to be critically assessed. Yet these buildings remain little known and uncelebrated. Devon continues to publicise its attractions as a bucolic idyll fossilised sometime in the eighteenth century while its fragile twentieth century heritage is systematically eroded by an unthinking and ignorant generation. Devon's architects, builders and patrons deserve better; this architecture needs to be better known, studied and understood and the best of it carefully preserved.

INTRODUCTION

1 For example in the history of modernism presented by J.M. Richards, *An Introduction to Modern Architecture*. Harmondsworth: Penguin, 1940 and later editions. Richards was assistant editor of *The Architects' Journal* and *Architectural Review* in the 1930s and editor of *Architectural Review* after the War. Both magazines published buildings of the Modern Movement to the exclusion of other contemporary architecture. Richards' views were influenced by Nikolaus Pevsner, *Pioneers of the Modern Movement*. London: Faber and Faber, 1936 (reprinted as *Pioneers of Modern Design*) and Sigfried Giedion, *Space, Time and Architecture*. Cambridge: Harvard University Press, 1941.

2 See Alan Powers, 'Liverpool and Architectural Education in the Early Twentieth Century' in Joseph Sharples, Alan Powers, Michael Shippobottom, *Charles Reilly & The Liverpool School of Architecture 1904 - 1933*. Liverpool: Liverpool University Press (Exhibition Catalogue), 1996.

3 *The Builder* published steel engravings of architects' drawings from the 1860s. From the 1920s the magazines *Country Life*, *The Architects' Journal*, *The Architectural Review*, *The Architect & Building News*, *The Journal of the Royal Institute of British Architects* and *Architecture Illustrated* and books published by The Architectural Press, Country Life, Batsford and Victor Gollancz amongst many others provided good quality photographs, drawings and technical drawings of contemporary buildings.

EDWARDIAN ARCHITECTURE

1 See Robin Clutterbuck, *Buckfast Abbey - A History*. Buckfast Abbey Trustees, 1994. The monks were expelled from La Pierre-qui-Vive in 1880 and took refuge in Leopardstown, Dublin. The first monks arrived at Buckfast in 1882 and Walters' work dates from 1883. The first drawings for the Abbey Church are dated 1886 (see *The Builder*, 30 October 1886) and are based on Cluny with a pyramidal roof to the squat tower. The triforium was added in 1908 and the final design dated 1909. Working drawings commenced in 1910 and continue through into the 1950s by Walters, Whitby & Kerr Bate and Walters & Kerr Bate. The firm were involved in all aspects of the design including the altars, furnishings, sculptures, coats-of-arms and vestments as well as houses and a primary school. The presbytery transept roof drawing of May 1930 shows steel roof trusses.

2 Belfast City Hall (1897-1906) by A. Brumwell Thomas and Colchester Town Hall (1897-1902) by John Belcher with J.J. Joass as assistant. Belcher & Joass rebuilt Tapeley Park near Bideford (1898-1916) in a formal Renaissance style and Bicton (1908-09) was rebuilt by Sir Walter Tapper.

3 There was also an open arcade leading up Union Street. This was filled in by the Borough Architect, P.W. Ladmore, on the building of Electric House and the new Library in Lymington Road in 1937.

4 The drawings are held in Torre Abbey Art Gallery. The project was to be funded by a private syndicate which received Royal Assent for its Bill in July 1907. The syndicate failed to raise the capital and the scheme was abandoned.

5 The Borough seems to have been fortunate in its choice of Surveyor & Architect. Garrett had also designed the entrance kiosks to the Torquay Recreation Ground (1910) in a spikey, Art Nouveau manner (information from John R.A. Wilson).

6 Sir Edwin Lutyens to Lady Emily Lutyens, 3rd August 1910. Quoted in Peter Inskip, 'The Compromise of Castle Drogo' in *Architectural Review*, April 1979, pp. 220-226.

7 See Peter Inskip, *ibid.*

THE ARTS & CRAFT MOVEMENT

1 See Jill Franklin, 'Edwardian Butterfly Houses' in *Architectural Review*, April 1975, pp. 220-225 and Christophe Grillet, 'Edward Prior' in *Architectural Review*, November 1952, pp. 302-308. The house was rebuilt after a fire in 1905 with a tiled roof. The Sedding family were from Cornwall but E.H. Sedding (1863-1921), J.D. Sedding's nephew, practised from Plymouth.

2 From *Transactions of The National Association for the Advancement of Art and its Application to Industry* (1889) quoted by Alastair Service, *Edwardian Architecture - A handbook to Building Design in Britain 1890-1914*. Thames & Hudson, 1977, p.24. This remains the best general guide to the architecture of the period.

3 These buildings are described in Nikolaus Pevsner & Bridget Cherry, *The Buildings of England - Devon*. London: Penguin Books, 1989 which remains the only comprehensive guide to the buildings of the county. The Barn was for a Major Weatherall; Penlee for Arthur B. Rendell, a London surgeon; Coxon for Basil Young, Gimson's blacksmith. There are many other examples including Hannaford Manor, Widecombe-in-the-Moor (1904) by A. Wickham Jarvis for Major Bolitho, of the Bolitho banking family, La Tourelle at Salcombe (c.1898) by C. Harrison Townsend, Home Orchard (1909, now Windmill House) at Sidmouth by M.H. Baillie Scott and Tuckett's Farm at Lower Netherton (1904) by W. Curtis Green for Debell Tuckett, the electrical manufacturer. Kingdon House (1906, the printing works) at Tavistock is a rare example by a local architect, Southcombe Parker.

4 Information on Fred Harrild from his son, Peter (b.1922), Diana Ward and John R.A. Wilson.

5 Livermead was for Wilfred Nicholson of the distilling family, Little Tor for Frank Swift, a local tobacconist.

6 Moult End at Salcombe has an arcade of Tuscan columns and the drawing for this and Casa del Sole by Cyril Farey turn South Devon into Lombardy. Harrild had travelled in Italy before the War and was a very competant watercolourist.

7 For example, at Beer by Walter Tapper in stone and thatch (*Architectural Review*, December 1928, p.254); Sherwood House, Budleigh Salterton (c.1932) by A.C. Martin also thatched but rendered; Victory Cottage (1945) at Broadhembury by Philip Tilden for Cedric Drewe, third son of Julius, in thatch. Also, the bus shelter (1925) at Broadclyst by Randall Wells, a minor masterpiece in stone and thatch. Wells had been clerk of works for Prior at St. Andrew's, Roker and for Lethaby at Brockhampton Church. There are many other houses by Fred Harrild at Salcombe, East Portlemouth and Thurlestone - for example, The Thatched House (c.1925, now Landpath), Thurlestone (*Country Life*, 30th May 1925, pp.887-888).

8 See Alan Powers, *Oliver Hill - Architect and Lover of Life 1887-1968*. Mouton Publications, 1989. Houses in Hill's Arts and Crafts mode include Woodhouse Copse, Holmbury St. Mary, Surrey (1924-26); The Thatched House, Knowle, West Midlands (1923-29); Boxhurst Farm, Sandhurst, Kent (1927-28).

9 The house was for Brenda Girvin and Monica Cousens, the playwrights. Sybil Thorndyke was a visitor. A separate Housekeeper's house was added in 1927 and a series of walled gardens. The main house was destroyed by fire and a new, smaller house constructed in 1944 and 1951-55.

10 Hill admired Scottish architecture. He published *Scottish Castles of the 16th and 17th Centuries* in 1953.

11 It is not the purpose of this essay to examine gardens in detail but Devon has many important twentieth century gardens. See Todd Gray, *The Garden History of Devon*. University of Exeter, 1995 and Stephen Pugsley, *Devon Gardens: An Historical Survey*. Alan Sutton, 1994.

12 Now called Castle Tor. The house is simple Arts and Crafts designed for Horace Pickersgill, the son of a successful Leeds bookmaker. The Viceroy's Garden is illustrated in Robert Grant Irving, *Indian Summer - Lutyens, Baker and Imperial Delhi*. New Haven & London: Yale University Press, 1981.

13 For example, No.4 Park Avenue, Farnborough, Kent (London Borough of Bromley) for G.H.R. Fawcett (1935) and is white, flat roofed modern with standard 'horizontal' metal windows. See *The Building Times*, July 1936, pp. 5-6.

14 Milne designed the separate Motor House with chauffeur's flat, where the rear elevation has standard metal 'horizontal' windows. Coleton Barton Farm (c.1927), the farm manager's house, is neo-Georgian with a symmetrical elevation and large sash windows with external shutters. He also designed workers' cottages for the Estate.

15 See *Architectural Review*, December 1928, p. 297.

16 For example, at Little Knowle, Budleigh Salterton; houses at Saunton and Croyde; Gray Croft, St. Budeaux, Plymouth (1953) by Sydney R. Edwards; all listed in Pevsner & Cherry, *Devon, op.cit.* Lupton Park, near Brixham (1955) is by O.P. Milne for Lord Churston. It is neo-Georgian with a straightforward, rectilinear plan - a simplified version of Coleton Fishacre.

17 See Maurice de Soissons, *Welwyn Garden City: A Town Designed for Healthy Living*. Publications for Companies, 1988. A.E. Malbon, general manager of Welwyn Builders, became manager of Staverton Builders, the construction firm set up by Dartington.

18 The Estate was developed by Staverton Builders and was intended to occupy all the land to the south west of Topsham Road with Earl Richards Road becoming a crescent, similar to layouts at Welwyn. Staverton

Builders also commissioned houses from de Soissons at Dittisham (1933-35) and Cliff Park Avenue, Churston Ferrers.

19 The full scheme is shown on sketches now in the RIBA Drawings Collection LUT[33] 1-6 but it is difficult to relate the drawings to the topography of the village. There is a completed perspective dated 1933 by Cyril Farey showing thatched cottages around an arcaded market building. The project was the first on which Lutyens worked with his son, Robert. Cockington was owned by the Mallock family who were developing the land on the edge of Torquay and trying to preserve the village.

20 See Reginald Snell, *William Weir and Dartington Hall*. The Dartington Hall Trust, 1988.

THE MODERN MOVEMENT

1 Technical magazines of the early 'twenties illustrate many of these inventions. There were also prefabricated building systems in timber and asbestos sheet marketed by manufacturers.

2 Grose was the son of the hotel's owners and had qualified as an engineer before the War. He became the chief engineer of the Irish Lights for Trinity House. The hotel was extended again in the same style in 1933-34 and a third floor added by - Archer, architect of London. See Peter Pugh, *The Thurlestone Hotel - A Century of Family Enterprise*. Cambridge Business Publishing, 1996.

3 Sir Ernest Petter (the inventor of the Petter engine) and Lt. Col. Peter N. Nissen. The houses are 'Nissen-Petren Non-Parlour Houses' designed in association with D.J. Dean, the surveyor for Bampton Urban District Council. The drawings are in the Devon Record Office. There are similar, contemporary houses at Yeovil and West Camel in Somerset.

4 William Walter Wood, letter to the author 9.10.72.

5 Wood was friends with Pierre Vago and André Bloc, the founders of the *avant garde* architectural magazine *Architecture d'Aujourdhui*. W.W. Wood, letter, *ibid.*

6 It was called 'The Mystery House' and 'The House without a Chimney'. W.W. Wood, letter, *ibid.*

7 Seathwaite (1931), opposite Oversound House at Down Thomas, and a house at Roborough, Plymouth. Seathwaite and Roborough have been altered beyond recognition, White Walls was demolished in the 1960s. White Walls, at least, was built of 'concrete units' and it appears that Oversound House has cavity walls (probably also of concrete blocks) and a concrete frame.

8 This is illustrated and put into its American context in Robert A.M. Stern, Gregory Gilmartin and Thomas Mellins, *New York 1930*. New York: Rizzoli, 1987. Lescaze moved his office to New York in 1934. The curved corner is a favourite motif and recurs on many building types.

9 The house was intended to be constructed from reinforced concrete but this was changed to suit local construction methods and capability. Lescaze had designed the Frederick V. Field House, Connecticut (1930-31) with a steel frame and lightweight plastered cladding. It is stylistically very similar to High Cross.

10 Sir Edwin Lutyens to Lady Emily Lutyens quoted by David Dean, *The Thirties: Recalling the English Architectural Scene*. London: Trefoil, 1983, p.129. Gropius quoted by Colin Penn in Andrew Saint, 'An Interview with Colin and Virginia Penn' in *Thirties Society Journal* No.4, 1984, p.35: *'[Gropius] said that he could remember the plan of every 'functional' house ever built but he couldn't remember the plan of that one!'*

11 Gerald Heard in 'The Dartington Experiment', *Architectural Review*, April 1934, p.122.

12 Gerald Heard, *ibid.*

13 Kurt Jooss, the ballet dancer, had visited Dartington in 1934 and returned as a refugee in 1935. The house, 10 The Warren, was built into the steep hillside and had a ballet practice room.

14 Robert Hening, letter to the author, 23.10.72.

15 For Gropius' work in England, see David Elliott, 'Gropius in England: A Documentation 1934-1937' in Charlotte Benton, *A Different World: Emigré Architects in Britain 1928-1958*. London: RIBA Heinz Gallery, 1995.

16 L'Exposition des Arts Décoratifs et Industriels Modernes in Paris (1925) from which the Art Deco style developed; the *Weissenhof Siedlung* at Stuttgart (1927) directed by Mies van der Rohe with buildings by many architects including Le Corbusier and J.J.P. Oud; the Stockholm Exhibition (1930) designed by Erik Gunnar Asplund.

17 For an account of Shrinkhills house, see Peter Wickham, 'Points of Entry - Shrinkhills' in *History Today*, Vol.42 November 1992, pp.62 - 63. Tozer had been Fred Harrild's assistant in the Totnes office. Vitacop so

named because its glass was patent 'Vitaglass' and its (flat) roof of copper. Sunpark is very similar to houses at Hendon and Luton by Simmons & Grellier. The Daily Mail published standard plans of houses, many of which were exhibited at the annual *Ideal Homes Exhibitions* at Olympia, London. For a full list of these houses in Devon and elsewhere, see Jeremy Gould, 'Gazetteer of Modern Houses in the United Kingdom and the Republic of Ireland' in *The Modern House Revisited*. London: The Twentieth Century Society, 1996.

18 Le Corbusier's *Vers une Architecture* was first published in English as *Towards a new Architecture* in 1927 by John Rodker, translated by Frederick Etchells. Gropius' *New Architecture and the Bauhaus* was published by Faber & Faber in 1935.

19 For example at Goodrington, near Paignton; Livermead at Torquay for the Mallock family of Cockington (with some houses designed by Gerald Lacoste at Cockington); at Sweetbriar Lane, Heavitree, Exeter (1933 onwards) also by W.F.R. Ham for T.B. Keate.

20 Henry Wright was one of the founders of the regional planning movement in the United States with his report on Regional Planning for New York State (1926). Wright and Clarence Stein were the planners for Radburn, New Jersey (1929) which advocated a city made up of 'civic nuclei', or neighbourhoods, grouped around the school, playground and swimming pool. Churston Ferrers can be seen as a small Radburn nucleus.

21 The scheme is illustrated in Dean, *The Thirties*, *op.cit.*, p.130 and may be compared with Oliver Hill's Midland Hotel (1932-34) at Morecambe and his project for Frinton-on-Sea (from 1934).

22 From *Churston - South Devon*. Staverton Builders Ltd., 1935. The brochure compares the qualities of the proposal favourably against traditional houses and planning and shows the layout plans of various house types. These are based on High Cross (shown as 'a £4,500 house by the Churston architect') and the photographs illustrate High Cross and its interior as well as the first houses actually built. The project eventually failed through public uncertainty caused by the political situation in Europe and disputes over ownership of land. Only ten houses were built. Curiously, part of the scheme appears to have been finally completed (1958-59) to a layout by Louis de Soissons with O.P. Milne and A. Underhill as architects for the houses. Drawings are in the RIBA Drawings Collection 31/F/21 1-3. These are the houses on Brunel Road/ Broadsands Road corner; those on Tor Close may be contemporary.

23 The Empire Exhibition at Wembley from which the most celebrated survivor is the Wembley Stadium by Simpson.

24 These, in their turn, brought new building types - the petrol filling station and the roadhouse public house. Filling stations could be in any style and were often thatched. Roadhouses, for example, the Countess Weir Hotel at Exeter by Lucas & Roberts of Exeter followed the Arts and Crafts with big gables and tiled roofs. The bus station at Moretonhampstead is 'thirties modern with a rendered front and porthole windows.

25 Archibald Nettlefold owned the Comedy Theatre in London and his wife was an aspirant opera singer. It was she, when widowed in the early 'thirties, who converted it into an hotel. It was much visited by the London 'set'. The hotel was damaged by a wartime bomb and the bay window only partly rebuilt, giving it a more 'thirties look than the original. Information from Tony Porter. Agatha Christie was a visitor and Christopher Nicholson, the architect brother of the painter Ben Nicholson, landed his glider there on 17th April 1938, establishing a British distance record.

26 A.J. Seal was known for his racy, streamlined modern buildings in the Bournemouth and Poole area. His Palace Court Hotel, Bournemouth, although larger than the Queen's, had very similar balconies with glazed screens. See *The Architect & Building News*, 10 January 1936, pp. 65-69. Information from Warren Lever.

27 The others are the Babbacombe Concert Hall (1937-39) and additions to the Pavilion (1939). The additions to the Pavilion were demolished in 1986-87 when the Edwardian structure was restored.

28 The installation was carried out by Pollards Ltd. of London, the leaders in this type of shop fitting. The windows are by Henry Hope and are sherardised (rust-proofed), a very early example of this treatment.

29 Oscar Faber (1886-1956) was one of the leading structural and mechanical engineers of the 'thirties. He was founder of Oscar Faber & Partners and published many books on concrete structures and the heating and ventilating of buildings.

30 Thomson (b.1902) was an Australian and had been partner to Amyas Connell (later of the firm Connell, Ward & Lucas) who had designed the house High and Over (1929) at Amersham, the first reinforced concrete house in England. The stone was provided by Walter Jenkins Ltd. of Torquay who had offices in the building.

31 For other cinemas in Devon and elsewhere, see Richard Grey, *Cinemas in Britain*. London: Lund Humphries, 1996. The perspective drawing (now lost) for the Odeon, Exeter is shown in David Atwell, *Cathedrals of the*

Movies. London: Architectural Press, 1980, p.153.

32 The Tivoli was for Gregory Eastmond and J.E. Hamlin, local entrepreneurs. This and the house, Shrinkhills also for Eastmond (see note 17) were Saunders' only ventures into modernism. Information from Peter Wickham.

33 Anthony Chitty was one of the founder members of Tecton, the leading modern architectural firm of the 'thirties. He had built two timber houses at Churt, Surrey (1935) for Lloyd George. Also various small timber buildings in Devon with Robert Hening including an extension to a workshop at Shinners Bridge, a labourer's cottage and the summer house, all at Dartington, and the Youth Hostel at Lownard. Chitty wrote: '*We gradually became aware of the fact that modern construction and finishes had less margin of safety against weather, decay etc. than more 'traditional' materials...In 1936...some of us felt our work too bald, too ill-finished and in need of enrichment with colour, shadow, modulation and even applied ornament.*' Anthony Chitty, letter to the author, 23.10.72.

34 See *Architectural Review*, September 1938, pp.95-98. The Straight Corporation also developed the airports at Plymouth, Inverness and Ipswich. The buildings at Ipswich by Hening & Chitty are Listed. For the history of Exeter Airport, see Geoff Worrall, *Exeter Airport - In Peace and War*. Exeter: Devon Books, 1988.

36 These are 8 & 9 Warren Lane, Dartington (1938) of painted brick next to similar, but rendered, houses by Lescaze.

LARGE BUILDINGS AND EXETER UNIVERSITY

1 Adams Holden & Pearson specialised in hospital design. The Hospital Board commissioned Percy Adams as early as 1921 but the scheme did not proceed until 1925 when Hengrave House and its land was purchased from Major R.P. Kitson and funds were given by Mrs Ella Rowcroft and her sister, Violet Wills, of the Wills tobacco family. They owned a villa in Torquay and would have known of the Bristol Royal Infirmary. See F.J. Payne, *The History of Torbay Hospital 1844-1980*. League of Friends of the Torbay Hospital, nd. The Chapel was originally designed to be Gothic and drawings now in the RIBA Drawings Collection show the gradual change to the final design.

2 For Ashcombe Tower, see Alan Powers, 'Ashcombe Tower, Devon' in *Country Life*, 12th December 1996, pp.40-43 and *Country Life*, 13th February 1937, pp.172-177. For RMS Orion, see *Architectural Review*, October 1935, pp.130-138 and 155-158. The 'decisive influence' on the choice of architect was Mrs Rayner, née Courtauld.

3 The University became autonymous in 1955. Copies of the University plans are in the University collection. The first plan is less ambitious and uses less of the overall site. There are two fine perspective drawings in the RIBA Drawings Collection (RAN 2/N/3 1-2) which may relate to this scheme showing stone faced Baroque buildings. An undated project for Dartmouth Town Hall (RAN 3/I/1) is also at the RIBA. The continuing influence of Lutyens on Harris may be seen at the Bristol Council House (from 1938) with entrance pavilions borrowed from Thiepval and the Viceroy's House.

4 The only example in Devon is the addition to Mothecombe House (1922-25) for Alfred Mildmay. The Mildmay family also owned Flete.

THE MODERN CHURCH

1 Very little has been written on the architecture of the new churches of this period. The best contemporary references are *Fifty Modern Churches*. London: Incorporated Church Building Society, 1947 and *Sixty Post-War Churches*. London: Incorporated Church Building Society, 1956. See also Neil Bingham, Elain Harwood, Kenneth Powell, Alan Powers, *The Twentieth Century Church*. London: RIBA Heinz Gallery/The Twentieth Century Society (Exhibition Catalogue), 1997.

2 Keble Martin (1877-1969) better known as author of *Flora of Devon* (1939) and *The Concise British Flora in Colour* (1965). The architect was his brother, Arthur Martin of London. The length, breadth and height of the church are 1000 inches complying with the proportions of the city of Revelation 21.16. See *The Dream Church*, brochure of St. Luke's Milber, nd.

3 This is by no means a complete survey of the modern churches of Devon. Edward Maufe designed St. George, Goodrington (1939-62) at Paignton derived from Lethaby and the Arts and Crafts. Also by de Soissons (under the name of Louis de Soissons, Peacock, Hodges, Robertson & Fraser) is St. Teresa, Efford (1958, now derelict) and the Baptist Church, Crownhill, both Plymouth; Walls & Pearn's St. Margaret Mary (1959), Plymstock is outstanding with its strong, concrete framing and stone infill; Christ the King (1961-62)

Armada Way, Plymouth was built posthumously to a design by Giles Gilbert Scott in brick; St. James, Stoke Hill (1955) in Exeter by Gordon Jackson & Partners is also brick with a concrete structure.

4 See *The Twentieth Century Church*, op.cit. Sir John Ninian Comper (1864-1960) trained in the office of George Frederick Bodley who, in turn, was a pupil of Sir Gilbert Scott. St. Philip (1937) had a central altar.

5 The Astor window by Piper and Patrick Reyntiens was completed in 1958. Further windows followed in 1965. Hans Feibusch (b.1898, Frankfurt-am-Main) came to England in 1933. See, David Coke (ed.), *Hans Feibusch - The Heat of Vision*. London: Lund Humphries, 1995. The St. Sidwell's mural is *Christ in Glory* (1957-58), with the artist and family lower left, and George Street Baptist Church, *Baptism of Christ* (1960). The west window of St. Sidwell's is by Hugh Patterson, the principal of Bideford School of Art.

THE PLANS FOR PLYMOUTH AND EXETER

1 Maxwell Fry, *Fine Building*. London: Faber & Faber, 1944, p.44-45. Fry was chairman of the MARS (Modern Architectural Research) Group who had presented their plan for London. He is writing of London, but the remarks are clearly aimed at any large town in England.

2 Ralph Tubbs, *Living in Cities*. Harmondsworth: Penguin, 1942, p.18. Tubbs was a member of the RIBA Reconstruction Committee and secretary of MARS. The book was a sequel to the 1940 travelling exhibition 'Living in Cities'.

3 See Le Corbusier and P. Jeanneret, *Oeuvre Complete 1934-38*. Zurich: Girsberger, 1945. Most of Le Corbusier's work of this period involved town planning and the insertion of major new *quartiers* into old cities - Rio de Janeiro, Paris, Nemours, Algiers etc. Frederick Etchells' translations of Le Corbusier's *Urbanisme* (*The City of Tomorrow*) had been published in 1929.

4 The CPRE was founded in 1926. Important to it was Clough Williams-Ellis' treatise *England and the Octopus*. London: Geoffrey Bles, 1928 which was an emotive attack on the uncontrolled spread of towns. Patrick Abercrombie, Honorary Secretary to the CPRE, wrote an 'Apologica' to the book. The *Architectural Review* published many articles on the subject. For example, 'Cry stop to Havoc' in *Architectural Review*, May 1935, showing Gropius & Fry's proposals for flats on St. Leonard's Hill, Windsor and Christopher Tunnard's 'The Case for the Common Garden' in *Architectural Review*, September 1938, pp.109-116 showing the redevelopment for Claremont Park.

5 J. Paton Watson and Patrick Abercrombie, *The Plan for Plymouth*. Plymouth: Underhill, 1943. The Plan covered the suburbs of Plymouth and Devonport but this essay will discuss the city centre only. The politics of the Plan are well described in Brian Chalkey and John Goodridge, 'The 1943 Plan for Plymouth: War-Time Vision and Post-War Realities' in Brian Chalkey, David Dunkerley, Peter Gripaios, *Plymouth - Maritime City in Transition*. David & Charles, 1991. For Abercrombie's theories on planning, see Partrick Abercrombie, *Town and Country Planning*. Oxford University Press, 1933 (2nd edn., 1943). Abercrombie was professor of town planning at University College and was working simultaneously on plans for London, Hull, Edinburgh, the Clyde and the West Midlands. He was influenced by the Garden City Movement (Sir Frederick Osborn was a friend), was an advocate of regional and local zoning and an early promoter of the bypass to relieve city centres of through traffic. He was a member of the Barlow Commission on industrial population (1937, published 1945) which exposed the conditions of urban concentrations and greatly influenced Town Planning legislation for towns and cities. Abercrombie had been professor of civic design at Liverpool University (1915-35) which had strong connections with America.

6 The War Memorial (1920-24) by Sir Robert Lorimer to a standard design was previously concealed from the city side by a terrace of houses. The Memorial was extended by Edward Maufe after the War.

7 John A. Brodie, the City Engineer of Liverpool, was on the New Delhi Planning Commission (1912) and it is probable that Abercrombie knew of the early plans. Abercrombie, together with C.H. Reilly and S.D. Adshead his co-editors of *Town Planning Review*, published a critical review of the New Delhi plan in 1913. See Robert Grant Irving, *Indian Summer - Lutyens, Baker and Imperial Delhi*. London and New Haven: Yale University Press, 1981. pp.143 ff. Coincidentally, the topography of the main axes at Plymouth (Armada Way) and New Delhi (Kings Way) are similar in that views are hidden by the undulating contours.

8 Abercrombie, *The Plan for Plymouth, op.cit.*, p.77.

9 For the Glasgow Exhibition see, J. Neil Baxter, 'Thomas S. Tait and the Glasgow Empire Exhibition 1938' in *The Thirties Society Journal*, No.4 (1984), pp.26-30. There were existing examples of Tait's pylons in front of St. Andrew's House, Edinburgh (1936-39).

10 The perspective drawing submitted with the Planning Application in March 1946 is by J.D.M. Harvey. The podium was built first and the upper floors added from 1947 onwards. The concrete cladding was partly used because bricks were in short supply but Sir John Burnet Tait & Lorne had used precast concrete on their flats at Amhurst Road, Hackney (1933-34).

11 Norwich City Hall (1932-38) by C.H. James and S. Rowland Pierce. Nikolaus Pevsner (*Buildings of England - North East Norfolk and Norwich*. Penguin, 1962, p.260) identifies its portico as derived from Ivar Tengbom and the façade from Ragnar Östberg. He states that '*Norwich City Hall is likely to go down in history as the foremost English public building of between the wars.*'

12 Willem Marinus Dudok (1884-1974) was municipal architect of Hilversum where he built many major buildings including the Town Hall (1928-31). He was awarded the Royal Gold Medal for Architecture in 1935. His work was very influential in England in the 'thirties particularly on Sir John Burnet Tait & Lorne. For example, their Hammersmith School for Girls, Curzon Cinema in Mayfair, Royal Masonic Hospital and Paisley Hospital for Infectious Diseases.

13 William Crabtree was a graduate of Liverpool University where he was taught by Patrick Abercrombie. Crabtree won the competition for the Peter Jones Department Store, Chelsea (1933-35) which he executed in association with Slater & Moberley and Professor Charles H. Reilly, professor of architecture at Liverpool. He was also planner for Southampton (1944-45).

14 The buildings completed by 1952 are illustrated in *Architects' Journal* 12 June 1952, pp.716-732. This includes most of Royal Parade, Old Town Street and New George Street. Other Royal Parade buildings are: Spooners by Healing & Overbury of Cheltenham; Pophams by Easton & Robertson, Cusdin Preston & Smith of London. Old Town Street buildings are: Marks & Spencer by Lewis & Hickey; Burtons by N. Martin. New George Street buildings are: W.H. Smith by W.G. Norris; Woolworths by H. Winbourne; six shops east of Woolworths by W.H. Watkins & Partners; shops to the west of Woolworths by De Metz & Birks, Percy V. Burnett & Partners and Taylor & Bracken.

15 Examples of buildings by Tait in this style are Adelaide House, London Bridge (1920-25), St. Andrew's House, Edinburgh (1936-39) and the pylons for the Sydney Harbour Bridge (1925). Tait's work of this period is discussed in a Scottish context in 'The Architecture of 'Mass': Burnet, Tait and the Beaux-Arts Legacy' in Miles Glendinning, Ranald MacInnes, Aonghus MacKechnie, *A History of Scottish Architecture*. Edinburgh University Press, 1996, pp.394-400. This traces Tait's architectural connections back to Alexander Thomson and via his brother-in-law and office manager, Gordon Farquhar, to the Chicago office of Raymond Hood. Lorne too had worked in America and in the 'forties became the chief architect to the Anglo American Corporation in Johannesburg. The firm had designed its headquarters in the late 'thirties in a style similar to the Plymouth buildings. The pylon-ends of St. Andrew's House are very similar to the towers of Dingles and Pearl Assurance.

16 Erich Mendelsohn (1887-1953) with his Schocken Department Store, Stuttgart (1927). Tait was an admirer of Mendelsohn's work and awarded him first prize in the competition for the De La Warr Pavilion in 1934. See Russell Stevens and Peter Willis, 'Earl De La Warr and the competition for the Bexhill Pavilion, 1933-34' in *Architectural History*, Vol.33 (1990).

17 The Museum of Modern Art by A. Aubert, J.C. Dondel, M. Dastugue and P. Viard - one of the permanent buildings from the International Exhibition of that year.

18 The office of the City Architect produced other interesting buildings. For example, the Building & Engineering Block of the Technical College (1954), Ernesettle Residential Care Home (1955) and the Woolster Street Flats (1956, now Vauxhall Street) amongst many others.

19 Stockwell Garage (1953), London by Adie, Button & Partners and Brynmawr, South Wales (1951) by the Architects' Co-Partnership. Other interesting structures include the Whitleigh Footbridge, Plymouth (1950-53, demolished) by Denys Lasdun of Drake & Lasdun and Oscar Faber's Grain Silo (1941-43) in Milbay Docks described by Pevsner (*Devon*, 1st. edn.) as *'a secularised Albi Cathedral'*. The first three are illustrated in Trevor Dannatt, *Modern Architecture in Britain*. London: Batsford, 1959.

20 Sharp had been an academic and had worked for the Ministry of Town & Country Planning but had entered private practice in 1945. He was to prepare plans for Oxford, Salisbury and many other smaller towns.

21 Thomas Sharp, *Exeter Phœnix*. London: The Architectural Press, 1946, p.109. Again, this essay discusses the proposals for the city centre only.

22 For example, Maxwell Fry's Ramsay Hall for London University and Ralph Tubbs' YMCA Indian Students' Union and Hostel (1951-54) in Fitzroy Square, London. This was a larger version of Erno Goldfinger's

houses at Willow Road, Hampstead (1937-39) for which Tubbs made the drawings. Its publication in the *Architectural Review* in April 1940 made it a very influential building for young architects who were otherwise engaged.

23 The architects for Princesshay are: north side - Percy V. Burnett & Partners (Bedford Street end); Jack E. Dalling of London (adjacent to arcade); Lionel H. Fewster & Partners of London (east end and High Street block). South side: P. Morrey & L. Blease of London (Bedford Street end); Jack E. Dalling; Redfern & Gilpin of Exeter for Hughes Garage (east end). Eastgate House (1957) is by J.E. Dalling.

24 Lucas Roberts & Brown's shops were Willsons and Wymans and were designed before the conversion of Colsons. The rear of Colsons has a curved corner similar to that of Alec French. Colsons and Willsons & Wymans were united in 1961 by Beech & Curnow Cooke to form what is now Dingles.

25 This contrasts with their Barclays Bank, Plymouth (1949-52) on the corner of Armada Way and Notte Street which is neo-Classical in Portland stone, illustrated in *Architects' Journal* 12 June 1952, p.728. The original perspective (now lost) shows a five storey building but the upper storeys were not completed. The banking hall in Exeter is now obscured with recent decoration and only the diagonal entrance gives a hint of the quality of detail which has been lost.

26 McMorran worked for Vincent Harris from 1927-35 when he left to form his own practice in London. The shortlist of architects recommended by the president of the RIBA, Howard Robertson, was McMorran (of Farquharson & McMorran), Messrs. Denman & Sons of Brighton, Julian Leathart of Sunningdale, Sir Hubert Worthington of Manchester, S. Rowland Pierce of London and Louis de Soissons. Information from Devon County Council. Vincent Harris had won the Royal Gold Medal in 1951 and one assumes that his voice was influential. The partner-in-charge for County Hall was George Whitby.

27 Ragnar Östberg's Stockholm Town Hall (1911-1923) which is composed around two courtyards. McMorran's use of Doulting stone to the rear wall of the Council Chamber and timber panelling elsewhere in 'stonework' patterns is similar to decorative schemes by Erik Gunnar Asplund, for example at his City Library, Stockholm (1920-28).

28 The University at Aarhus (from 1932) by Kay Fisker, C.F. Møller and Povl Stegmann is in yellow brick set in parkland. Holford's job architect, Bernard Cadd, had been visiting student at the Royal Danish Academy in the early 1950s. The Holford groups of buildings closely resemble the block plans of Aarhus in their geometry and relationship to the contours. The Assembly Hall (post-War, by C.F. Møller) has similar windows, pitched roofs and a very similar curved screen wall to the Queen's Building. Also important was Alvar Aalto's MIT Senior Dormitory (1947-48) at Cambridge, Mass. also of brick with a regular pattern of small rectangular windows.

Dartington - A Modern Adventure

David Jeremiah

NEW SOCIETY - NEW LANDSCAPE

> If you are in the neighbourhood of Dartington Hall during the summer you should not fail to see this unusual experiment in operation. Conducted tours of the Estate afford you an opportunity of spending an enjoyable morning or afternoon in a particularly beautiful corner of Devon and at the same time of extending your knowledge of the countryside, its produce and crafts.[1]

Such was the invitation extended to readers of the *Rural Industries Quarterly Magazine*, Winter 1935. Beautiful Devon, with its coastline and moor, cathedral city and historic naval port, now had a new major tourist attraction.[2] A modernized country house estate, that owed something to the spirit of the model industrial villages and garden city movement of the late nineteenth century, the Dartington experiment was more than unusual, it was unique (Fig. 65).

In the ten years since its founders, Leonard and Dorothy Elmhirst,[3] had discovered the derelict hall and its estate, it had grown into a utopian vision of Britain. There were new farms and new methods of farming, a new school, a gardens department, a sawmill, a textile mill, the largest building company in the south-west, a retail shop and growing mail-order list, working class housing estates and executive housing, craft workshops, dance and theatre companies, and artists. It had completed a programme of restoration, and moved from arts and crafts, neo-Georgian, to modernist architectural styles. There were new roads, new services, and a new sports field for the estate cricket and football teams. It was with good reason that it was seen to have grown from a derelict estate 'into what is probably the most modernized and widely-known square mile in the British Isles'.[4]

From the picturesque ruin of Francis Bedford's *Devonshire Illustrated* (Fig 66), Dartington had become the image of progress and the icon of the progressive. Little of the original enterprises has survived, but walking the landscape continues to provide a good way of exploring the meanings of the Dartington reconstruction.

When, on 4 March 1925, Leonard Elmhirst, armed with the Land Agent's notes on the historic associations of the Hall, drove tentatively up a Devon lane he was travelling back in time. The modern world was about to encounter medieval England, hidden behind Victorian taste and contemporary decay. Not that Dartington Hall had missed the beginning of the technological revolution, after all it had a garage for three cars, it had simply been left behind.

At the time that Leonard discovered Dartington Hall, he and Dorothy Whitney Straight had been edging towards marriage. Leonard, then in his early thirties, still had no obvious career pattern, other than that he knew he did not wish to become a parson, and had a prolonged interest in agriculture and good works. Dorothy, widowed since 1918, with three young children, remained uncertain what to do with her wealth and life. United by a desire to add meaning to their lives, the construction of Dartington was the means for its realisation, Leonard through management, Dorothy through creative experiences.

Secluded on three quarters of its boundaries by rivers and extensive woodland, its intimacy was even more pronounced in the 1920s. The road from neighbouring Totnes had not been constructed, and the route from Dartington village was a single track un-made road. The original estate had been dismembered in three separate sales in July 1919, October 1920 and June 1921. The contents of the Hall had been sold off in December 1921,and the property and estate, with its two surviving farms, had subsided into further decline. It was an extreme example of the widespread problem of the British rural depression. Not quite a wilderness, the estate was sufficiently decayed to stimulate the imagination, it offered an 'old world atmosphere'[5] and economic potential. It was out of 'easy reach of a big industrial town',[6] but had good communication links with the GWR line from Paddington to Penzance, stopping at Newton Abbot and Totnes, ideally meeting its social and commercial needs.

The estate offered the opportunity to experiment in the practicalities of the everyday. Its landscape was the stuff of an English romance. Leonard's first reaction was to speak of it as a 'fairyland', Dorothy described it as 'heavenly', while one of their first American visitors, overwhelmed by the place, recalled it as 'a true Alice in Wonderland experience'.[7] This perception of stepping into and out of real time played an important part in the lifestyle of Dartington, and in its representation of a new society.

Formed and protected by the Elmhirsts' patronage, the experiment in rural reconstruction never achieved the commercial viability and economic independence that was expected, but it was a new model that brought the arts and industry together in a way that could not be ignored by the contemporary planners and politicians. As a social experiment it was about England, the decay of English rural society, and Leonard's belief in the need to generate a new and revitalised role for the Country House estate in modern society. Started at a time of industrial unrest and economic uncertainty, Leonard saw Dartington as a scheme,

> wrapped up in the breakdown in England of the big estates as economic units, not because the unit is unsound, but for external reasons -attack on the privileges of landlords by Lloyd George's Death Duties - the war - breakdown of inherited responsibility- and our feeling that instead of breaking up these estates they should be given a new social sanction, with a sounder economic basis, organised as industrial units and companies, and no longer depend on death of owner or agent. Dartington Hall stands for the exploration of a new technique of land management through-
>
> (a) Land Holding Company or Land Trust
>
> (b) Operating Company which rents to tenants or pays managers, or operates a Federal or a Cooperative Farming system.[8]

In this way he sought reform, without being a revolutionary. Although he was associated with socialist thinkers and ideals, Leonard determinedly sustained a position of political neutrality for himself and Dartington, and secured a far more conservative social framework for the estate than might at first seem the case.

Dartington's history falls broadly into three phases, the early years, post-war reconstruction, and the post-founder years. This account is primarily concerned with the early years, and the manner in which the arts, crafts, design and architecture were used to develop and represent the new society.

As a Trust, Dartington had six organisational divisions dominated at one extreme by Dartington Hall Ltd., and at the other by Education and the Arts Department. Heavily dependent on friends and a long list of recommended professionals for advice, in practice the arts and education were for Dorothy, industry and agriculture for Leonard. At times Dartington operated in the manner of a large company, but more often drifted between federalism and an enlightened monarchy. The Hall was at the centre of the enterprise (Fig 67).

> Everything is going well with us here. We have a gorgeous old place which we are gradually converting into a school, and losing none of the old character of the surroundings I think in doing so. There is an endless amount of renovating and restoring still to be done, and of course, we have only just begun to touch the garden and general surroundings.[9]

When the process of restoration began in 1925, the Elmhirsts never envisaged that they would embark on the large scale building development that became Dartington. The estate offered the pre-industrial pastoral landscape of woodlands, pasture, orchards and riverside. In the process of modernization, the Elmhirsts were anxious not to lose its beauty, but utilise it in the creation of a rural paradise. There was no plan, in the sense of a prepared 'town' plan, but critical to the overall development was the desire to protect the immediate landscape of the Hall.

Initially the modernisation of the Parsonage and the private house of the Hall had little direct impact on the landscape, but as Sir Henry Tanner[10] began a restoration programme on the interior and external elevations of the Hall, effectively removing the Victorian modifications, one of the most popular images of Dartington started to take shape. With the deserved attention given to the restoration of the Great Hall, the importance of the structural changes to the private house are sometimes overlooked. A conservatory was removed and replaced by a loggia, the nineteenth century Gothic porch pulled down and the front wall of the extension raised to hide the roof. But, most important of all, it was the replacement of all the windows and insertion of new windows in the basement to create a library that authenticated a twentieth century reinterpretation. It introduced a new order and spatial simplicity that has become the hallmark of the Hall complex and gardens (Fig. 68, 69).

With Avray Tipping[11] to advise on the gardens, William Weir[12] on the Great Hall, and Rex Gardner[13] on the general building programme, Dartington initially aligned itself with those commited to the movement for the preservation of Rural England. It was Leonard with his need for a modern farm that brought the first major changes to the Dartington landscape.

The first moves to restore the Hall courtyard had been implemented with the removal of the Barton, or Home Farm, into a new farmhouse built on adjacent land.[14] At the same time pressure was being put on the tenant farmers of Shinners Bridge Farm, until eventually they moved out, leaving the farmhouse to be restored and the site to be exploited for industrial and commercial purposes. To replace it a new neo-Georgian farmhouse by Oswald Milne,[15] was built next to the Parsonage, along with new farm buildings for modern farming methods. It was with these agricultural buildings and the digging up of hedgerows to convert fifteen fields into Dartington's own prairie that the estate encountered the first large-scale changes to its landscape. Traditional and modern farms now faced each other across the Dartington landscape.

The restoration of the Great Hall, and redesigning of its gardens and courtyard were the Elmhirsts' most satisfying projects and enduring legacy. The result of rewarding personal relationships, involving the contributions of William Weir, Beatrix Farrand[16] and Elizabeth Peacock,[17] it produced the image most readily associated with the new Dartington, a harmony of traditional and modern expression at its most English (Figs. 70, 71, 94).

At the outset Dartington had declared its ambition to see the Hall revived as a 'dynamic centre for the hamlets and villages of the immediate neighbourhood',[18] but increasingly preoccupied with its own identity, this objective was not given the attention that the neighbours might have expected.[19] As the Dartington village witnessed the expansion it was to find itself distanced from the pleasures of the new age. There was a continuing recognition of the importance of the new jobs created by the estate, but also the limited local patronage. Approaches from the managers of the local village school received a minimal response and as the new estate buildings surrounded the school and the prefabricated village hall, the differences of privilege were exposed.

In the first instance the scale of development was in a distinctly rural English tradition, with Rex Gardner's designs for workers cottages, the redesigning of Shinners Bridge Farmhouse, the cottage conversions of stables and cowsheds at Lownard and a barn conversion at Yarner (Figs. 72, 73). He was to design a thatched nursery school adjacent to the hall, and a bothy with six bedrooms for the Garden Department. However, events were changing around him.

Having opened the first Boarding School for boys and girls, aged between 8 - 14, in the Hall courtyard, two years later, in November 1928, plans were being prepared by Rex Gardner for a new school building, 100' x 30', that was to include study rooms, a workshop, a science room and garden house. The intention was to use 'all the natural materials for teaching that the Estate offers in such a way that visiting teachers can themselves see how to link up the education of the Village school with all that is going on round them.'[20]

But, even as this announcement was being made, Dorothy's attention had already turned towards the creation of a different kind of school. Based on work that she had seen in America, it would act as a research centre for child education and the development of knowledge for nursery school practice and parents. Consequently the new building was abandoned, leaving the existing school in the courtyard.[21] At the beginning of 1929 planning for a nursery school and kindergarten at Aller Park commenced under the direction of the American architect, Van der Gracht.[22]

Marking the beginning of Dartington's monumental phase of architecture, during which the search was on for the most effective architectural expression of its ideals, it created the first major change in the social framework of Dartington. A decisive moment in the formation of the new society, it broke with the original concept of education and community. Vaguely Tudor revival in style and on a grand country house scale, the Aller Park School had some wonderful interior details, including highly colourful mosaic bathrooms, and inspiring fireplaces, but the layout and setting was institutional rather than domestic (Figs. 74, 82, 83).

This development in Park Lane set in motion an escalating battle of styles that almost ran out of control. It may be argued that there was a tenuous link between the original cottage style boarding houses by Fincham at the head of the lane, and the new school, but the siting and design of the three modernist boarding houses, 1934-37, by Lescaze made no pretence at continuity (Fig. 28).[23] It was an argumentative piece of planning, and not altogether convincing in its lessons on the new social order. At the other end of the estate Leonard had his English model school, neo-Georgian collegiate, designed by Oswald Milne (Fig. 79).

Despite a never-ending sequence of change, which at times involved disconnected and conflicting projects, one of Dartington's central ideals concerned the well being of the modern family and the freedom of children. Expressed in terms of home comforts and the means for a new lifestyle, even as the 'new' was being embraced established social models were replicated in the designs. For example, determined to provide all its employees with the opportunities to 'build for themselves and their children an abundant life through education, recreation, and the creative use of leisure', the housing programme continued to follow the conventions associated with professional and working class provision.[24] Similarly, while moving to a radical stance on education, the school boarding houses utilised the 'nanny' model, arranged around a housemother, rather than houseparents.

The commitment to improve the quality of life, owed much to American ideas on modern living with their emphasis on efficiency and household management. Leonard and Dorothy had arrived at Dartington with knowledge of Cornell's developing interest in home economics, and in June 1928 a start was made on an apprenticeship scheme, opening a training centre for domestic science at the Parsonage, with eight girls from the locality. Leonard was keen to develop this project on the latest American lines, and at the same time have American-style kitchens installed at Dartington.

So a start was made; Leonard invited his Cornell contact, Alice Blinn, who was working for the Delineator Home Institute in New York, to design the Dartington kitchens and their new domestic 'training centre'. She visited the estate in the summer, 1928, preparing designs and a report on a range of Home Economics initiatives. Commenting on higher and elementary education, apprenticeships, and a household equipment laboratory that would work with manufacturers testing 'household labour-saving equipment', there was even a proposal for a 'Demonstration Cottage' for students to practise and visitors to observe, to 'be built on a strictly modern plan of house planning - modern kitchen and equipment, modern laundry and equipment, bath and plumbing, etc.'[25] The model American home, and lessons in home-making, appeared to be destined for the Dartington estate. But, unable to persuade Blinn or any of her contacts to come over to run the training centre, interest waned and before the end of its second year it was closed as being uneconomic.

Despite this setback, Blinn designed the kitchen and cafeteria for the school, her ideas of domestic efficiency and home management were imposed on Milne's design for Foxhole's school, and it was Leonard's hope to see them introduced into Lescaze's High Cross House for Bill Curry, the new headmaster.[26] The intention was to incorporate a demonstration kitchen designed by Alice Blinn, which in layout and equipment would employ the latest American thinking and be used as a showhouse by Staverton Builders[27] as British agents for the product range. An extraordinary idea, it came to nothing as the headmaster's wife disliked the proposed design, even though she wanted the waffle iron, food mixer and dishwasher. In the end American innovation was 'combined with typically English arrangements'.[28]

Against the national housing crisis, the urban slums and primitive conditions of rural housing, Dartington's record holds up well. Even so its interpretation of living spaces and siting of buildings sustained the conventional social order, the executive houses contrasting with the worker's cottages. For example, in Warren Lane the Lescaze house for Kurt Jooss[29] with its dance studio, servants' rooms, nursery and beautiful view, is set alongside the modernist workers' cottages, with their living/dining rooms and backyards.

The workers' housing shows Dartington trying to interpret government guidelines on the minimum housing requirements, particularly on questions of the location and facilities of bathrooms, and the number of living rooms. Cottages designed by Gardner in 1928 were criticised for lack of space, but Dartington continued to opt for a minimum standard. From the Milne cottages of 1931, with parlour and living room, and a bathroom with washbasin, the accommodation at Huxhams Cross and Broom Park designed by Louis de Soissons[30] was reduced to one living room, and the bathroom to a bath and WC. It would seem that Leonard was reassured that working-class people much prefered to get washed in the kitchen.[31]

The siting of these workers' cottages on the edges of the estate have raised comments that are worth further consideration. There had been a point in 1930 when things might have turned out differently. De Soissons had been invited to carry out a survey and formulate recommendations on the estate's housing needs, and in May 1930 he provided the Elmhirsts with a preliminary indication of his ideas on the location of the 'Village'.[32] Estimating that Dartington had some 300 workers of whom two thirds were in the Building Department, he thought it necessary to provide 200 new houses. Initially there had been no intention of creating this large workforce, it had simply grown out of Leonard's desire to keep the ever expanding building programme out of local hands. The task now was to stabilise this development through new housing, anticipating that it would generate a commitment to the culture and life of the country house estate.

At the beginning of June de Soissons' survey was presented as a detailed report. It argued against using the land immediately adjacent to Totnes as it was thought possible that the workers would have divided loyalties between the town and the estate. The preferred choice was for the housing development to take place further along the road at Shinners Bridge, using the existing Dartington village around which to establish 'a real home village under the influence of Dartington and loyal to its purpose'.[33] De Soissons recommended that the Elmhirsts should buy the hamlets of Yarner and Week to ensure that the proposed development would benefit the Estate and complement the home area that was Dartington Hall.

By March 1931 the recommended purchases had been completed, but the village concept was never developed. Instead Dartington opted for two new workers' housing estates isolated on the fringes of the estate, at Huxhams Cross and Broom Park (Fig. 75). The village, with its school, village hall, almshouses and shop, became the focus for the industry, retail and administration of Dartington Hall Ltd. Considering that Shinners Bridge was the junction of the Exeter and Plymouth roads, it seems likely that with the steady expansion of motorised transport it was seen to offer the best location for Dartington's commercial activities. It also overcame any lingering anxieties over questions of the workers' loyalty to the estate, and protected the inner heartland from further erosion.

For good economic reasons Dartington also found itself in a position to consider building utopian landscapes in other parts of the south-west (Fig. 76). Making efforts to provide long term security for its building department, Dartington began negotiations for the purchase of building land which within three years resulted in the development of five separate sites for domestic housing, four on the coast and one on the edge of Exeter (Figs. 21, 31, 77). Colonisation of rural Devon was underway, with Leonard believing that they would 'make an outstanding contribution to seaside residential planning'.[34] As events turned out it resulted in a range of speculative housing projects which in scale, design and location were to expose Dartington to public criticism, dividing opinion on the estate, and undermining the economics of its operations.

Intent on selling the good life in a beautiful landscape, Dartington had seriously underestimated the growing support for and strength of the conservationist movement through the work of the Council for the Preservation of Rural England. Even the formation of the Devon branch of CPRE at a meeting in Torquay in November 1930, registered no effect on their plans. Convinced of their good intentions, and the quality of their architectural design, Dartington felt immune from criticism. This was to prove to be a costly mistake, and only one of their housing schemes, that at Cliff Park, Paignton, was to be completed to anything like the original plan.

It was the scheme at Churston, a short distance along the coast, which was to create the greatest discomfort. Originating out of the contact with Milne, in June 1932 de Soissons was invited to visit the Churston site and produce a plan for its development. Dartington finalised the purchase in July and submitted de Soissons' plans to Totnes Rural District Council in October.

At this stage the intention was to have a café, bathing huts, a semi-permanent camp of twenty chalets, ornamental and paddling pools, a site for camping and guest houses. The domestic houses were zoned according to cost, offering three types of houses. The plan was approved on the understanding that there would be houses of a cottage class for those 'who will be employed as garden labourers, chauffeurs and wage earners in connection with cafés and shops'.[35]

De Soissons continued to work on the designs for the cottages, and the first twenty received approval in June 1933. What neither the authority nor de Soissons knew was that in January 1933 the plan for Churston had been attacked by Lescaze, who, after a meeting with Leonard, had been invited to produce an alternative scheme (Fig. 31). There had also been discussions with Gropius.[36]

When, two weeks after local authority approval had been given for the cottage designs, news of a change of plan and architect reached the local press, the first signs of local disquiet at the scale of the development broke out. On 8 July 1933, the *Totnes Times and Devon News* carried a report of Lescaze's interview with the *New York Herald-Tribune*, detailing how an American architect was to build a new town of 400 modern houses on a 200 acre waterfront site in Devonshire.

The functional modern architecture attracted criticism, but was not the major issue. Devon was losing a stretch of unspoilt coastline that still provided the opportunity for bathing in rural surroundings. The fact that it was American money and now an

American architect that was seen to be imposing this plan on rural Devon made matters worse. Dartington made great efforts to play down the American contribution, but the damage had been done. Its vision had been seduced by Lescaze who had misunderstood the lessons of High Cross (Fig. 27).[37]

A brief but vigorous exchange of letters in the local press, brought to the surface all the disquiet over the loss of extended areas of natural coastline. The proposed new land development on the River Dart at Dittisham, the industrial building at Staverton as well as the buildings on the Dartington estate all came in for criticism.

In defence of Churston, Dartington explained that they were going Continental, drawing on the lessons of the South of France to ensure that the estate was a true part of the English Riviera. At the same time it was intended to apply lessons learnt from the American experience by providing labour-saving layout and equipment for those who could no longer afford domestic servants. Landscaped, with traffic free walks, it was an estate considered to be ideal for the retired civil servant, ex-naval and army officers, retired business people and public officials.

Their defence was far from convincing, and not only did it damage the commercial viability of the project, but divisions on the Dartington estate were opened, with Staverton Builders being blamed for the fiasco. Not unexpectedly the company pointed out that the scheme was very much influenced by the Trustees, who should have realised that no matter how carefully the development had been planned, an area of great natural beauty would be spoiled. As Trustees, the blame was being directed back at the Elmhirsts.

Considerable efforts were made to unify support for the development and with its modernism under attack, Lescaze was brought over at the end of 1934, to present a paper on 'Why we have adopted Modern Architecture'. This went some way towards reassuring the estate, but the commercial prospects showed no improvement. By February 1935 only six houses had been sold, and the plan for a new hotel on the headland had failed to attract any investors. For a scheme that had the potential for up to 500 houses, it was an alarming position to be in. It was also confusing.

In High Cross, Dartington had a design that was selected to represent the latest development of domestic architecture in the *Architectural Review*'s 'Progress of Architecture in England for the Twentieth Century', in April 1934. The following month it was on the front cover of *Design For Today*, and referenced in Thomas Sharp's essay 'The Changing Landscape', as the expression of modern civilization in a changing landscape.

Reassured, Dartington decided that its problems were the outcome of a local conspiracy instigated by local businesses and the Church because of its aversion to the progressive stance of the school. Certainly Dartington had its opponents, but the economic reality was that the houses on the new estates were substantially more expensive than those of their competitors. Starting prices were from £1260, when the majority of new home owners were looking for houses priced between £500-£800. The fact was that Dartington was building an estate on a scale for which the market did not exist, and on a site which continued to attract criticism. Unfortunately it was an experience repeated across all of their land development schemes, with Dartington torn between experimenting and producing ready sales.

Having built the first six houses at Churston, but with no signs of improved sales, a decision was taken to modify the design, and produce a sales brochure explaining the benefits of the site and the pleasures of living in Devon. A place 'where the winds are warmer and the sun more generous', and where 'architecture is as it should be', the claim that the houses would soon become part of the landscape was difficult to believe.[38] The graphics created an image of the romance of the Devon coastline, but the photography of the existing houses, exposed on the hillside, instantly defeated the argument (Figs. 31, 78). The clumsiness of the siting and crude formal massing were all too visible. As with the Central Offices and modern houses on the Dartington estate, they could offer arts and crafts gardens designed by Beatrix Farrand, but these did little to hide the limitations of Lescaze's design. The final appeal was to offer a share in the Dartington ideal, suggesting that in buying a Dartington house, built by local labour with local materials, new home-owners would be contributing to Dartington's commitment to rural reconstruction.

None of these manoeuvres improved sales and panic over the economic failure of the project began to impact on Dartington's every move. In a last attempt to save the dream, de Soissons was re-engaged to design twelve houses. These were approved in March 1936, and subsequently de Soissons was asked to design some semi-detached houses and to develop a revised plan for the estate. The final move was taken in February 1938 when approval was given for 'pitched roof houses to be built in the Flat Roof Area, and also for thatched cottages in the area below the viaduct'.[39] Brought to a standstill by the second world war, and with no chance of reviving the plans in the period of post-war restrictions, in June 1945 Dartington sold the land to Paignton District Council. By commercial miscalculation and world events, rather more of the Devon coastline had been preserved than might have been originally expected.

The Dittisham development was just as problematic. A questionable venture from the start, Dartington was aware that the National Trust was trying to raise money to buy the headland. Persisting with its purchase, the attraction was to build dream houses in the Devon landscape, on sites that were 'virgin in their sun-bathed and open aspects and in their scenic surroundings'.[40]

De Soissons was the architect, and the speculative housing made well-planned conventional use of the site. But, even with a thatched roof alternative, the houses proved difficult to sell. The problem this time was not architectural style. A beautiful site, it was substantially inaccessible with an inadequate ferry and surrounded by single track unpaved roads. Electricity had yet to reach the village. To open up the area to new development Dartington needed close collaboration with the County Council and service industries, and this was not forthcoming. In an attempt to exploit the commercial possibilities of the site, the original manor house had been opened as a Guest House, but by 1938 efforts were being made to sell it and the substantial areas of undeveloped headland.

These continuing difficulties were not widely known, and at a national level opinions on Dartington's experiments remained positive. The architectural press consistently provided Dartington with good copy and images to match, praising the simple expressions of purpose seen in High Cross and Foxhole, and remaining enthusiastic over Dartington's pursuit of the 'Ideal Unit', its modern spirit, its modernity.[41] The traditionalists appreciated the romantic idealism of Dartington and the architectural landscape that had created a 'paradise' for the children (Fig. 79).[42] Even the workers estates and speculative building projects were regarded as models of quality development, well sited and in harmony with their surroundings.[43]

The dilemma was distinguishing the myth from the reality of the mission. The popular press was happy to carry images of the new Utopia (Fig. 80), but the commercial market remained sceptical of Dartington's intentions. In retrospect it is possible to see that the Elmhirsts became over confident in the quality of professional advice and the ability to transfer the experiments of the Dartington estate to the business world. At the core of these problems was the misunderstanding of the lessons of the Dartington landscape.

In an essay for *The Book of the Modern House*, 1939, Geoffrey Jellicoe, Vice-President of the Institute of Landscape Architects, wrote

> Dartington Hall, set besides the River Dart, in one of the loveliest of English landscapes, contains so many adventures in art and industry that it is not surprising that an attempt has been made to understand the new landscape. We may feel that the house on the right in the illustration does not suggest the culture of living so much as that on the left, but no one can fail to appreciate the beautiful harmony that exists throughout the landscape as a whole.[44]

The comparison was between Lescaze's High Cross House and Milne's Foxhole School (Figs. 27, 79). The new landscape was the harmony of forms and styles. Of course it was important that the selected viewpoint supported the thesis, but at least the Dartington landscape offered a range of possibilities. In contrast, Lescaze's modernist village at Churston and de Soissons' garden villages at Exeter and Dittisham lacked the variables of the architectural expression of Dartington, and the plans dominated rather than integrated with the landscape.

Soon the modern was to be absorbed into the mainstream. In the first post-war annual of the *Daily Mail Ideal Home* there was a double page illustration of 'Typical English Houses'. That it included the work of de Soissons and Milne is not surprising, but the same cannot be said of the inclusion of Lescaze's High Cross House. In this context Milne would have been appalled by the juxtaposition of his house with that of Lescaze. In *Ideal Home*, August 1942, Milne had written about his misgivings of the flat-roofed, white, modern house, 'It looks bald and uncomfortable. In a word, it is un-English'.[45] Nevertheless, having attempted to popularize modernism through its Churston project Dartington's modernism had become typically English.

Despite some of the disappointments surrounding Dartington's new society idealism, the other aspects of the Elmhirsts'patronage had long term social implications. Prompted by their friendship with Kenneth Lindsey,[46] in 1931 they funded the setting up of the Political and Economic Planning Group. It was to open its first offices in October, and go public in March 1933. The following month it published the first of its broadsheets. It was these papers, 48 in the first two years, and its reports on subjects such as Social Services, Health, British Press, Housing, and in the post-war period, the Arts and Household Appliances, that turned it into a highly influential research group. In its search for a harmonious social order it brought Leonard into contact with Israel Sieff,[47] out of which developed a lasting friendship. Likeminded, when Sieff wrote to Leonard '...it is the spiritual which determines the material',[48] he would have understood such sentiments, except that Leonard would have expressed it as a unity, for that was what he believed Dartington represented.

As the second world war progressed Dartington began to turn its attention to the process of social renewal and national reconstruction. The war years, with the influx of evacuees, had a formative influence on Leonard and particularly on Dorothy, as they developed a more direct understanding of social needs and community.

In March 1944 Dartington hosted a confidential weekend of visits and discussions with representatives from the Ministry of Town and Country Planning, during which time they considered the future development of Devon in the light of Dartington

Hall's experiences. Questions and problems of industry, tourism and domestic developments formed the agenda. Dartington's unease over its relationship with local authorities was apparent, but so was its positive awareness of the importance of National Parks and coastal developments in the next planning phase for Devon.

The following month Dartington launched a national competition for cottage architecture through the architectural press. The results were published in January 1945, the first prize of £150 being won by the Preston architects Grenfell Baines Group, and the model as well as those of the runners-up was displayed at the Housing Centre, London and at Dartington. The intention had been to erect two model cottages on the estate, but although a site had been identified this part of the scheme was not realised.

In the post-war rebuilding programmes Dartington was unable to secure any major new contracts, and in terms of its own society found itself having to start all over again as it began the long process of reconstruction. The principles that underpinned the foundation remained in place, but there was no longer a desire to carry on the mission to create a new social order. Dartington never fully realised the synthesis between the arts, industry, agriculture and education that it so much desired, but it remained a key objective.

In 1931 Kenneth Lindsey had described Dartington as a model of 'rational planning based on a spiritual idea'.[49] Events have shown that it was far more intuitive than rational. As for the spiritual it is impossible to identify it as an idea, but in the broadest sense, as Dorothy understood, it was the spiritual that gave meaning to the whole enterprise.[50] With the arts fulfilling much of this function it is not surprising to see that it was the arts within a rural setting that became its most influential post-war contribution.

NEW PATRONAGE - NEW ENTERPRISES

Dartington's early experiences with art, crafts and design were very much a paradigm of national debates concerning patronage and industry, as ideological differences, commercial confusion, and professional rivalries were exposed.

Pleasure and usefulness were the guiding principles. As benefactors, collectors, entrepreneurs and investors the Elmhirsts were prepared to experiment, but they also wanted to succeed. Consequently they preferred to work with practitioners, recommended by friends and family, whose reputations were already established. They had a persistent desire to be seen to get things right, and often did, but insecure in their own opinions they were often too reliant on experts.

Amongst Dorothy's scrapbooks of cuttings from *Country Life* was an essay, 'A Plea for the Modern Spirit in Decoration in England', 4 December 1926. Explaining how the old can be made to mix with the new, it was a blueprint for Dartington. Leonard, referring to Dorothy's cuttings as a great game called *Snip and Stick*, recognized that it had wider implications for the restoration work. It was a good example of the enthusiasm with which they set out to understand the historic and cultural boundaries of their new life.

For the furnishing of the Hall the Elmhirsts favoured antiques, from the middle ages through to the eighteenth century, with a strong representation of 16th century Spanish furniture and decorative art. Heals were used to furnish the schools, and as the reconstruction progressed furniture was bought from Betty Joel, Gordon Russell, Finmar, Gerald Summers (Fig. 81), and Thonet, reflecting the range of taste of those working at Dartington.[1]

Their early phases of collecting was dominated by patronage of the English crafts which they bought variously as gifts, for their own use and decorative arts collection, and in the case of ceramics, to form a teaching collection for the students. There was considerable support for Bernard Leach[2], whom Leonard had first met in September 1925. In turn he had a pronounced influence on the ceramics collection, and their understanding of the object as an expression of the inner self, a philosophy that they came to apply across the arts.

Leach played an influential role in the appointment of Jane Fox-Strangways[3] as artist-potter and teacher at Dartington, and in the purchase of work from Michael Cardew, Norah Braden and Katherine Pleydell-Bouverie. Considering the ceramic debate of the 1920s it is also interesting to note their acquisition of work by Staite Murray. In the process of collecting the Elmirsts developed close contacts with the Little Gallery, Sloane Street, and The New Handworkers Gallery, Percy Street. They sought the advice and bought work from Ethel Mairet, Enid Marx and Elizabeth Peacock, as well as work by Barron and Larcher.[4] This association with the rural English romantic movement was completed with work from Eric Gill and David Jones.[5]

Crafts were the core of the new building and restoration programme, and the manufacturing base of the Dartington enterprise. In the areas of pottery and textiles, in which they had expected to construct major new industries, they experienced nothing but frustration. Similar difficulties were confronted in the building and furniture production of Staverton Builders, but it remained one of Dartington's more successful commercial ventures.

In 1927 three appointments were made that marked the formal commitment to crafts, as art and as industry. Jane Fox-Strangways, arrived in January to be head of the Art Department and art advisor and to establish a pottery studio.Toby Fitzpatrick[6] came in April to set up hand-loom weaving as a rural industry, followed in October by Rex Gardner as artist-craftsman appointed to head the Building Department. For varying reasons each of these individuals was to be overwhelmed by the impossibilities of a brief that sought to match creative freedom with commercial constraints. This unrealistic demand was at the root of most of Dartington's problems.

The pottery was opened in September 1927. To promote the study of design, Jane Fox-Strangways was to organize a series of 'Design and Workmanship' exhibitions that showed work from across the estate, demonstrating the values of art and design in the everyday object. She wanted to see her department extend this unity of purpose to drama and music, but this was not to be. She had no teaching experience, and in a short time gave up her struggle to deliver the educational provision.

Her output as a potter barely survives, but it was one of high quality, as can be seen in a range of tile designs for a series of fireplaces on which she collaborated with Rex Gardner. Starting with the designs for the restoration of the Parsonage, her ceramic tiles embody a graphic freedom of mark-making that took nature to the edge of abstraction. Similar qualities are to be found in her designs for the fireplaces in the Aller Park school (Figs. 82, 83).

Eighteen months after Fitzpatrick commenced his weaving workshop, Dorothy became aware of the broader work of craft textiles through her contacts with Enid Marx, Ethel Mairet and Elizabeth Peacock. Attempts were made to lure Elizabeth Peacock to run her workshop at Dartington, but with no success. Fitzpatrick continued to research into the home and rural textile industries, and the development of a new loom suitable for home weavers, but patience in the quality and volume of the weaving output was fast running out.

After two years of further frustration, Leonard made an unsuccessful attempt to secure the services of the Norwegian craft weaver, Gerd Bergersen,[7] and still preoccupied with the problem when they visited Berlin in January 1933, they returned with designs by Otti Berger, a student at the Bauhaus, for further consideration. Again nothing emerged from this contact, and they seemed unable to find a satisfactory solution for textiles.

Dartington's staple commercial product was country tweeds, admired for their quality of finish but little else. In the autumn of 1934, Fitzpatrick was replaced by Hiram Hague as manager.[8] Within months Hague was ill and was to be absent for most of 1935, leaving the textiles in confusion. It was at this point that Bergersen renewed her contact with Dartington, proposing to set up a scheme 'to create a new modern sportsline with woven and knitted goods to be worked out together'.[9]

She had her contacts in London, and wanted full responsibility for manufacture and marketing. In September 1935 she started work at Dartington, and three months later was given a year's contract, but not with the range of management responsibilities that she sought. In January 1936 Hague returned, and began discussions with Crysede Ltd on the possibility of them using designs produced by Hein Heckroth.[10] Nothing came of this move but it aggravated an already difficult situation. Confusion continued, and by October Bergersen decided to leave. It was said 'that she did not fit into the organisation'.[11]

Hague's plan was to move manufacture from craft to industrial production. As an interim measure he had entered into an agreement with Wilks and Cohen of Manchester, arranging for them to weave tweed for 300 overcoats for the American market, to be marketed as 'Dartington Standard'. The struggle 'to keep in touch with the times and to make cloths which are useful and of good design to sell at a reasonable price' continued.[12]

Rex Gardner found himself in a similar position. Moved out of architecture, he set about establishing a workshop for industrial design that would 'gather together all the small efforts of individuals to a common focus for teaching, for exhibitions, and for sales'.[13] Organised as a Craftsmen's Studio, rather than resolving problems it exposed Dartington's confusion over issues of production and marketing even more. It attracted the support of Dartington's recently formed Arts and Crafts Advisory Group, which highlighted the contradiction of the studio being expected to 'maintain a high standard in design and workmanship, and also follow up every prospect of making revenue by catering for the needs of any and every passing customer'.[14] Attempts were made to develop cooperation between artists and craftsmen, and it was suggested that there was an urgent need for well thought out toys and educational apparatus. The proposal was not taken seriously, although some time later wooden toys were added to Staverton's Dartside Furniture catalogue. From the time that the Craftsmen's Studios had been opened it played an important role in marketing, capitalizing on the tourist trade. It worked closely with the Rural Industries Bureau, stocking rushwork, wrought-iron, hand-quilting and turnery, as well as the pottery of Bernard and David Leach, and Michael Cardew of Winchcombe, and eventually material from the Textile Mill.

Although Gardner never resolved his personal differences with the Dartington management, and in 1934 left to work part-time for the Rural Industries Bureau, he produced two highly successful designs. There was his illustrated map of the estate (Fig. 65), which was available as a plain or hand coloured print, framed or unframed, and his designs for the popular garden furniture. Available by mail order, the garden furniture was designed to be flat packed for home assembly (Fig. 84).

As Gardner left, planning for design went off in another direction. It was decided to establish a committee, based in London, that would advise on designs and designers, and carry out market research on products and sales. Meeting on 19 September 1934 at the Little Gallery, Leonard Elmhirst and William Slater from Dartington, were joined by Miss Rose, Jack Beddington and Noel Carrington.[15]

Carrington had prepared a paper for the meeting, identifying the problems and the task facing the Committee. The objective was to ensure that Dartington products were as good as their competitors, with a distinctive quality of design, material and workmanship. With no record of any further meetings the brief remained unanswered.

In a climate of uncertainty Dartington displayed a recurring lack of confidence in the design work of Staverton Builders. The company had gained a wide range of expertise through its involvement with restoration and new building work across the estate, and through the Elmhirsts' social and political connections obtained some important contracts for building and furniture. By 1933 it was in a position to exhibit a bedroom suite at the Dorland Hall Exhibition and had furnished the showhouse on its new housing development at the Priory site, Exeter (Figs. 21, 77). It was also involved in new building at Holne, Cockington and Bath. The following year it commenced work on Ashcombe Tower and the Electric House at Torquay (Figs. 32, 37), and was working on furniture contracts for the University Hall of Residence at Exeter and the Pioneer Health Centre, Peckham. Ongoing was the consideration of a whole range of housing developments in addition to those already started in Devon and Cornwall, including Abersoch in North Wales, Dawlish, Cockington, Bournemouth, and Northwood. For a variety of reasons, mainly organisational, none of these projects were taken on, but they provide an indication of the growing reputation of the company.

Despite its successes, the company found itself at the centre of arguments over style and technique. The tension between tradition and the modern was the cause of the cultural migraine from which Dartington persistently suffered, it was to have considerable bearing on the manner in which Dartington approached its relationship with Gropius.

Nancy Ross, a long time friend of Dorothy's, having formed the view that Dartington had similar aspirations to those embodied in the Bauhaus, wrote to the Elmhirsts for their help in meeting its escalating financial problems. The approach failed to produce the necessary backing for the Bauhaus, but when the Elmhirsts visited the Ross's in Berlin in early January 1933, it stimulated their interest in the work of Gropius, and raised the possibility of Mies van der Rohe and Oud working on the Churston housing project.[16]

Despite these developments, by March 1933, the Elmhirsts opted to give the Churston project to their American connections, Henry Wright,[17] Lescaze and Beatrix Farrand. However, Henry Wright, who had been in Berlin at the same time as the Elmhirsts, had confirmed Gropius' desire to spend 'time somewhere where experimental work was being carried on'.[18] This was sufficient encouragement to prompt Slater to invite Gropius to spend time at Dartington looking at their housing and land development. It was anticipated that in return for Gropius seeing a beautiful corner of England he would give some of his views on modern architecture.

Gropius and his wife made their first visit to Dartington in the week commencing 29 June 1933. To Gropius it was an encouraging start,

> many details and the kind of human relationship between the members of your staff remembered to me the first times of the 'Bauhaus' in Weimar. Likewise the junction of all parts and details and their bringing them into relation to the whole life was my principal aim too.[19]

They had talked of design, the work of Dartington's London office, and the plans of the Churston development, with Gropius showing much more than a passing interest. Believing that they were on a similar mission, he was to send Leonard a copy of Moholy-Nagy's *New Vision*, and encourage them to visit his exhibition in London. At this stage Gropius was unaware that the Churston project had already been given to Lescaze. When Gropius found out he was understandably disappointed not to be involved, as also was Breuer.

Contact was re-established with Gropius at the time of his exhibition at the RIBA, but it was not until 14 December 1934, when he and his wife spent the weekend at Dartington, that he was commissioned to redesign the Barn Theatre. This visit coincided with developments at Dartington concerning furniture design. In November 1934 there had been a discussion over the possibility of employing a specialist designer for Staverton's 'Dartside' furniture range (Fig. 85), and a memorandum of 18 December, talked of the need to engage an architect with knowledge of furniture design and interior decoration to head a design team. With this proposition in mind Slater wrote to Gropius, on 3 January 1935. The response was fascinating, but not what Dartington expected.

Gropius proposed a one year contract during which he would build up a collaborating group of designers, and 'secure a unified character for the Dartington products'.[20] To do this he would study the English market and English taste, draw up a scheme for the kind of furniture and its price, bring together a group of young architects, establish links with industry and organize critical discussions on the designs. The intention was to commission five or six young architects to design a room, which would be constructed by Dartington and then shown in London under the name of the designer, with an indication of what was made by Dartington and what was on the market. This proposal was too experimental for a company that wanted immediate commercial results.

Still hoping for a major contract, Gropius refused the £100 consultancy fee as inappropriate to the work that he had in mind. However, excited by the project, he was willing to select the right architects and review designs for no fee. The proposal was again considered on his visit to Dartington on 6 February, but a subsequent management meeting decided that Gropius would be too expensive to head a panel of designers for their scale of operation. The following month further discussions took place, and again Gropius was considered and turned down, this time on the basis that 'his style was too modern and would probably not sell, and it was doubtful if he would see the value of the traditional styles'.[21]

Gropius' reputation was also an additional complication for Dartington to cope with when it was still coming to terms with the impact of the arrival of the Ballets Jooss. The work of the arts had been destabilised, and Christopher Martin, appointed in 1934 to coordiate this work into an Arts Department, had hardly had time to formulate a new policy paper.[22] The presence of Gropius on the estate would have been an added problem. Nevertheless he continued to work on the Dartington theatre project, but even this presented difficulties. His preferred scheme was turned down on grounds of cost and he had to develop a compromise to meet new specifications. The final and unrealised project for Gropius at Dartington was the re-designing of the Open-Air Theatre in October 1935 (Fig. 86).

The Elmhirsts were not indifferent to the reputation of Gropius, or unsympathetic to his professional difficulties.[23] It had not helped that the contact coincided with the unresolved tensions between hand and industrial production, and the continuing difficulties surrounding the land development at Churston, but professional rivalries and fears were at the core of the problem.

Lescaze was openly concerned over the arrival of Gropius on the Dartington scene. Writing to Curry, 19 January 1935, he said 'You, no doubt, know that Gropius has been at the hall, and I do realise that, what with his charm, his Bauhaus reputation and his friendship with Jooss, the situation may be very dangerous for me.'[24] Leonard gave Lescaze the necessary reassurances. Gropius, with the help of Jack Pritchard, was left trying to convince the Elmhirsts of alternative schemes.[25]

In the meantime Dartington continued to fret over its lack of a design policy. In January 1936, Staverton received a report on cheap modern furniture for 'young people of small means but of some education'.[26] The report, produced by David Booth who had previously worked for Gordon Russell, argued against the use of laminates and veneers. Believing that the public did not share the views of the 'extreme architectural left', the report proposed that their furniture should be 'based on the intelligent use of solid timber'.[27] Discussed at the point when Gropius made his last recorded visit to Dartington it positioned the future development of 'Dartside' furniture, and closed off the final opportunity Gropius could have had to work at Dartington.

The language of the 'Dartside' furniture brochure (Fig. 85) encapsulated this conclusion. Marketed as heirlooms of the future, craft products from 'the cream and cider land', the furniture was 'made by hand by a group of skilled workers who understand the traditions of Chippendale, Sheraton and Hepplewhite, but who also absorb the genius of modern design...a peasant industry...reaching the highest standard of modernity'.[28] This furniture was seen as appropriate to the modernism of High Cross, and the designs show obvious links with Heals and Gordon Russell, the fitted furniture of Lescaze, and the work of Gerald Summers. However, just when it seemed that Dartington had finally resolved its design position with a modern eclecticism, another variation took shape.

At the end of November 1936, having formed a new Committee for Design to consider matters of marketing, fashion and good design, Dartington decided to 'select an artist in whose emotional response they had confidence, and to leave him to work out his ideas on design, or on a particular series of designs'.[29] Hein Heckroth, at Dartington since July 1935, surrealist artist, designer for the Ballets Jooss and teacher in the school, was the Committee's choice.

Taking up the post of chief designer in December 1936, he had responsibility for textiles, advertising and display, furniture and interior design. The practical problems of the appointment soon emerged. The Design Studio had difficulties translating Heckroth's furniture designs into working drawings, aggravating the task of producing modern furniture through traditional methods of construction.

The one tangible outcome of this development was the design and marketing of the 'Lamda' chair (Fig. 88). There are questions regarding the extent of Heckroth's contribution to the design of the chair. The fabric came from the textile mill, and Bob

Hening[30] has suggested that the major design input came from Hiram Winterbotham. Initially the intention had been to produce a chair using laminated tensions, but this had to be modified to a conventional construction because of the limitations of the workshop. Nevertheless, the 'Lamda' chair was the first product of departmental collaboration. It was marketed with great flair, supported by a catalogue notable for Heckroth's design and expressionist photography (Fig. 89). He was to design Dartington's stands for the 1938 British Industries Fair, but soon afterwards was moved from the Design Studio back to the Arts Department.

In design terms neither Dorothy or Leonard were modernists, but as demonstrated by High Cross they could be persuaded of its ideological benefits; and through the reconstruction of their flat, 42 Upper Brook Street, London, in 1933 -1934 by Serge Chermayeff,[31] Dorothy became personally identified with modernism. The original intention had been to carry out a programme of redecoration and furnishing, with Staverton Builders commissioned to make the new bedroom furniture. There is no record of the point at which it was decided to implement a total redesigning of the flat, but on 14 October 1933 the Elmhirsts had their first formal contact with Chermayeff, discussing possible design alternatives. By the end of the first week of November he had produced preliminary sketches. He was to open up the interior space by removing the wall between the dining room and the living room, and by moving the bedroom wall created additional living space out of an existing corridor (Fig. 90).

The Elmhirsts had to exert considerable pressure to keep the costs near to their budget, and retain some say in the design. They made it clear that they were not fond of the use of steel in furniture, and insisted that some of the bedroom furniture made by Staverton should be used. Chermayeff accepted their preferences, but in all other matters, the flat was as he wanted. There were to be no ceiling lights, and copper bronze doors to the service and dining rooms were introduced to add 'elegance' to the whole. Furniture was by Pel and Summers, lighting by Best and Lloyd, rugs by Marion Dorn and Marian Pepler. The flat was completed in June 1934, and photographed for the architectural journals. Dorothy had a much publicised 'modern' flat (Fig. 91).

Six months later Dorothy invited 'The Little Gallery' to redecorate the flat. The living room was refitted with old bleach linen curtains with box pleated valance, and a fitted Axminster. The same old bleach linen was also used for fitted covers for furniture in the living-room and the main bedroom. It was one thing to patronise the modern, but living with it was another matter.

Their earliest acquisition of contemporary British art was a marble figure by Henry Moore, acquired in March 1928, and *Snow Scene* by Duncan Grant, was bought in March 1929. Pleasure rather than scholarship was at the root of their art collecting, showing a preference for narrative, and perhaps in response to their travels, an attraction to oriental and exotic landscapes.

Mark Tobey[32] as resident artist added to Dartington's romance with the arts, although his murals, completed after a recent trip to Italy, strain credibility as representative of a new renaissance. It is interesting to track his move from expressionist works into abstraction, and the critical importance that Dartington and its patronage played in this process. Professionally he gained much from this relationship, but his contribution to Dartington was much more limited, although he did introduce Ben Nicholson to the Elmhirsts.

The only occasion that the Elmhirsts assembled a coherent and high quality collection of work was at the beginning of the 1930s. The artist was Christopher Wood.[33] It was very much Dorothy's collection, working from the advice of Jane Fox-Strangways. Begun in November 1930 with three paintings selected from the exhibition at the Wertheim Gallery, including the *Man in a Cart*, there are no clear records of the order in which the collection was built up. Three paintings were purchased in 1932, including the *Dancing Sailors*, which Dorothy had specially installed in her London flat, and then in 1934 the watercolours were bought from the exhibition at Alex Reid and Lefevre. By 1935, when they bought *Fish in a Basket* (Fig. 92), the Elmhirsts had assembled a substantial collection and contributed ten oil paintings and four water-colours to the 1938 exhibition of the work of Christopher Wood, arranged by the Redfern Gallery at the New Burlington Galleries.

Their collecting brought them some important new contacts, amongst whom Jim Ede,[34] at the time an assistant-curator at the Tate Gallery, not only contibuted to their developing interest in the work of Christopher Wood, but tried to interest them in the idea of running a contemporary art gallery. His letter to Dorothy of 11 October 1935, makes fascinating reading.

> The Heckroths came in and spoke of your thinking of starting a picture gallery at Dartington. It seems to me a most vital idea and I wondered if apart from having some kind of permanent exhibition of Contemporary painting you had considered the possibility of having Special Exhibitions of such outstanding quality and idea that people would just have to come there to see them.[35]

Dorothy was interested, but Ede's estimate of running costs of £2000 a year was initially off-putting. This would not have been a sufficient deterrent on its own, particularly as the climate of change at Dartington seemed appropriate to the plan. However, the recently established art department under Christopher Martin had not had time to sort out its organisation and priorities, and this was one proposal too many for it to handle. Caution prevailed and the proposition was never realised. This also explains another lost opportunity, when they declined Ben Nicholson's offer of the 'Abstract & Concrete' travelling exhibition.[36]

Rather than painting and sculpture it was the crafts as art that provided Dartington with its most effective modernist statements of a twentieth century reconstruction. There was the grey green abstract formality of Beatrix Farrand's Hall courtyard and the monumental geometric simplicty of the open-air theatre, but it was in the Great Hall that Dartington acquired its great modernist statement. In this space Elizabeth Peacock was inspired to create a series of woven banners that can be claimed to be innovative pieces of modern art. Despite the symbolic associations with the estate departments, the abstract shapes and colourings hint at other possibilities in much of their visual language. It was little wonder that Leonard should exclaim that 'everyday they take on more meaning'[37] (Fig. 93).

Elizabeth Peacock first visited Dartington in October 1929, but it was in July 1933, after the reconstruction of the roof of the Great Hall had been completed, that the commision for the banners was undertaken. Intially the proposal had been for one large banner to be woven for display over the fireplace, but as the discussion took place in the Great Hall it was agreed that the spaces between the windows were more appropriate. Soon it was also accepted that the banners should hang at right angles to the side walls, on wrought iron wall brackets. But once the medieval associations had been established, the banners were clear modernist statements. Captivated by the experience Dorothy wrote to Elizabeth Peacock of the way in which they were 'the link between ancient and modern which brings everything else together in the perfect whole. Mr Gropius was profoundly impressed with the banners'[38] (Fig. 94).

Ten banners in all were produced, six were completed between the summer of 1933 and the end of 1934, and four in the period 1936 to 1938. Technically it was a formidable undertaking, the scale, texture and colours each presenting unique problems. Apart from the 'Farms' banner, which was constructed out of five pieces, all the other banners were woven as one piece. The iconography ranges from the explicit symbolism of 'Textiles' and 'Buildings' to the abstract 'Gardens' and 'Orchards'. Exhibited at the Whitechapel in 1935, the Whitworth Art Gallery, Manchester in 1938, and the Little Gallery, London, in 1939, they had taken craft weaving out of the constraints of the arts and crafts movement, and located it within modernism.

Elizabeth Peacock could have transfered her workshop to Dartington, but chose not to. Similarly, Bernard Leach enjoyed the patronage of the Elmhirsts, shared many of their ideals, but would have preferred not to move to Dartington. That he did was down to his financial and personal difficulties, rather than any commitment to its ideals. Once there he made effective use of its reputation and support, but to gain his creative freedom he had to ensure that his work was seen as art, thereby keeping it outside of the commercial demands imposed by the Dartington managers.

What came from Leach was not just the idea of the 'beautiful' pot as the manifestation of beauty and utility as one, but the appreciation of the object as a spirit of unity between Eastern and Western craftsmanship. It was not a uniformity of style but of imagination, with the inner becoming the outer, the expressions 'of their makers and of race culture' that transcended international barriers.[39] Constantly making comparisons between East and West, Leach admired the annonymity of the Japanese pot, and despaired of the self-consciousness of much of western craft pottery.

In December 1938 Dartington experienced at first hand a comparative introduction to this East-West relationship, with an exhibition organised by Leach. Chinese and Korean pots of the Sung dynasty were alternated with the work of contemporary English and Japanese studio potters. Accompanied by a weekend conference, it was an event that established contacts between Dartington and regional studios and industries, and through its continuing links with the Rural Industries Bureau maintained an association that was to have long term benefits for the crafts at national and local level.

Convinced by Leach's teaching on the art of the pot, in July 1941 the Elmhirsts commissioned him to make 'the five most beautiful pots he had ever imagined making'.[40] His response was surprising. In April 1942 he was to send them ten pots of varying sizes. Some he liked better than others and, as only one or two were large, Leach suggested that they choose at least eight. An ambiguous reply, it left the question regarding the 'most beautiful' to be answered by the Elmhirsts (Fig. 95).

Considering the work of the artists either supported or bought by the Elmirsts, it is apparent that style was less important than the qualities of hidden meaning. Mystery or mysticism, it did not seem to matter. An expression of the inner self was what Dorothy expected from the arts and the crafts, and for this the artists were protected from Leonard's obsessive demands for facts and figures. It was a difference of treatment that was not without its critics on the estate, and in 1937, when faced with the exhibitions of the work of Mark Tobey and Cecil Collins, tolerance finally disappeared. Collins' exhibition came in for vigorous criticism, and Dorothy had to come to the defence of the expressive freedom of the arts.[41]

Philosophically the arts and the crafts was now reaching a synthesis of purpose. There had been evidence of this thinking in the Craftsmen's Studio and the Design Studio, but it was the the formation of the Dartington Hall Art Studios in 1939 that provided a tantalising glimpse of what might have been but for the advent of the second world war.

For Christopher Martin 1939 had been an oustanding year for the Arts Department. It had an established Dance School, had recently opened the Art Studios under Hein Heckroth, and was in the process of opening a music studio. Attempts were made to keep things running, but when South Devon was declared a prohibited area for aliens in 1940 (Fig. 102) it effectively brought everything to a halt, although the art studios lingered on with a handful of students working with Cecil Collins.

The Art Studios were to offer a three year year course run by Heckroth, Leach, Collins and Willi Soukop.[42] Heckroth, who had been running classes for life and landscape, and art history, was full-time, the others were to be paid according to the classes that ran. Considering the philosophical differences, Martin considered it a great achievement to have got these individuals to align themselves as a group. Structured as an atelier system, with a master to apprentice relationship, the intention was to support the personal vision of the students, while giving them a working knowledge of practice and basic principles as these have existed in all art from ancient to modern masters'.[43] A three week summer school, offering painting, sculpture and a general course, provided the momentum for the launch of the new school in autumn 1939, but Martin was disappointed that they had started with only twelve students, some of whom had been allowed to register with reduced fees. In the circumstances the surprise is that they actually managed to start at all.

There were few opportunities for any further development of art practice, but this did not mean that there were to be no new initiatives at Dartington. With the onset of war Roland Penrose and E.L.T. Mesens of the London Gallery, had decided to locate their picture collections at Dartington, allowing for them to be arranged into public exhibitions. Initially it was planned to hold six exhibitions, but in the end only two took place, 'Panorama', a survey of modern art from 1900-1940, 10 March - 21 April 1940, and 'Before Cubism, Negro Art, Cubism and Chirico', 12 May - 9 June of the same year. Together the two exhibitions provided the first major showing of surrealist work in a British provincial gallery.[44]

Although these were isolated events, they confirmed a growing understanding of Dartington's commitment to Modern Art, and did much to ensure that when Christopher Martin put forward a proposal to instigate an 'Arts Enquiry into the position of Drama, Music and Visual Arts in Britain', it was taken seriously by the government bodies. It was to be an objective and fact-finding survey that would help find a place for the arts in post-war Britain and encourage the inclusion of concert halls, theatres and art galleries in the new town plans.

The Enquiry's first committee meeting was held on 6 November 1941, but in September 1942 its personnel and direction underwent a significant change. Christopher Martin was seriously ill, and his chairmanship was taken over by Julian Huxley, who immediately set about forming a specialist Visual Arts Group.[45] Determined to put forward recommendations alongside the report, it split the group with Miss Glasgow, Secretary of the Council for the Encouragement of Music and Arts, resolutely opposed to this development. The disagreements eventually led to the resignations and disbanding of the Central Committee, but by then the key stages of the work were complete. Although the report was not published until 1946, and then under the authority of the Dartington Trustees, it had played an important part in forwarding discussions that shaped both the Arts Council of Great Britain and the Design Council of Industrial Design.[46]

Integral to Dartington's growing desire to contribute to a new phase of national reconstruction, less attention was given to its identity as a new society, and more to its role in national and regional planning. Alongside the Arts Enquiry of 1941, Dartington took on the responsibility for the Area Film Library of the recently formed Film Council of the South West. It kept alive Dartington's interest in documentary and educational films, in which they had been involved since 1933, and influenced their decision to establish a new Film Unit in August 1946.

A more pragmatic climate now enveloped Dartington. There were still moments of patronage, but nothing on the scale of the earlier years. The one exception was the memorial to Christopher Martin, a reclining figure by Henry Moore.

Much of the character of Dartington of the early period had been formed by appointments that would now be described as Artist in Residence. There would be some teaching, but primarily it was patronage for the artists to further their own practice. After the war serious consideration was given to reviving this system, but Peter Cox[47] was able to convince Dorothy of the merits of the plans that Christopher Martin had started to formulate, whereby policy and objectives would be set out and then posts would be created to fit these plans. In this context Cox made it clear that he did not want the responsibility for the Jooss-Leeder Dance School. The outcome was that in art and music there was a re-examination of the links with community, and Dartington entered a period in which its influence was exercised through the work of Imogen Holst for music and Peter Cox's organization of major exhibitions and the international conference for the crafts.

Occasionally craft work was purchased, in furniture, pottery and textiles, but it was the exhibitions, 'Teacher and the Arts',1949, 'Made in Devon', 1950, 'International Crafts', 1952, and 'Made for Pleasure', 1957, that were the focus of Dartington's patronage and shaped the post-war perception of its work. In Devon it was a programme that fostered new relationships as a centre for teachers, and a crafts patronage that led to the setting up of the Devon Guild of Craftsmen. Paintings and prints were purchased or commissioned, but within the visual arts it was the crafts as art with which Dartington became most closely associated, returning to the ideals that had been integral to the foundation years. In this climate Dartington's industrial ventures have steadily been closed, leaving the Shinners Bridge retail centre as the major survivor and success of the early years.

To Dorothy the core values of the Dartington community were constructed from the arts. They were integral to the whole and in some form essential to the individual. From the success of their sponsorship of Maurice Browne's production of *Journey' End* at the Savoy Theatre, 1928-1929, the arts played an extraordinarily important part in the construction of a public image of Dartington as a radical and progressive experiment. What is worth re-emphasising is that Dartington was about rural Britain, a modernization process intent on reversing the population exodus, bringing about a new relationship between the city and the country, and providing the cultural experiences readily associated with city life within a rural community. By ignoring the role of dance and theatre in this early period, this account of the arts within the Dartington experiment is incomplete, but this can be remedied by reference to the Ballets Jooss theatre programmes, designed by Hein Heckroth.

The arrival of the ballet company in 1934, had pulled the Dartington experiment out of shape, but Leonard had realised that it was the unique relationship of modern dance and agricultural economy that gave Dartington its radical profile. Through its publicity it catapulted Dartington on to the international stage, the marrying of images of the Dartington landscape with those of the avant-garde performances of the Ballets Jooss providing a powerful political statement for the international audiences in London, Paris and New York (Fig. 87).

The theatre programmes brought together modernism and the arts and crafts. Positioned in the middle of Leonard's programme notes on Dartington Hall was Rex Gardner's lino print of the reconstructed courtyard at Dartington. Expressionist in its treatment, it captured the mood of Leonard's text, a manifesto to the new world being born out of the Dartington experiment.

> The fact that Dartington Hall is not only the home of Mr Jooss's International School, but also of the International Conference of Economists shows something of the catholic, the ideal and the practical nature of the Dartington Hall enterprise. Here are two roads that cut right across national boundaries and that both lead to the same end - the building of one commonwealth of nations recognizing one common weal, but expressing in a variety of ways different aesthetic and economic means of reaching a common goal.[48]

That was the position in 1939. The belief in a new society, a new world order born out of a unity of science and art, facts and imagination, patronage and enterprise was as strong as it had been at the outset of the Dartington adventure. It remained so in the post-war reconstruction, but has been less obvious over the recent past.

In April 1974, the month after Leonard died, attention turned to ways in which the meanings behind the appearance of Dartington could be best explored, and the seeds of what was to become the Elmhirst Centre were planted. So was the central concept that has been pursued in this essay: 'Dartington is not one thing, nor yet one thing and another thing, but a complex unity of activities'.[49]

NEW SOCIETY - NEW LANDSCAPE

1 Advertisement. *Rural Industries Quarterly Magazine*, Winter 1935.

2 From the semi-formal permit system introduced in 1931, Dartington moved to a twice-daily organised tour which in the first six months of 1935 recorded 3675 visitors. An article in *The Times*, 13 April 1936, giving a cautious welcome to Dartington's 'social experiment', noted that over 5000 had visited during 1935. Rex Gardner's illustrated map that had been first produced for the visitor's permit, was available as uncoloured large, 9^{d}, small coloured, 6^{d}, and large coloured in oak frame 5/6.

3 Leonard Elmhirst, 1893-1974. By the time that Leonard returned to England in 1925 he had been out of the country for almost eight years. Struggling financially at Cornell University, he had sought a purpose for his life, resolved not to return to his family estate on the edge of Barnsley, and determinedly pursuing Dorothy for marriage.The initial energy for the Dartington experiment was provided by Leonard, but in time he settled into a life of committees. Professionally he saw himself as an Agricultural Economist.
Dorothy Elmhirst, 1887-1968. Widowed 1918, with three young children. Well travelled, attracted by the radical, member of New York Society. From the early 1920s in search of the spiritual in her life, which was one of the key factors in taking on the challenge of moving to Dartington. Starting a new family, two children, in her late thirties, gives an indication of her personal strength. The initial years at Dartington were difficult, but she was to discover creative freedom through the Checkov Theatre, the arts in general, and garden design. Dartington through the experiences of Dorothy is the work that needs to be researched.
Michael Young, *The Elmhirsts of Dartington*, republished 1996, provides an invaluable introduction.

4 Roger Morel, 'Letter from Dartington', *Garvin's Gazette*, Jan/Mar 1942, p.26.

5 *Outline of an Educational Experiment,* Dartington, 1926.

6 L.K. Elmhirst, *Dartington*, The Report of the International Conference of Craftsmen in Pottery and Textiles, 1952, p.2. The Dartington estate is some 10 miles from Torquay and the Devon riviera coast, 24 miles from Exeter, and a similar distance from Plymouth.

7 Letter from Alice Blinn to Leonard and Dorothy, 29 October 1928. LKE USA 1.

8 Letter from Leonard to Berta Asch, Brookings Institute, Washington DC. LKE USA 1 A. 30 Oct 1934. The Devon Trade Directory listed Leonard Elmhirst as the new Lord of the Manor.

9 Letter from Dorothy to Helen Page, Colorado Springs, 16 Mar 27. DWE Gen 8.

10 Sir Henry Tanner, 1849 - 1935. Principal Architect and then Chief Architect in the Office of Works. After

retiring in 1913 he joined his son's architectural practice which had a growing reputation for large scale commercial projects in London. It could be that Tanner's illustrations for *English Interior Woodwork* (1903) and *Old English Doorways fron Late Tudor to the Eighteenth Century* (1903) had some influence on his appointment. First meeting with the Elmhirsts 4 June 1925, London, followed by visit to Dartington on 10 June.

11 Henry Avray Tipping. Had written for *Country Life* since 1907 on craftsmanship and English homes. Garden designer and wrote important work *The Garden of Today* . Advised on the first phase of clearing the formal gardens, and opening up the Tiltyard. Occasional visits to Dartington from February 1927 through to September 1928. Died 16 November 1933, aged 78.

12 William Weir. The contact was first made in October 1925. His reputation for restoration work and as a committee member of the Society for the Protection of Ancient Buildings, were sufficient reassurance. Commenced work on the courtyard buildings and the private house in August 1926, November 1928 selected timbers for Great Hall and in April 1931 work starts on the restoration. See R. Snell, *William Weir and Dartington Hall*, Dartington Hall Trust,1986.

13 Rex Gardner. Had worked for Gimson. Autumn 1927 commenced his designs for new workers cottages, restoration and conversion work. His conversion of Yarner Barn and re-designing of Shinners Bridge Farmhouse are quite outstanding. It was a working relationship that picked up directly from the one that Elmhirst had had with Fincham (see note 23) in the building of the Barton Farmhouse. Appears not to have been able to establish a satisfactory working relationship with William Weir. Set up the Craftsmen's Studio in 1930. In I934 Gardner became part-time regional organiser for the Rural Industries Bureau, and one year later was full-time. Died 1970.

14 Letter from Leonard to John F. Bowden, Land Agent, 3 July 1937. T. Estate 10. Properties 1 C.
"I remember so well the first year that we were here, when we stood with you there, and you suggested that all the dividing walls should be taken down and the courtyard restored to one big unit. It is not easy to visualize it as it was in 1925, but your vision, I think, foresaw something of its present state."

15 Oswald Milne, 1882 -1968. Articled to Blomfield, assistant to Lutyens, set up own practice 1903. Recommended to the Elmhirsts in October 1929. Made his first visit to Dartington at the end of April 1930, and almost immediately was engaged on a wide range of projects. Included workers cottages, farmhouse, school, Textile Mill, the Saw Mill and three executive houses at Staple**.** The last mentioned houses, in the grand home counties style, significantly broke into a new area off the estate heartland, and for the first time the expansion of the estate impacted on the character of Dartington village.

16 Beatrix Farrand. American garden designer, friend of Dorothy's, advised from 1933 through the 30s. Important work included the courtyard path, and the paths through the woodland.

17 Elizabeth Peacock. 1880-1969. Student at the Herkomer School of Art, Bushey. Extended period living at home until 1916 when she joined Ethel Mairet to learn weaving, together moved to Ditchling. By early 1920s established her own workshop at Clayton, Sussex, living with Mollie Stobart.

18 *Prospectus,* Dartington Hall, 1926, p. 8.

19 To facilitate a greater understanding of the whole, and develop sense of common ownership, Dartington put great trust in its *News Of The Day*. A news sheet first issued on the 8 December 1927, it was an important source of information and debate of life and work on the estate, and of its plans and idealism.

20 *News of the Day* 6 Nov 1928, p.2.

21 At this stage it had been planned that the Hall and courtyard buildings would be the centre for the Arts and Education, with Leonard and Dorothy intimately involved in the day to day activities. The site and foundations of the building started by Rex Gardner were used by Milne for the Dance school.

22 Ides van der Gracht. From the New York firm of Delano and Aldrich. There were endless problems with the building programme, as it was sited over an underground water course, and the School did not open until 1931.

23 August 1925, Alfred Fincham had started as clerk of works. 24 October 1925 he wrote to Leonard, 'As a small contribution to your educational scheme, I would like, - with your permission, - to design one of your cottages to be erected on one of the sites recently selected for your approval, by Mrs Elmhirst.' (T. Est.1) W. E. Lescaze 1895-1964. Introduced to the Elmhirsts by the new headmaster, W.B. Curry. See L.W.Lanmon, *William Lescaze, Architect*, Art Alliance Press 1987.

24 *News of the Day*, 30 Sept 1931, p.1. The flavour of the early years is most effectively expressed by Dorothy in

a letter, 11 February 1927, to her friend Frances Livingstone, 'I think you would be amused at our social activities. We have a dancing class every Tuesday night which is great fun. It consists of the older boys in the school, the school staff, some of the workers on the Estate, the maids in the house, and one or two outsiders…Then on Wednesday evening we all sing together in a big chorus...before Christmas, we as school staff, gave a play, The Importance of being Earnest,...for all our own workmen with their families. It was great fun...we see very little of the neighbours, but for the time being we are concentrating on building up a community life among ourselves.' (DWE Gen 7. L.)
In terms of estate activities, it is worth reading through the *News of the Day* reports of the talks given to the 'Sunday Evening Meeting' which were started in 1931. Open to the estate, it was a social evening with an impressive list of speakers, including politicians, historians, educationalists and those from the arts. They are important enough to be worth reprinting as a set.

25 Letter from Alice Blinn to Leonard, 24 Jan 1929, p.2. LKE USA 1.

26 William B Curry, 1900-1960, Trinty College, Cambridge. Headmaster of Oak Lane County Day School Philadelphia.
Milne had begun the planning for the senior school at Foxhole, and in July 1930 discussed the designs, and those for the headmaster's house with Curry. In August Curry took these plans back with him to America, where he showed them to Lescaze. When Curry returned to Dartington he had Lescaze's preliminary designs for High Cross, and alternative proposals for the school. Unwilling to change the plans for the school, even though they accepted the argument linking modern architecture to progressive education, it was the possibility of having a model American home on the estate that finally persuaded the Elmhirsts to go modern. In its siting and configuration it was a house for the lover of large American cars
For Curry's ideas on education see his *The School and a Changing Civilisation,* John Lane, 1934.

27 Staverton Builders, began life in 1927 as the Engineering and Building Department, and was established as a company of Dartington with its own share issue in July 1930.

28 Letter from Alice Blinn to Lescaze, 15 October 1931. T. Sch 31-57. 13

29 Kurt Jooss, founder of the Ballets Jooss which was achieving international recognition through *The Green Table*. The building and siting of the Lescaze house for Kurt Jooss, and the purchase of a large house on the edge of Totnes for the dancers and students, were indicative of the importance that the Elmhirsts attached to the relocation of the ballet company to Dartington.

30 Louis de Soissons. 1890-1962. The important connection was his work at Welwyn Garden City. Leonard first considered making an approach to de Soissons in December 1929, a time when he referred to Dartington as 'our embryo Welwyn in Devonshire', (Letter, 2 December 1929. C.Stav. 1). This was as close as the Elmhirsts came to establishing their own garden village at Dartington.

31 Despite reservations these developments compare favourably to the national framework shaped by the 1926 Housing Rural Workers Act and the 1930 Housing Act.
The workers houses at Huxhams Cross and Broom Park were started in May 1932 and completed by the following October. Building materials were modified, and the overall costs were reduced by a third of the price of the Milne cottages, with the new houses costing just over £500 each to build. In terms of local authority housing this was not unusual, indeed it would have been applauded for sound economics.
Robert Hening produced a report for the estate *Minimum Standards for Housing*, (21.12. 33) which if fully implemented would have run counter to policies on reconstruction and restoration. A committed modernist he sought to build less substantial buildings which could then be demolished in 25 or 30 years as cheaply and quickly as possible. (T 3 Estate 1.)

32 Letter from de Soissons to Leonard, 14 May 1930. T.3. Estates A. The location of a 'village' is the primary interest of the survey, and indicates that the preliminary inquiry points to Shinners Bridge.

33 *Report on the Dartington Estate*. 4 June 1930, p.4. T.3.Estate A.

34 Letter from Leonard to Mr Davidge (Chief Advisory Officer of the South Devon Regional Planning Committee), 18 May 1933. T.3.Estates A. Leonard was lobbying on behalf of the Churston plan. It was modernism seen as the antidote to jerry-building. See argument outlined by William Walter Wood, 'Glorious Devon', *Architectural Review* , September 1929, p. 109-113.

35 *Managing Director's Report* 1932 -3. C. Stav. 2.

36 See section two.

37 Curry was convinced that he had plans for a house that would 'almost rival the Hall itself as a showplace'.

(Curry to Lescaze, 1 Sept 31. T.Sch 31-57. 13).
It was to be an expensive experiment, costing three times that of a Milne house, going 60% over budget. As building got underway on High Cross, problems steadily emerged over the interpretation of Lescaze's instructions and drawings. For all its functional claims and image of modern living, it had its shortcomings. Designed with four bathrooms, separate stairs and entrance for the servants, substantial dressing-room for the main bedroom, no thought had been given to the possibilities of it having to accommodate a growing family or the needs of young children. Only as the Curry family adjusted to the arrival of their new baby did they realise that the interior wall finish was not suitable for young children. Unwilling to give up the guest wing or encroach on the servants rooms for additional living space, Curry was faced with the prospect of his family fitting into a two bedroom wing. He considered the possibility of building an extension, but had to be satisfied with covering in the first floor sleeping porch.
Delineating the family accommodation from that of the guests and servants wings with the blue/white divide raised a range of technical problems that were never effectively overcome, and as Lescaze was ambivalent about this part of the scheme, it leaves unanswered the cultural significance of this division. Curry would have prefered the house to remain plain white, but in the end Lescaze decided that the servant/guest block should be painted a light shade of blue-grey. When eventually it was painted blue, Curry found the colour too dark, and had it repainted. Even then Curry did not like it, but decided to leave it as it was. In a short time the colour began to wash off, and when the new boarding houses by Lescaze were being painted with an improved white paint, the house reverted to all white.
A difficult house to build, it was also problematic in its maintenance. Water seepage from the roof steadily increased, until in 1947 it was decided to carry out major repairs, at which point it was found that the felt flashings had rotted. It was a novel, and to the Elmhirsts a rather daring design. It was by an architect they considered to have an international repuation, whose work had been included in the 'Modern Architecture-International Exhibition' at MOMA, New York, February- March 1932. What they failed to recognize was that the qualities of High Cross lay in it being site specific, its formal limitations off-set by the landscape. It was not a house that could be readily translated into a model for speculative development.

38 *Churston, South Devon*, Dartington Hall Ltd, 1935, p.2. The brochure was issued in November. Devon was exploited by Staverton Builders as a haven for the retired, a playground for the sportslover, and a paradise for children.

39 *Minutes.* 16 February 1938. C. Staverton Minutes 1938.
Over this period national opposition to the erosion of the English coastline through building development had intensified. Locally the arguments had gained renewed credibility with the publication in 1932 of W. Harding Thompson's, *Devon: Its Coast, Moors and Rivers* for C.P.R.E.; considered to be pointing to the need for control of landowners, see *The Builder*, 2 September 1932, p. 353. In October 1936, this position was reinforced when C.P.R.E. held its annual conference at Torquay on the theme, *'The English Coast: its Preservation and Development'*.

40 *The Joy of a Home*, publicity leaflet, Staverton Builders, nd

41 Gerald Heard, 'The Dartington Experiment', *Architectural Review*, April 1934, p.119-122.
Gerald Heard was a regular weekend guest of the Elmhirsts.
'The New Rural England', *Architect and Building News*, 30 June, 7 July, 14 July, 21 July, 1933.
Comprehensive coverage of architecture at Dartington, but excludes Huxhams Cross, Broom Park, and the Aller Park School.

42 Christopher Hussey. 'A Modern School, Dartington Hall, Totnes'. *Country Life*, 27 May 1933. p. 548-553. In praise of Oswald Milne.

43 'The Architect and Housing by the Speculative Builder-vi. Some Estates in Devon'. *Journal of the RIBA*, August 1936, pp.975-984. Review of de Soissons work for Dartington, referencing his work at Churston, but making no mention of the Lescaze designs.

44 G.A. Jellicoe, 'The House in its Suburban and Country Setting', p. 211, in P Abercrombie (ed.) *The Book of the Modern House,* London, 1939, p.211.
Dartington houses were illustrated in three of the fourteen chapters. Claimed to be a survey of the best houses of the previous twenty-five years, reference was made to Oswald Milne's house at Staple in the chapter on 'The Country House', the work by Louis de Soissons at Dittisham and Churston was in 'The Ready Built', and the Lescaze High Cross House and Louis de Soissons' houses at Exeter were included in 'The House in its

Suburban and Country Setting'.

45 *Ideal Home*. August 1942, p.64.

46 Kenneth Lindsey, 1897-1991. After service in First World War, went up to Oxford. President of Oxford Union Debating Team, which visited New York 1922, where he established friendship with Dorothy, and enjoyed her patronage for a year. Member of the Labour Party, and in 1933 became MP for Kilmarnock. The Elmhirsts would have liked him to join them in their work at Dartington. They had to be satisfied with supporting the plans that brought PEP into being with Lindsey as its first secretary. A group had been invited to spend the weekend of 18 April 1931 at Dartington to carry forward ideas that had been oulined in Max Nicholson's article 'National Plan for Great Britain', in *Weekend Review*, 14 February 1931. A further meeting was held at the Royal Society of Arts at the end of June, and its office opened in October.

47 Israel Sieff, then vice-chairman of Marks and Spencer, together with the Elmhirsts financed PEP. He was the chair from 1933-39, Leonard then taking over. The level of trust between Leonard and Israel Sieff is well illustrated by Leonard's renting of a secret hideout for Sieff and his family on the Gower, in the event of a German invasion.

48 Letter from Sieff to Leonard, 12 February 1940. LKE PEP 5.

49 Letter from Lindsey to Dorothy, nd, 1931.

50 Letter from Dorothy to Ruth Morgan, 28 May 1928, DWE Notebook 1928-29.

NEW PATRONAGE - NEW ENTERPRISES

1 The furniture deserves more research. Many twentieth century pieces are no longer at Dartington. The first order from Heals in December 1926, was for bedroom furniture for the school. Furniture from Betty Joel was ordered in April 1929, and a dressing table commissioned in December. The furniture from Summers was for Michael Straight's rooms at Cambridge, the Heckroths' flat, and the Checkov studio at Dartington.

2 From their first major purchases of Leach's work show at Paterson's, Old Bond St. in Spring 1927, they never wavered in their support, giving him freedom from commercial constraints throughout the1930s, and providing the funding for his year long trip to Japan in 1934. It allowed him the time to explore his ideas on the art of the pot, and produce *A Potter's Book*, Faber, 1940.

3 Sylvia Fox-Strangways, but always known as 'Jane' at Dartington. Trained at the Central School of Arts and Crafts, the RCA and Camberwell. Worked briefly for Bernard Leach. Exhibited with the Potters' Guild in London, Paris and Leipzig, and in 1928 at an International ceramic show in New York. Close and continuing relationship with Dorothy.

4 Most of the work was purchased for use as curtaining and covers, or as gifts, usually at Christmas.

5 Eric Gill. Collecting commenced in 1927 with work from St George's Gallery and Golden Cockerell Press in November 1927. The latter purchases also included the David Jones engravings of 'The Deluge'. Gill prints were purchased from the Goupil Gallery in 1928 and 1929, and books from Golden Cockerell Press. In March 1931 they purchased stone carving by Gill from the New Handworkers Gallery, but it is no longer in the Dartington collection.

6 Toby Fitzpatrick. Hand-loom weaver working at Willand, north of Exeter, when discovered by Dorothy. Understood that his department should show that it was 'possible to manufacture textiles economically on so small a scale and so simple a system as to come within the capabilities of the rural worker, i.e Villagers, Small Holders, etc.' 14 May 1929. Tex C. 1. A.

7 Gerd Bergersen. Norwegian craft weaver. At the time that Dartington made contact she was working in Bilbao. After visiting Dartington, worked for the Rural Industries Bureau in Wales for a year and a half, and then moved on to work for a mill in Huddersfield. Heard of Dartington's problems through Clough Williams-Ellis.

8 Hiram Hague. Carried out review of textiles in October 1934, and shortly after was appointed to run department. Absent from August 1935 through to the end of the year, producing a new policy statement for the Textile Department in January 1936. Highlighted problems over quality production, and lack of concern for markets. The Mill was to be mechanised, but this did not solve the problems. October 1937 Hague came into an inheritance, the following month changed name to Winterbotham. 1939 left to run family business.

9 Letter from Gerd Bergersen to Leonard. 21 March 1935. p.2. C.Tex 1 A 1.

10 Hein Heckroth. Arrived at Dartington in July 1935, left June 1940. From 1938 was teaching life class, history of art, and landscape drawing classes for the estate. July 1938 students from the life class held an exhibition,

and in their catalogue notes explained 'drawing and painting are enjoyable activities and those who practise them will develop a perception and a skill which will be of value to themselves, to their jobs, and to the world at large'. February 1939 Heckroth presented paper to Sunday meeting on Modern Art.

11 *Managing Director's Report*. October 1936, p.3. C. Tex. 1 B 1935-45.

12 Letter from Hiram Hague to Margaret Isherwood, 2 April 1937. T. Sch 1931-57. B.

13 Letter from Rex Gardner to Leonard, 17. 6. 1930. C.D.H.Ltd 1926-45. 9. (A)

14 *Memorandum*. Advisory Group on Craftsmen's Studio. 16 Nov 1933. C.D.H.Ltd 1926-45. B

15 William Slater was a chemist who had come to Dartington in 1929 to set up the Science Laboratory, but soon after he was also appointed as Managing Director of Dartington Hall Ltd. Jack Beddington, Publicity Director for Shell-Mex and Noel Carrington, critic and writer, author of *Design and a changing civilization*. With Muriel Rose representing the crafts. It could have been a stimulating committee if Dartington had sustained its interest.

16 Letter from Charles Ross to Leonard, 25 January 1933, T. Estate 7 D

17 Henry Wright. American landscape architect and planner, brought into the scheme on the initiative of Lescaze, visited Dartington at the end of January 1933, suggested 'constructional programme should centre around an idea rather than marketability' (Memorandum. T. Estate 7. F.) His appointment was confirmed March 1933.

18 Letter from W.K.Slater to Gropius, 3 May 1933, T. Estate 7D

19 Letter from Gropius to W.K.Slater, 21 July 1933. T. Estate 7 D

20 Letter from Gropius to W.K. Slater, 6 January 1935. T. Estate. 7. D

21 *Minutes*. 20 March 1935. p.1. C. Stav. 1.

22 Family connections had brought Christopher Martin to Dartington. Had been President of Oxford Union, worked in the city, grandfather had been vicar at Dartington, uncle was the current vicar, family connected to the Champernowne's by marriage, wife's family connected to the Elmhirsts' lawyer Gwatkin of Mckenna & Co. It was Gwatkin's recommendation that brought about the appointment in 1934. Martin died of tuberculosis in August 1944.

Looking back to this period Christopher Martin talked of the problems of having to shape their policy around the influx of artistic refugees, (Admin Rep 21 Nov 1941. T Arts Admin 1). Individuals were also the casualties of these changes. At the beginning of the decade Dartington had been satisfied with the pioneering dance/ drama work of Margaret Barr in promoting a spirit of unity between the arts and rural life for its own community. With its later emphasis on the international audience for its message of the new society, Barr was out and the partnership broken.

23 The delays in arranging a major project were putting Gropius in financial difficulties.To alleviate his problems and their conscience, after yet another visit to Dartington on the 27th March 1935, the Elmhirsts sent money as a token of respect 'for the work of the Bauhaus' under his leadership.

24 Letter from Lescaze to Curry. 19 Jan 1935. T. Sch 1931-57. 14

25 It was Jack Pritchard who first took action on his behalf, anticipating that while no work had materialised at Dartington the Elmhirsts would wish to be associated with plans to keep Gropius in England. Pritchard had come up with a scheme to launch a share issue for ISOKON (Windsor) Ltd to build and operate blocks of flats at St Leonard's Hill, Windsor. To be designed by Gropius and Fry, the aim was to provide all the amenities of living that were to be found in a really comfortable country house. With a planned share release on the 27 June 1935, Gropius discussed the project with the Elmhirsts on the 21 June. Intially prospects looked good, but two weeks later Leonard declined to invest in the scheme, and although Pritchard persisted with his approaches throughout 1935, there was to be no change of mind. At the end of the year he was to come up with an alternative scheme linked to the village college programme being put together by Henry Morris for Cambridgeshire. On 6 March 1936 Pritchard set out the details of the scheme, accompanied by a copy of Morris' letter of 3 March outlining the ambitions for the new village colleges to be designed in terms of modern architectural possibilities in structure, design, materials, decoration and hygiene. For this he wanted the best of modern European practice combined with a realistic English appoach, he wanted Gropius and Fry. The question was how to raise the £1200 needed to cover the architectural fee. Leonard decided to give £120, and persuaded his friend Israel Sieff to donate £100. The work commenced and in 1938 the models and plans were finished, and the building finally opened in September 1939. Money problems had never been resolved, and Pritchard continued his efforts to get more financial support from Leonard, but seemingly losing patience he would not increase his contribution unless the other subscribers increased their original financial support by

25%.

26 David Booth, *Notes on cheap quality produced furniture*, Jan 1936, p.1. C.Stav 1.

27 ibid p.15

28 *Dartside*. Furniture catalogue. nd.

29 *Memorandum. The Commercial Department at Dartington*. 24 November 1936. p.2 C DHLtd 26-45. 9. Design

30 Robert Hening ran the estate drawing office from 1930, and was directly responsible for the interpretation and implementation of Lescaze's designs. Each week Hening was allowed one three minute telephone call to Lescaze in New York to clarify any points raised in correspondence. After some initial dificulties, the relationship flourished at a personal and professional level. The drawing office was closed in December 1936, with Hening entering into partnership with Chitty, and continued to play a major advisory role in the building programme through to the 1960s.

31 Serge Chermayeff, 1900-1996, at the time of the commission he had recently completed studios along with Coates and McGrath for the new BBC building, had begun to develop friendships with a wide range of artists, and was entering into his partnership with Mendelsohn, with whom he was to design the De La Warr Pavilion at Bexhill.

32 Mark Tobey had come to Dartington as a visiting artist in September 1931. It was for art and education that Ben Nicholson first visited Dartington with Adrian Stokes in the early 30s, probably 1932, to meet Tobey. On Tobey's recommendation the Elmhirsts had developed an interest in the work of Ben Nicholson, purchasing one of his paintings for the Hall.

33 Christopher Wood, 1901-1930. Despite his visits to Cornwall and connections with the Seven and Five Society, there appears not to have been any direct contact between Wood and the Elmhirsts. In making their first purchases shortly after his death, there was a distinct note of determination to acquire good examples, and when faced with a misunderstanding over the availability of the *Man in the Cart*, eventually agreed to meet the asking price, £450.

34 Influential in their collection of Alfred Wallis and expansion of the Christopher Wood collection, there is no doubt that the Elmhirsts were surprised and disappointed when Ede decided to move to the continent at the end of the 1930s. An astute collector since his days at the Tate Gallery, when eventually he moved to Cambridge in 1957, he had a collection, which with his home, Kettle's Yard, was given to the University in 1966. It provides a special insight into art of the 1920s and 1930s, and leaves open to conjecture what might have happened if Ede had been able to develop his ideas at Dartington.

35 Letter from Jim Ede to Dorothy. 11. 10. 1935. DWE Arts 1.

36 There seems a suggestion with these responses that Dartington was not sure how it wanted to position itself in relation to modern art. Certainly in any relationship it did not wish to lose its identity, which may offer some explanation of the reaction, later in 1936, to Barbara Hepworth's invitation to Curry to write an article for a new review that was to become *Circle*, published 1937. She explained that they were not interested in personalities, but in good work done, and its relation to the whole social structure and to life in general. Curry needed to know more before he would make a commitment. No essay was forthcoming, and the opportunity to reinforce the progressive image of Dartington with the cause of modernism was missed.

37 Letter from Leonard to Elizabeth Peacock, 13 June 1934

38 Letter from Dorothy to Elizabeth Peacock, 25 May 1938

39 Bernard Leach, 'Report of talk', *News of the Day*, 9 December 1938. p.4. Also see *The Integration of the Craftsman*, and *The Contemporary Potter*, papers in Report of International Conference, Dartington 1952,

40 Letter from Leonard to Bernard Leach. 21 July 1941.

41 Cecil Collins had first met Tobey in 1934, and two years later moved to Dartington, staying there until 1944. It made no demands of him, and in the small amount of teaching that he took on he appeared content to be responsible to Heckroth. Protected by Dorothy's patronage, when faced by the hostile reception to his exhibition Collins felt obliged to mount his own defence in a letter to the *News of the Day*.
'My works are visual music of the kingdoms of the imagination. There is, in all human beings, a secret personal life. It is this sensitive life which my art is created to feed and sustain - this real life deep in each person. Thus my art is truly functional'. (25 June 1937, p.3).

42 Willi Soukop. 1907-1995. Came to Dartington in April 1934 through contact with Mrs Kay Starr, private secretary to Leonard. Taught in the school.

43 *Dartington Art Studios.* Publicity Leaflet, nd. Arts Visual 2.

44 The first exhibition included work by Agar, Braque, de Chirico, Max Ernst, Magritte, Miro, Picasso and Man Ray. In the foreword to the catalogue Christopher Martin talked of modern art as the mirror of 'the thought and emotion of the age in which it finds itself'.

45 The Visual Arts Committee held its first meeting 18 November 1942; R.P Bedford, Misha Black, Kenneth Clark, Barnett Freedman, Philip James, Audrey Martin, Henry Moore, Eric Newton, John Rothenstein, E.M. O'R Dickey, Philip Hendy were present. Peter Cox was the secretary, and the compilation of the final report was substantially his work.
Of the discussion papers produced for the group, two are worth noting, Misha Black's *'Notes on the Associations concerned with the Economic and Political Problems of Artists and Designers'*, and Nicholas Pevsner's *'Memorandum of the Position of the Designer for British Industries After the War'*.

46 It remains an important piece of documentation on issues of education, patronage and commerce, both in its review of the existing provisions and recommendations. *Report on Film* was published 1947, and *Music* in 1949.

47 Peter Cox came to Dartington in 1940 through his contact with Christopher Martin. He was to see the Arts Department become the Arts Centre in 1955, and then in 1961, the Arts, Music and Drama departments brought together as a College of Arts, with himself as Principal. A development that lies outside the brief of this research, it remains an important area for inquiry.

48 Ballets Jooss Programme. 1939.

49 Maurice Ash, *The Future of the Private House*, 22 March 1974. T. Estate 10. Properties 1.

The Ceramic Heritage of Devon

Doug Fitch

INTRODUCTION

The county of Devon yields an ancient association with the production of ceramics, which dates back to the early Iron Age. A history of pottery manufacture in some form has remained uninterrupted to this day within the county, which still provides the provenance for a number of long-established makers, on both an industrial and studio-based scale.[1] Most of these potteries were founded as a consequence of the rich expanses of quality clay seams, found beneath the Devon top-soil.

Experiencing the most prolific period of manufacture during the middle of the seventeenth century, chiefly in the Bideford area, Devon's cottage industry supplied hand-made pots to the home market and for the American colonies.[2] As industrially manufactured wares[3] gradually took the place of the products of these potteries, surviving businesses concentrated the basis of their production into supplying specialist items which were not made by the industry. These small businesses became known as the country potteries and were at their most enterprising during the nineteenth century.[4]

With the outbreak of the first World War, much of the workforce was enlisted. The related economic restraints, combined with changes in the requirements of society and easier access to the products of industry, all contributed to the demise of the country potteries during the first half of this century.[5] This signalled the end of the British hand-crafted pottery tradition, with the exception of the work of the 'art potteries' and that which became identified as studio pottery.

Many visitors to Devon in the twentieth century would associate the county's pottery production with its well-known art potteries, which originated during the second half of the nineteenth century. The tradition of manufacture by some of these concerns continues to the present day.

C H Brannam of Barnstaple, for instance, produced hand-crafted, ostentatious, Victorian-styled pieces which demonstrated an apparent affinity with the Arts and

Crafts Movement. The Watcombe Pottery in Torquay, catered specifically for the tourist trade, establishing a huge range of 'souvenir' pottery, depicting naive interpretations of the Devon landscape. Typical pieces carry rural scenes of thatched cottages, or rhymes and phrases in sgraffito text, composed in phonetic, colloquial Devonian.[6] It was by the promotion of a stereotypical quaint and rustic Devon that such potteries marketed their wares, conjuring-up an image of a romantic, lost-in-time Britain, with an epitomising sense of pastoral escapism.

The work of these potteries, although commanding an important position in the ceramic heritage of Devon, is beyond the bounds and of divergent objectives from those of the studio pottery movement. Despite a hand-crafted element, they were primarily commercial enterprises with many of the ethics of small-scale industry.

THE STUDIO POTTERS

With the domination of industry all but destroying the last of the British tradition of hand-made pottery production, individual pots made by hand processes adopted the characteristic of a non-essential, even luxury item. Asserting themselves as the antithesis of industry, studio potters focused attention upon the hand-crafted character of their work. Their pots thus became fashionable status symbols, to be found in the homes of the middle and upper-classes. They were certainly comparatively more expensive than general industrial pottery. The studio potters initiated the transition of pottery making from what had traditionally been a working-class trade into a craft which was now in the domain of the intellectual. Studio pottery was not purely the adoption of a process and the practitioners were not simply makers, they were articulate commentators on their work. This work, which combined hand-made processes with a philosophical element, became a vehicle for assessment, analysis and debate in much the same way as critics, collectors and practitioners approached other aspects of the arts.

The birth of the studio pottery movement in the 1920s created an approach to ceramics which had never before been considered in the western world. The potter would become an 'artist-craftsman,' fusing a philosophy of practice with traditional elements of pottery style and manufacture from a diversity of cultures. The products made by the initiators of this movement may be described as: 'Work produced on a relatively small scale by a single person or small team, where the individual hand-made nature of the product and a consciously non-industrial stance are important characteristics.'[7]

Early in the development of the movement, two major trends became apparent. There were the traditionalists, who worked in a way established by Bernard Leach (1887-

1979) at St Ives and those who considered themselves to be more innovative, from the London colleges. The most highly revered potter of this latter tendency was William Staite Murray (1881-1962).[8] The creative philosophies of these two predominant 'schools', are exemplified in developments which occurred at Dartington Hall, from the 1930s onwards.

BERNARD LEACH AND DARTINGTON

In 1932, hoping to add a potter to the Dartington community, the Elmhirsts invited Bernard Leach to set up a workshop. This proposed pottery was to produce a range of domestic ware which was to be cheap, available in volume and designed for everyday use. Leach was to combine the development of the pottery with teaching at the progressive Foxhole School which was situated on the estate (Fig. 79). He was at the time working at the Leach Pottery St Ives, which he had established with the Japanese potter, Shoji Hamada, in 1920. Realising the advantages of better access to materials and customers which would be available to him at Dartington, Leach wrote in a letter to Leonard Elmhirst,

> ...the necessary amalgamation between science, machinery, organisation, distribution and the capital necessary, even for a small experimental venture cannot be expected of the hand craftsman working in complete isolation. At Dartington, this is the best environment I have seen.[9]

Leach worked in a style which became identified as the 'Anglo-Oriental' tradition, heavily influenced by Japanese ceramics, English medieval pottery and Chinese stonewares of the Sung and Tang dynasties (Fig. 95). He was born in Hong Kong and had spent much of his youth in the East. In Japan, he had become friends with Soetsu Yanagi, a philosopher and leader of the Mingei movement.[10] Yanagi introduced Leach to Zen Buddhism and the Buddhist concepts of beauty. Inspired by the philosophy of the Orient and with a wish to infuse this culture into British attitudes to pottery, Leach had returned to England in 1920, hoping to generate a combination of these two very diverse cultures. Leach shared this interest in the synthesis of East and West with Leonard Elmhirst, whose experiment at Dartington had been based upon the advice of a friend and mentor, Rabindranath Tagore. Tagore, quoted by Leonard Elmhirst in a Dartington Hall newsletter, proposed,

> ...you must open a craft-school of your own and be sure that your weavers and potters always keep in touch with your artists. The practical work of craftsmen must always be carried out in partnership with the

> divine spirit of madness - of beauty - with the inspiration of some ideal of perfection.[11]

The concept of the potter as an 'artist-craftsman' was at the time quite a novelty, as Bernard Leach emphasised in 1939,

> ...Very few people in this country think of the making of pottery as an art, and amongst those few the great majority have no criterion of aesthetic values which would enable them to distinguish between the genuinely good and the meretricious.[12]

Leach established a workshop at Dartington in 1932. There had previously been a small pottery sited on the estate, which had been started in 1927 by Sylvia Fox-Strangways (1900-1974). Here she had made slipware and also tiles, some of which may still be seen in several fire-surrounds in Dartington Hall (Figs.82, 83). A former student at the Leach Pottery, she had been invited by the Elmhirsts on the recommendation of Bernard Leach to establish the workshop and to carry out the teaching of pottery at the Foxhole School. Fox-Strangways had retired in 1929, however, due to ill health and the pottery had closed.

The existing workshop facilities were inadequate, so Leach built a replacement at Shinner's Bridge, situated within the woodland of the estate. The pottery in St Ives was failing financially and in desperation, Leach was considering transferring the production from St Ives in its entirety. Indeed, it appeared that the move would be the only salvation for the Leach pottery. His initial conception was that at Dartington he might,

> step out from the studio...towards a small factory where quality of design and material is preserved, whilst science and organisation are put at the service of the craftsman and not prostituted for the sake of easy sales.[13]

The Elmhirsts funded a trip to Japan for Leach and his friend, the resident Dartington painter, Mark Tobey. Later, they also supported him financially while he wrote his hugely influential study, *A Potter's Book*, which was first published in May 1940. Much of this book was written while Leach was living on the Dartington estate.

In Japan, it was Leach's intention to invest his energy into researching Japanese stonewares so that on his return he could implement a range of tableware at Dartington. The pots were to be,

> ...hard and fine and graceful, with a quality of clay and glaze (that) a skin of lead on bone china will in its very nature never yield.[14]

It is notable that Europe had not experienced a stoneware tradition, with the exception of Germany and its history of salt glaze production. Stonewares were considerably more durable than the earthenwares which had been traditionally used in Britain.[15] Furthermore, the quality of glaze and finish proved far more suitable to modern style. Leach highlighted the advantages of stoneware when he commented upon the production of traditional earthenwares,

> ...however much this ware (earthenware) expressed the English national temperament of one or two hundred years ago, it does not fit in with modern life. Its earthy and homely nature belongs to the kitchen, the cottage, and the country. Many refuse it because it only harmonises with the whitewash, oak, iron, leather and pewter of "Old England" - moods which have been creatively "worked out", however much I as an individual, or a few others, may have needed this experience as part of our personal growth. We cannot forgo those other qualifications, of thinness, hardness, non-porosity, and light toned colour.[16]

In 1933, Bernard Leach's son, David, began to teach at the Foxhole School and was assisting Leach with the development of the Dartington project. In the following year, the Elmhirsts paid for a course at Stoke-on-Trent Technical college for David Leach, intending that the experience gained there would instigate an improvement in production techniques. Their expectation was that this knowledge would enable Bernard and David Leach to realise the production of inexpensive utilitarian pottery at Dartington which had earlier been proposed.

Leach's initial reaction was outrage, fearing that his son's perceptions and sensitivities would be ruined. In a letter to Leonard Elmhirst, Leach protested,

> Stoke, the home of the industrial, devil! Why don't you send him out to Japan where he will get some sound personal conviction and direction about art; techniques he can pick up later as he goes along?[17]

In 1937, upon the completion of his course in Stoke, David Leach returned to St Ives and was making preparations to move to Dartington. This was interrupted by the war and his subsequent call-up in 1941. Upon the conclusion of the war, David Leach took his new-found experience and knowledge back to St Ives, forming a business partnership with his father, where he remained until 1955, when he left to establish his own pottery at Lowerdown Cross in Devon.

During the three years of David Leach's absence, Bernard Forrester (1908-1990), an employee at the Leach Pottery, was drafted in to Dartington to undertake David's teaching commitments at the Foxhole School. Although Forrester had assisted with the building of Leach's first kiln on the Dartington site in 1932, his role at Dartington was solely as a teacher and he did not undertake any further involvement with the developments at the pottery. He did however establish his own workshop in 1952 in

Broadhempston, Devon, where he produced earthenware, stoneware and latterly lustred porcelain (Fig. 101). Forrester was industrially trained, having completed an eight year apprenticeship with Mintons in Stoke-on-Trent. Although he had worked at the Leach Pottery, he was very aware of developments in contemporary art and this became apparent in his work,which had very little reference to the Anglo-Oriental tradition whose constraints he had found too restricting.[18]

Although the relationship between Leach and the Elmhirsts flourished, for a number of reasons any plans to move from St Ives were still-born. Primarily, Leach demanded total creative freedom from the authorities at Dartington and was unprepared to undertake the role of an employee of the estate with the restrictions which this might have implied. Furthermore, he would promise no profits for five years. His estimated running costs were considered financially unrealistic by Dr William Slater, managing director of Dartington Hall Limited, the company under which the affairs of the estate were managed. These factors, combined with the uncertainty which the war had instilled, ensured that all plans to transfer production were shelved. Nonetheless between 1935 and 1938, the Elmhirsts had invested the huge sum of £3500 into the modernisation of the Leach pottery at St Ives, which David Leach was able to revolutionise based on his new-found education. He effectively rescued the pottery from the brink of financial disaster.

Prior to this redevelopment, the St Ives workshop had conveyed the air of an artist's studio rather than that of a production pottery. With the introduction of the more efficient method of oil-firing, the dreadful kiln-losses, which Bernard Leach had accepted as an inevitability in the struggle to achieve the ultimate pot, were virtually eliminated. Machines such as pug-mills were introduced to speed up and improve the quality of clay processing, which until this time had all been carried out by the potter's hand. It was intended although never initiated that the pottery at Dartington would follow this example. Bernard Leach advocated the use of such labour-saving devices as pug-mills, although this was with some caution, stating,

> ...the tendency, as with the use of every new source of power, is towards abuse, or thoughtless over-use.[19]

A range of 'standard-ware' was produced (Fig. 96). The initial prototypes were designed by Bernard Leach, and then made with the assistance of the team which was working at the pottery. This range, evidently descended from bold medieval forms, combined with the influence of the style and materials of the Orient, was designed for daily use as a modern alternative to industrial tableware. Pared down to minimal decoration, with a hard celadon or tenmoku glaze,[20] the forms were designed for their functional practicalities, however great consideration was still paid to their simple aesthetic.[21]

It is significant that without the Elmhirsts' patronage, it is unlikely that Leach would have played such a major role in the shaping of the studio pottery movement. With support from Dartington, Bernard and David Leach had created pottery, in its own way distinctly modern, which rejected the highly decorated crockery with over-embellished forms and unpractical handles in production by the industry. Embracing purely relevant aspects of English and Oriental traditions, these works combined conventional hand processes with modern style and more durable, suitable materials.

SAM HAILE

During the same period as Leach was experimenting in the West Country, William Staite Murray, from the Royal College of Art, London, was establishing his reputation. Like Leach he drew influence from Oriental ceramics, sharing a corresponding interest in Zen Buddhism. However, he determined that the artist-potter should find his place in the contemporary world; as a consequence, he did not set out with the intention of producing 'utilitarian' work, the function of the vessels he created was coincidental and of secondary importance. Perceiving himself as a modern artist, he only exhibited his work alongside paintings and sculptures in the Bond Street galleries and it was his belief that pottery formed the meeting point of these forms of expression.

Leach by contrast argued the case for the 'utilitarian' or 'ethical' pot, over that of the 'art' pot, a view represented in a statement which was clearly an attack on Staite Murray's principals,

> What have the artist-potters been doing all this while? Working by hand to please ourselves first, and therefore producing only limited and expensive pieces, we have been supported by collectors, purists, cranks, or "arty" people, rather than by the normal man or woman. In so far as we have tended ourselves to become abnormal, and consequently most of our pots have become still-born: they have not a breath of reality in them: it has been a game.[22]

Yet surprisingly, it was a pupil of Staite Murray who followed Leach at Dartington. With the pottery at St Ives rescued from the brink of collapse, the workshop at Shinner's Bridge, Dartington was neglected and had fallen into disrepair. In 1946, Leach suggested to the potter Sam Haile (1909-1948) and his wife Marianne De Trey (b1913) that they should move to the Dartington Estate and take over the facility. Haile and De Trey moved to Devon from Bulmer in Suffolk where they had established and run a small pottery at Bulmer brickworks. Haile had met Leach and Hamada many times during visits to Cornwall and was well acquainted with their work and philosophy.

A former student of the Royal College of Art, Haile had studied under Staite Murray, sharing with him many of his opinions regarding the position of pottery within the arts. His pots were given titles, a practice initiated by Staite Murray, insinuating an affiliation with painting and sculpture. He was undoubtedly the finest student to come from the Staite Murray fold.

Haile first attended the Royal College in 1931 to study painting. An accomplished painter in the surrealist style, he grew frustrated and disillusioned, due predominantly to the negative response he received from the head of the Royal College, William Rothenstein, who disliked surrealism. Unable to overcome this criticism and facing the threat of failing his diploma, Haile began to develop a strong bias towards ceramics. During his final year of study, ceramics formed the dominant vent for his expression.

He did not lose his aspiration to paint and in 1936 his paintings were included in the International Surrealist Exhibition which was held at the Burlington Galleries in London. In this year, he also exhibited several pots in a group show at the Brygos Gallery, New Bond Street, entitled, 'Under £10 English Pottery.' His first major exhibition of ceramics was to follow in 1937, also at the Brygos Galleries. Despite the unconventional nature of the pots, both in form and decoration, the show was a considerable success. Sales were made to at least five British museums, the Contemporary Art Society and a number of discerning private collectors. It appeared that Haile was on the verge of establishing himself a niche as a major influence in the British studio pottery movement. The pots were a remarkable contrast to those of the Leach School which had dominated the movement, both in terms of style and their inherent philosophy.

Haile's work was characteristic of Staite Murray's in many ways, producing large, thick-rimmed vessels with deep, heavy footrings, the variation of line in the sometimes faltering, undulating forms, contrasting with the tightly springing profiles common in the linear pots of the Leach School. They differed however from those made by his tutor and mentor in the original fashion of their powerful decoration (Figs.97, 98). He drew influence from the works of Pueblo Indians, the Minoans, Cycladic and English medieval pottery and arts. Developing from Staite Murray's decorative approach, Haile adapted the style and subject of his paintings to adorn the surface of his pots, as described here by Patrick Heron.

> ...dancing nudes with bird-like heads being strung round the belly of an angular jar or spilt round the inside curves of a bowl. Ideographic in quality, Haile's images are cast in terms of nervous, vital, stringy line and they are employed as interchangeable units of design. Eyes; leaves;

> a group of purely abstract concentric rings; a figure with square breasts, fin-like hands and feet, eyes in its ears or, alternatively, a face-profile superimposed on a circle for its head, balanced on a single stalk, for a neck...his best pots created a new situation in contemporary English pottery - they were the first modern pots which bore any relation to modern painting...ten years before Picasso began to design and decorate pots at Vallauris, Haile was creating his essentially contemporary idiom in pot decoration...[23]

His forms were basically traditional, this because they were governed to a degree by function and tradition had evolved around ergonomics, but such use of decoration had not been seen before and was most certainly a sharp contrast to the work of Leach and his followers.[24]

In 1938, Haile married Marianne De Trey, a student in Textiles whom he had met while studying at the Royal College. De Trey reflected upon Haile's autonomy,

> Sam was a revolutionary; he loved the traditional things, but he wasn't at all bogged-down by tradition. He and Bernard [Leach] got on very well together, they liked each other, but of course their attitude was totally different.[25]

Haile was a pacifist and with the outbreak of war, left England for America with his wife. De Trey described the effect which his political convictions shed upon his work,

> They were imaginative paintings because he had to get it out of his system. They were about the terrible things that were happening in the world. It was all inside him and it had to come out somehow.[26]

This episode in his life denied him the opportunity to build upon the reputation which he had only just begun to form in Britain. It was in fact in America where the impact of his work was really felt.[27] In September 1943, Haile was drafted into the U S Army from which he was transferred to the British Army in 1944, leaving behind him an indelible influence upon the development of American studio ceramics, which had at the time not experienced the work of Bernard Leach. It was after his demobilisation in 1945 that he moved to Bulmer and finally to Dartington in 1947.

Finding the pottery at Dartington in considerable disrepair, Haile and De Trey carried out the necessary restorations. They converted Leach's updraft kiln to run on oil and set about the production of slipware and tin-glazed earthenware.[28] Although Haile had enormous energy and an incredible passion for ceramics, he had returned from the war suffering from a lack of creative inspiration as De Trey recalls,

> I think psychologically he just couldn't see his way ahead, so it was

> really a period of just waiting until he was ready...he'd had a bad time during the war, from sheer boredom, from not having facilities to do any drawing or painting. He wanted a period of consolidation so he was happy to go back to traditional slipware and wait until the right moment for being more creative again.[29]

Haile had begun to rediscover the vitality which had led to his success in America. Re-inspired and with new-found energy, he made plans to build a saltglaze kiln which was an avenue which had been virtually unexplored by studio potters. It seemed all was perfect to re-launch his life, career and reputation.

Tragically, Haile was never to build his saltglaze kiln. In March 1948, at the age of just 38, he was killed when his converted Jeep was in collision with a bus. Many of Haile's pots perished with him in the accident and consequently examples of his Dartington works are extremely rare.

It is only for us to speculate, on the fiftieth anniversary of his death, what effect Haile might have had upon the development of British studio ceramics had his life not been cut short. His juxtaposition of the traditional and the avant-garde, his energy of expression, his denial of pottery purely for the sake of purpose place him in a unique category during the short period of his creative life. He created a remarkable paradox with the execution of abstracted and surreal decoration by conventional slip-trailing or oxide brushwork on traditional forms, medieval-style jugs and huge chargers providing the carriage for his extraordinary images.

In a 1946 appraisal of Haile's work, A.C. Sewter commented,

> Confronted by pottery such as Haile's even a person not normally interested in the crafts is forced to realise that pottery is a craft with a range and power of expression not less than that of painting.[30]

MARIANNE DE TREY

Upon Haile's death, De Trey continued to develop the site at Shinner's Bridge. She made slip-decorated and tin-glazed earthenware which was fired in an electric kiln which had been built by Haile (Figs. 99, 100). The electric kiln guaranteed a regularity of glaze finish and evenness of colour which could not have been achieved in a kiln fuelled with wood or oil and the resulting pots had a surface comparable in quality to industrial wares.

De Trey introduced colour by the majolica technique,[31] which was well received, as it presented a brighter, less sombre product than those of the Leach school to a post-war public, who were deprived of decorated ware from industrial manufacturers.[32] Even in the studio pottery field, during the late 1940s there were very few people producing colourful pottery such as De Trey's.

In 1952, the pottery was expanded to employ three assistants who made an extensive range of domestic-ware to De Trey's blueprints. Although she was unaware of the earlier Leach/Elmhirst proposals, De Trey also emphasised volume production of a range which could be easily afforded and was therefore not too precious to use.[33]

THE DARTINGTON CONFERENCE OF THE CRAFTS

In 1952 Bernard Leach instigated the Dartington Conference of the Crafts at Dartington Hall. This conference sought to unite and engage the practitioners of the crafts from many nations in lectures and demonstrations, with the intention of defining the position and role of the craftsperson in the contemporary world. Work from the conference was toured nationally in a major exhibition and it was upon its arrival in London that Robert Melville launched a scathing attack upon Leach and his contemporaries in *Architectural Review.* He wrote,

> The whole air is of the remains of a lost civilisation, of a village and market town community of highly aesthetic peasants...Only the stoneware of Hans Coper and the porcelain of Lucie Rie remains outside the atmosphere of rural quietism. They alone make the point that the whole exhibition was intended to make. They show that the artist craftsman is not necessarily an anachronism in our time, that it is not impossible for him or her, so to speak, to be with us.[34]

Melville's damning assault on Leach's work represented the attitude of a sector of the pot-buying public who, by the 1950s were bored with the Leach ethic. They were hungry for an alternative to the Anglo-Oriental tradition.

Melville's comments however, typically disregard the innovative developments which Leach had, in the preceding decades, contributed to the studio pottery movement. Leach and his followers were not modernists in the purest sense, as their work drew few parallels with the art and architecture of the period; nevertheless, they insisted that without recognition of the effects of the modern world, that the craftsman was essentially play-acting and as a consequence his work could not be considered as sincere.

Leach endeavoured to place traditional elements of pottery into a more modern context. With an emphasis on utility (although his work is often displayed rather than used) he sought to strike a balance, by employing only appropriate traditional elements, combined with relevant influences from other cultures. Avoiding pure reproduction and ensuring that function would not be sacrificed to rational design, he maintained,

> The potter, in his concepts, must possess such a sheer love of the truth as will carry him past the dangers of revivalism on one hand and of futurism on the other.[35]

From this principled viewpoint, he set out not to continue a tradition, but to lay the foundations for a whole new tradition.

The painter Patrick Heron spent fourteen months working at the Leach Pottery. He defended Leach from the charge of revivalism, stating,

> ...he has demonstrated the aesthetic parallel existing between Sung and medieval pottery - thus creating a genuine East-West synthesis; and in doing this, he has given us a ceramic idiom very much in accord with aspects of modern art. One can compare him to Henry Moore in some ways: both by-passed the Renaissance.[36]

However, Leach's preoccupation with the production of pots for the 'common man,' combined with the denial of pottery as 'high-art', has done little to dispel the ruralistic interpretation of the man and his work, which has regularly served to overshadow his innovation. Indeed, although similarities may be drawn between some of Leach's ethics and those of William Morris and his fixation with the products of pre-industrial culture, common attitudes may be found between Leach and some modernist commentators. The emphasis Leach placed upon process, technique and the 'honest' use of materials sits sympathetically alongside certain modernist ideals.

In the pots he cherished, he sought soul and character from the marks of the potter's hands and tools, the accidents in the firings; every touch by the potter was considered to be physiognomic. Leach believed that,

> ...with insight and experience, the qualities of the man may be seen in the pot. We are more accustomed to the idea in the unapplied arts. To the trained eye, decision or hesitation, sensibility or dullness, breadth or narrowness, tenderness or sentimentality, nobility or the commonplace, are all nakedly exposed.[37]

Leach here demonstrates an assessment of the work of the potter more akin to the interpretation of modern expressionist painting. Similarly, Clement Greenberg's belief that modernism's break with the past is a dialectical move which is striving to, '...maintain or restore continuity...with the highest aesthetic standards of the past, to restore quality which in turn is to be preserved by constant renewal and innovation' might be applied to Leach's philosophy when implementing his rationalisation of traditional design.

The Leach tradition dominated the 1950's but by the 1960's Rie and Coper had established themselves in the mainstream of the movement, promoting the use of organic, natural forms, which emitted definite sculptural overtones. Theirs was truly modern work, which drew influence from sculpture, experimenting with form and texture. Other ceramists began to reject the Leach ethic and sought a freedom which the production of domestic-ware would not allow. Many of them, Coper included, were supported by teaching salaries and did not have to strive to produce vast quantities of pots to survive.

Although today, the demand for hand-made domestic-ware has dwindled, several renowned potters, who owe much to the Leach legacy, continue to produce tableware. With a few exceptions, these potters work alone and their pots command high prices. One of the last remaining workshops where hand-made pottery is produced on a semi-industrial scale, is at Dartington Pottery, on the now expanded Shinner's Bridge site.[38] Here the techniques of both craft and industry are combined in the production of reasonably priced tableware in volume for the 'common man.' Although the style bears no resemblance to that of the Leach tradition, perhaps Dartington Pottery finally represents the realisation, on the Dartington Estate, of the Leach/Elmhirst dream.

1 Many of the most celebrated studio potters of current times have established their workshops in the West Country, initially in Cornwall in the 1920s and since the 1930s, in Devon. The county is home to makers such as David Leach, Marianne De Trey, Clive Bowen, John Maltby, Svend Bayer and Nic Collins, among numerous others.

2 For a detailed study of seventeenth century slipware manufacture in Devon, see Alison Grant *North Devon Pottery: The Seventeenth Century,* University of Exeter Press, 1983.

3 In this study, references to industrially manufactured wares should be defined as ceramics produced by mechanical means or by a method of casting of ceramic in plaster moulds.

4 Country potteries typically produced hand-made, coarse earthenwares such as pitchers, ham salters, baking dishes and pickling jars, for use by local communities which were virtually self-sufficient.

5 The trade of the country potteries died out due to a lack of demand for their products. This was largely as a result of improvements in transportation, rendering towns and their facilities more accessible such that the products required for self-sufficiency were no longer a necessity.

6 Sgraffito is a decorating technique whereby lines are scratched through a surface slip of one colour to expose the clay body beneath of a contrasting colour. Bernard Leach *A Potter's Book,* London 1940, p. 274.

7 Oliver Watson *Studio Pottery*, London 1985, p.12.

8 The Central School in London experienced the development of studio pottery during the same period, under the guidance of Dora Billington. Much of the work from the Central School was influenced by Bristol tin-glaze of the eighteenth century.

9 Bernard Leach to Leonard Elmhirst, 11th December 1931, quoted in Bernard Leach, *Beyond East and West: Memoirs, Portraits and Essays*, London 1978, p.162.

10 The Mingei movement was responsible for the revival of the status of the Japanese crafts during the 1920s.

11 Quoted in Bernard Leach: *Beyond East and West: Memoirs, Portraits and Essays*, London 1978, p.163.

12 Bernard Leach *A Potters Book,* London 1940, p.1.

13 Bernard Leach to Dr Slater, 19th Sept 1935. Elmhirst Centre Archive, Dartington Hall.

14 Bernard Leach to Dr Slater, 4th Dec 1934. Elmhirst Centre Archive, Dartington Hall.

15 Stoneware clay, when fired, is impermeable and vitrified. Earthenware is porous when fired and may only be made impervious by covering with a glaze.

16 Bernard Leach. *A Potter's Outlook.* St Dominic's Press 1928. Republished in *Studio Pottery* Feb/Mar 1994 p.64.
17 Quoted by David Leach from a letter sent by his father to Leonard Elmhirst; in *Dartington 60 years of pottery 1933-1993*, Dartington Cider Press 1993, p.28.
18 Forrester continued to teach at the Foxhole School until his retirement in 1973.
19 Bernard Leach *A Potter's Outlook*, St Dominic's Press, 1928. Republished in *Studio Pottery* Feb/Mar 1994, p.66.
20 Celadon- A French name for a certain green applied to a large family of oriental stoneware and porcelain glazes. Tenmoku- A lustrous-black iron stoneware glaze sometimes running to a red rust on thinner parts. Bernard Leach *A Potter's Book,* London 1940, pp.264 & 281.
21 Standardware continued to provide the financial backbone for the Leach Pottery until 1983, when it was phased out in favour of one-off pieces made by Leach's wife, Janet Leach (1918-1997) and his final student Trevor Corser.
22 Bernard Leach. *A Potter's Outlook*, St Dominic's Press 1928. Republished in *Studio Pottery* Feb/Mar 1994 p.59. This statement is something of a paradox, as Leach himself produced a good many expensive, one-off pots, which he referred to as 'personal pots'. Their raison d'être however was no different from that of Staite Murray's 'art pots'.
23 Patrick Heron writing about Haile's Memorial Exhibition in 1951, *The Listener*, p.428. Daniel Rhodes wrote of Haile in a publication by the American Crafts Council, *Forms of the Earth*, 'Years ahead of his time, he created works of commanding importance both in scale and conception and his superb decorations belonged to the mainstreams of Modern Art rather than any debased tradition.'
24 George Wingfield-Digby commented in his book, *The Work of the Modern Potter in England,* London 1952. 'He brought the most original gifts to pottery and showed how an age-old art can be revisualised in purely modern surrealist terms.'
25 Interview between the author and De Trey, Shinner's Bridge, 7th February 1997.
26 Interview between the author and De Trey, Shinner's Bridge, 7th February 1997.
27 Upon arrival in America in 1940, Haile's work was seen by Dr W R Valentiner, Director of the Detroit Institute of Arts. Valentiner was hugely influential in the success which Haile was to enjoy. Impressed by the originality of the work, Valentiner brought it to the attention of his colleagues and acquaintances. This led to major exhibitions in New York and ultimately jobs, teaching at the New York State College of Ceramics at Alfred University in 1941 and in 1942, at the University of Michigan.
28 To supplement their income, Haile took a part-time position working for the Rural Industries Bureau, advising potters how to adapt their businesses to meet more contemporary demand.
29 Interview between the author and De Trey, Shinner's Bridge, February 7th 1997.
30 A.C. Sewter, *Apollo* December 1946, p.163.
31 The name given to Italian tin-enamelled pottery, being a corruption of the name of the island of Majorca. This stanniferous faience developed under the combined influence of Near-Eastern and Hispano-Moresque wares. The Della Robbias were its chief protagonists in the fifteenth century. Definition from Bernard Leach, *A Potter's Book,* London 1940, p.274.
32 Due to war-time restraints, the industrial potteries were legally restricted to supply decorated pots for the export market alone.
33 The pottery was burned down in 1957 and after its rebuilding De Trey implemented a range of stoneware. By 1960, this comprised pots glazed in black and white, which reflected the fashion of the late 1950s and early 1960s. The pots were regularly displayed at the Design Centre in London, as examples of good quality modern design.
34 Robert Melville, *Architectural Review* 112, November 1952, pp. 343-44.
35 Bernard Leach. *A Potter's Book,* London 1940.
36 Patrick Heron, *The Changing Forms of Art,* London, 1955, p.57.
37 Bernard Leach *A Potter's Book*, London 1940, p.124.
38 The Dartington Pottery Training Workshop was formed in 1976 at Shinner's Bridge to train potters in workshop practices. They produced a standard range, but time was allowed for the student/ employees to develop their personal work. This arrangement proved financially unviable. Under a new management, with support from Dartington Hall Trust and the Crafts Council, Dartington Pottery was formed from the old company. New designs by Janice Tchalenko were introduced and their colourful style proved fundamental to the survival of the pottery.

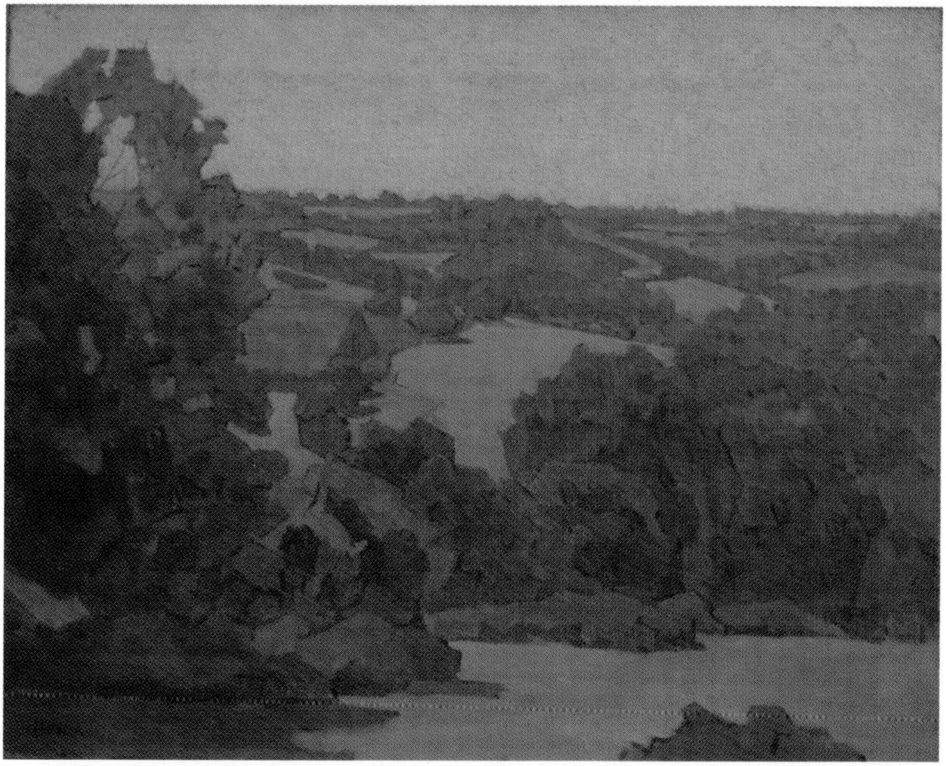

1. Robert Bevan. *Green Devon.* 1919. Oil on canvas. 44.5 x 54.8 cm. Plymouth City Museum and Art Gallery.

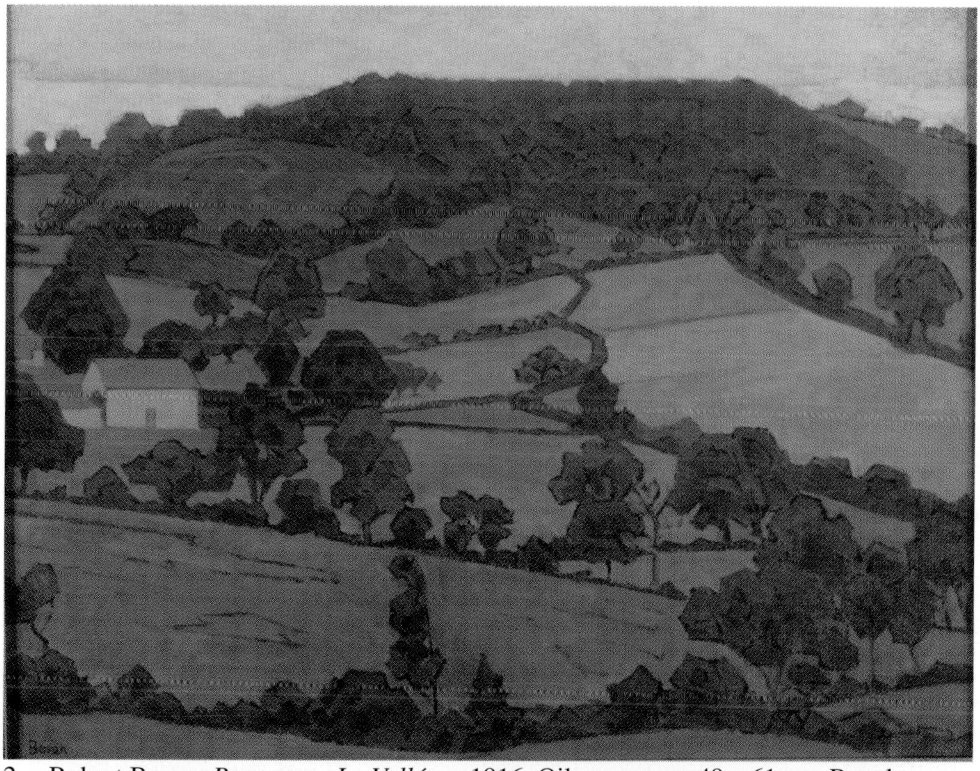

2. Robert Bevan. *Rosemary: La Vallée*. c.1916. Oil on canvas. 49 x 61 cm. Royal Pavillion, Art Gallery and Museums, Brighton and Hove.

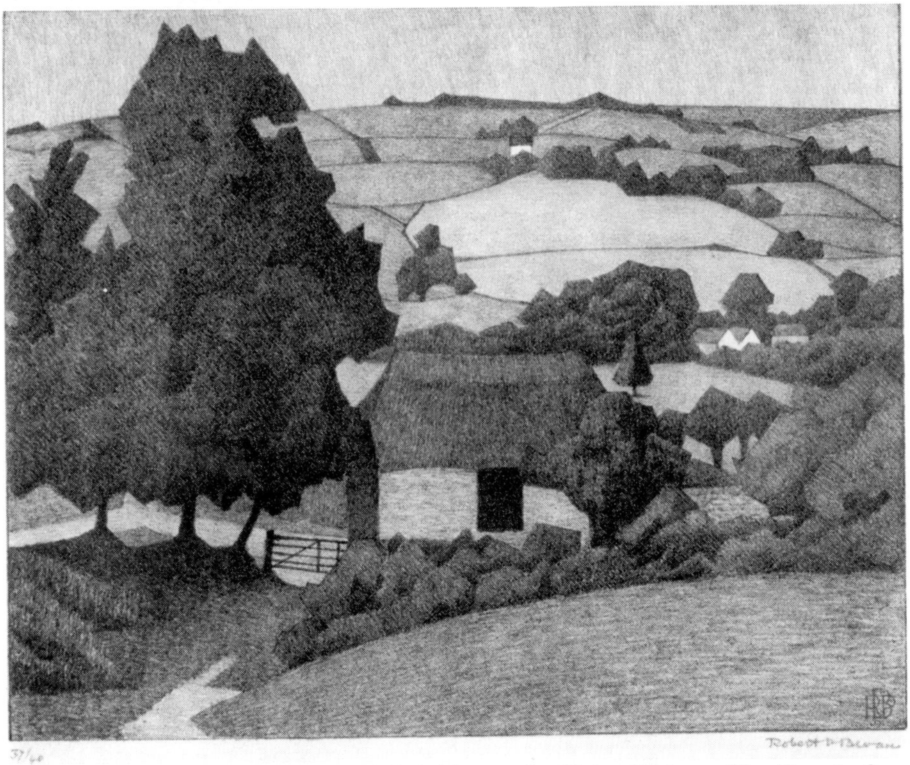

3. Robert Bevan. *Harts Farm.* 1922. Lithograph. 20.6 x 25.2 cm. The Board of Trustees of the Victoria and Albert Museum.

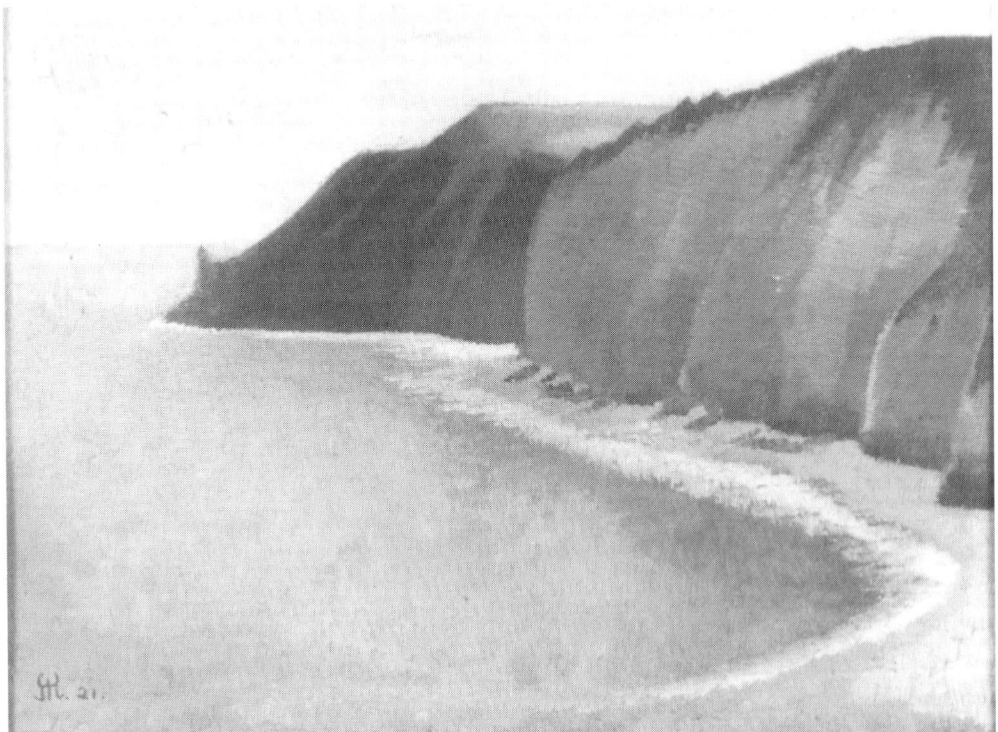

4. Winifred Knights. *Beer, Devon*. 1922. Oil on canvas. 13 x 16.7cm. College Art Collections. University College London

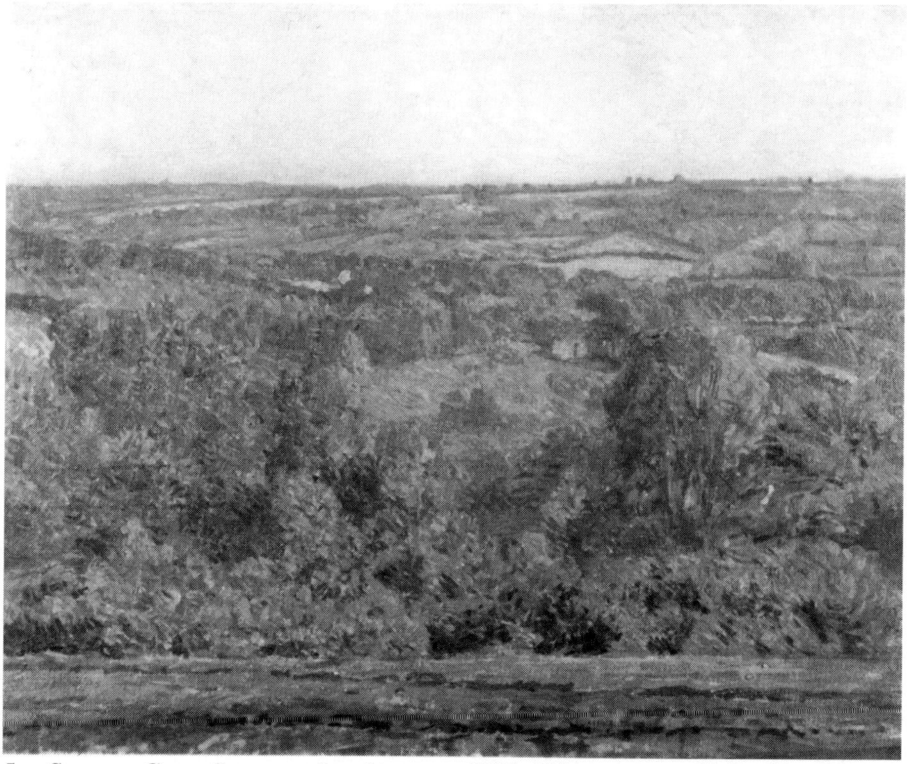

5. Spencer Gore. *Somerset Landscape*. c.1909. Oil on canvas. 50.8 x 61 cm. University of Hull Art Collection.

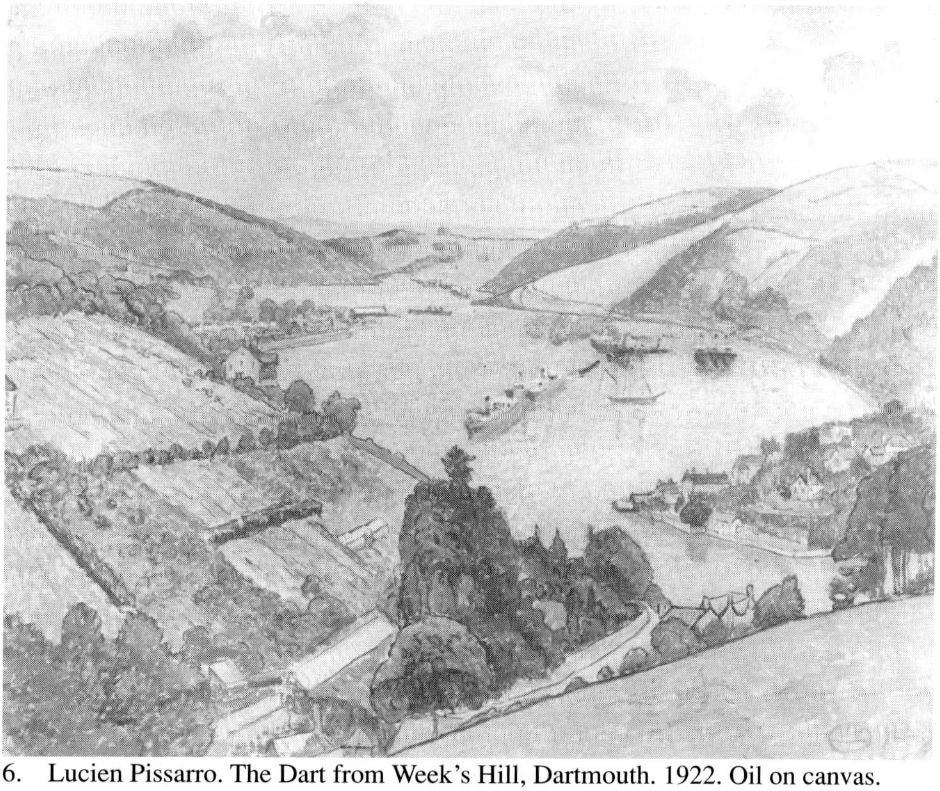

6. Lucien Pissarro. The Dart from Week's Hill, Dartmouth. 1922. Oil on canvas. 53.5 x 65 cm. © Manchester City Art Galleries

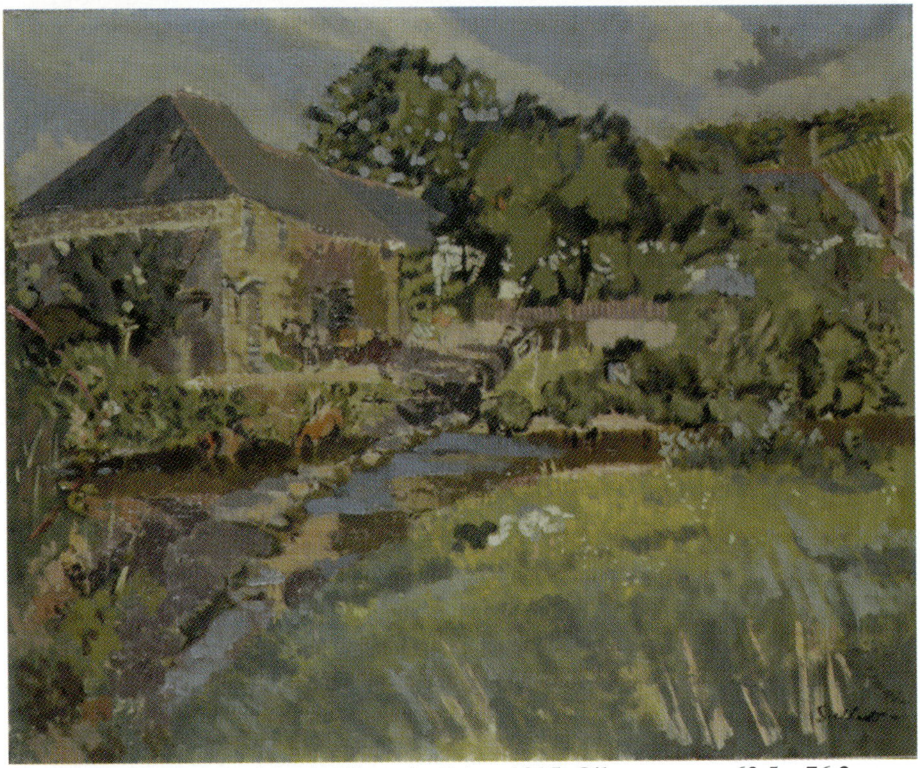

7. Walter Sickert. *Rushford Mill on the Teign*. 1915. Oil on canvas. 63.5 x 76.2 cm. The Syndics of the Fitzwilliam Museum. Cambridge.

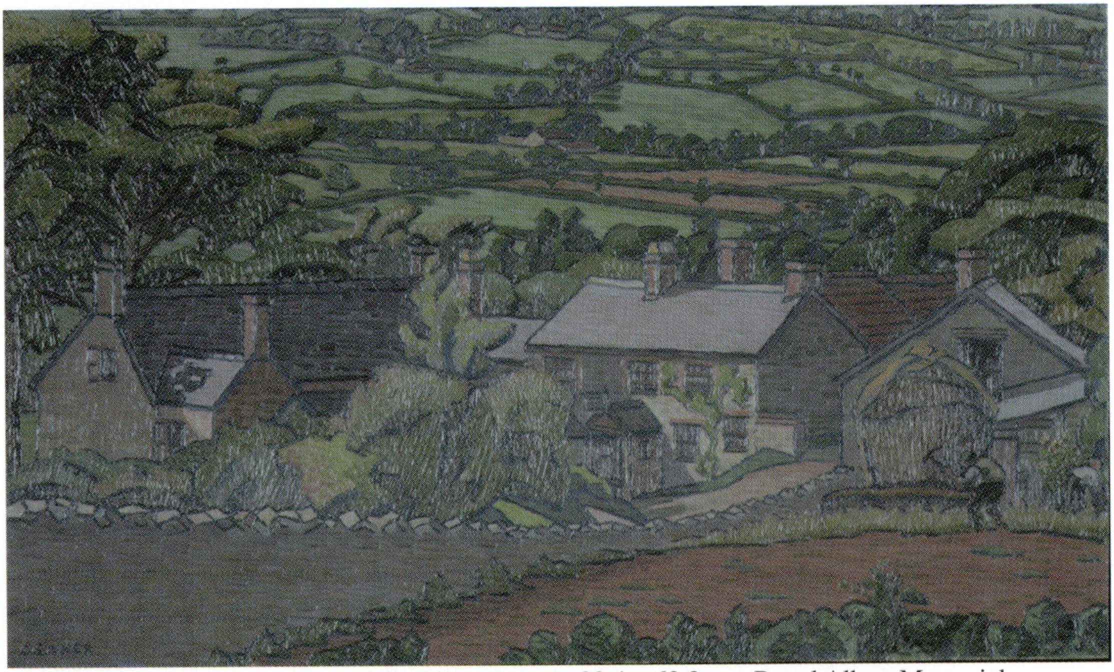

8. Charles Ginner. *Clayhidon*. 1913. Oil on canvas. 38.4 x 63.9 cm. Royal Albert Memorial Museum. Exeter.

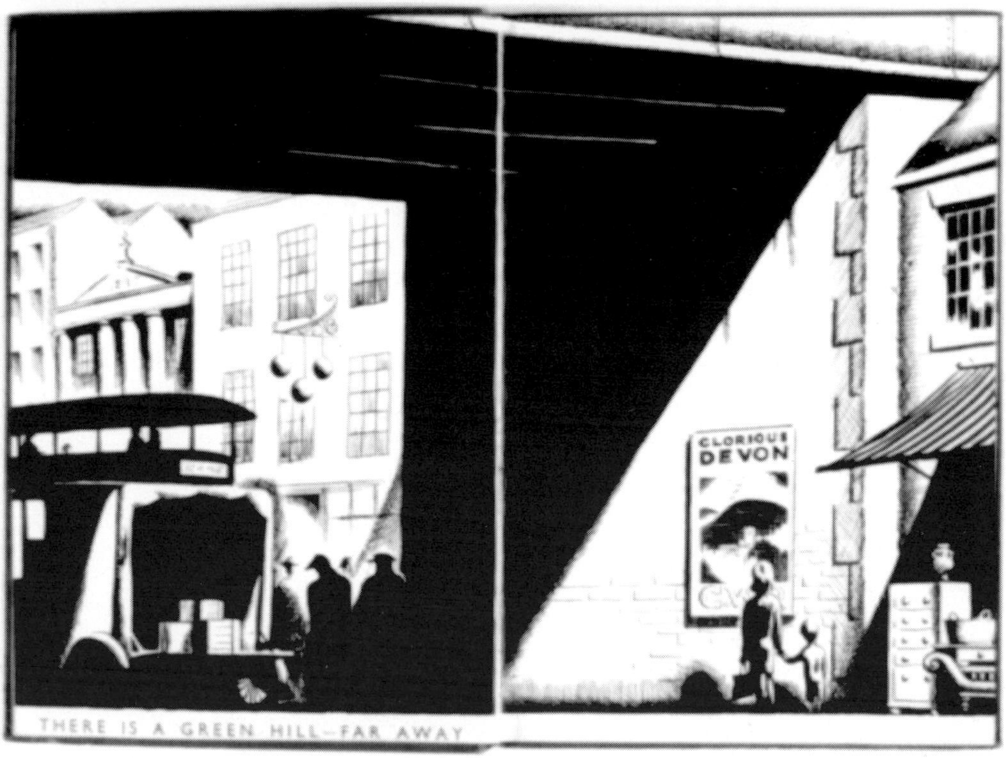

9. Arthur Wragg. 'There is a Green Hill - Far Away.' From *Jesus Wept, A commentary in black and white on ourselves and the world today*. London. 1935.

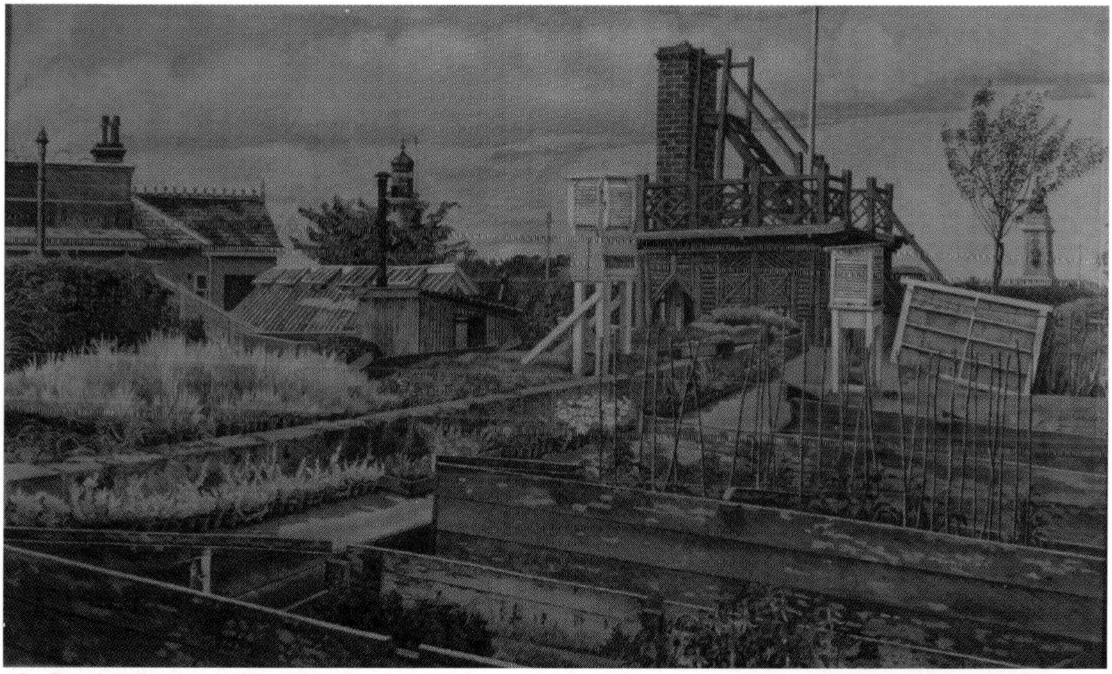

10. Stanley Spencer. *The Hoe Garden Nursery*. 1955. Oil on canvas. 67 x 108.8cm. Plymouth City Museum and Art Gallery.

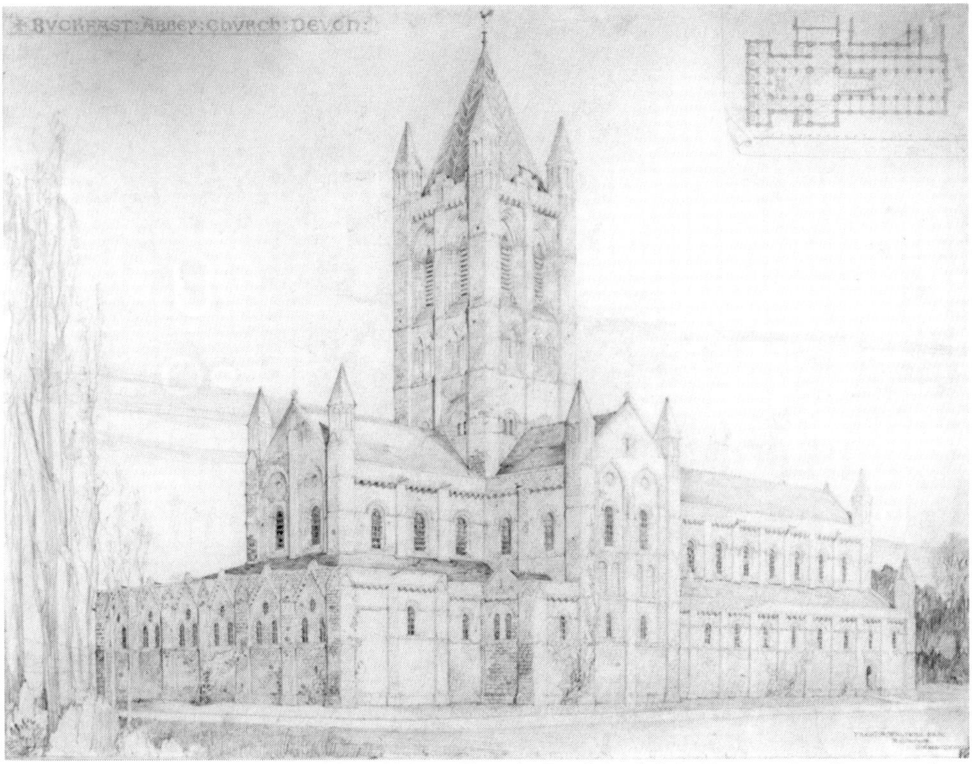

11. Frederick A. Walters. Buckfast Abbey Church, Buckfastleigh. Perspective from north-east. 1909. Built 1910-37. Pencil on paper. 80 x 98cm. Buckfast Abbey Trustees.

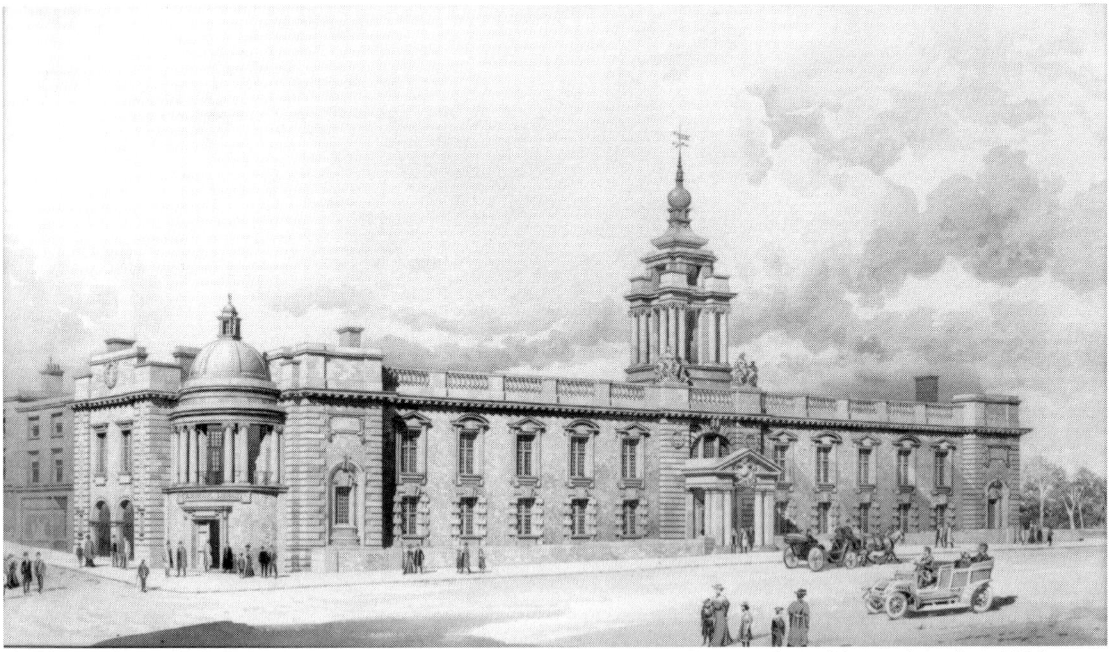

12. Thomas Davison.Torquay Town Hall. Castle Circus, Torquay. Perspective of front elevation.1905. Built 1906-07 and 1911-13. Artist unknown. Pen and ink wash. 36 x 62.5cm. Torre Abbey Art Gallery.

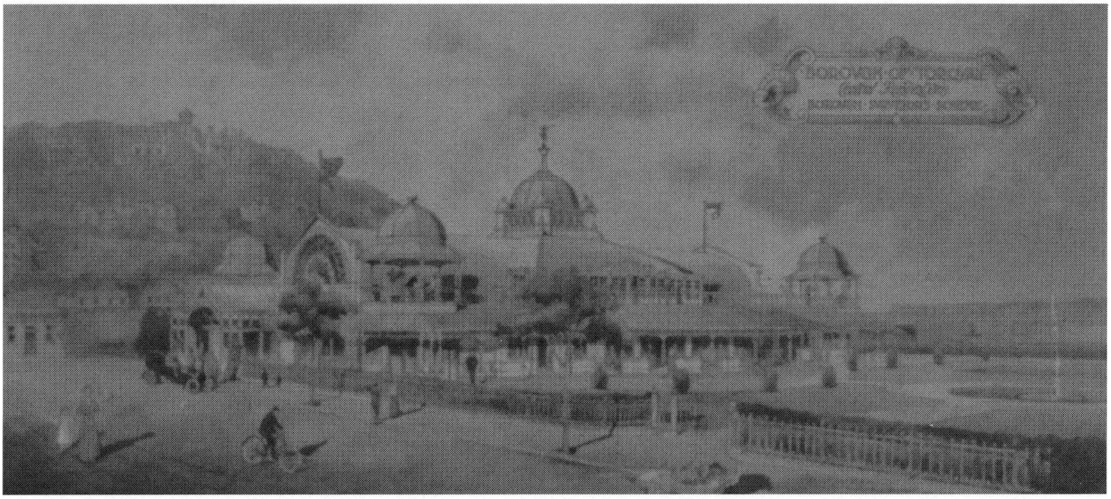

13. Major Harvey A. Garrett, Borough Engineer & Surveyor. The Pavilion, Torquay. Perspective. 1908. Built 1908-11. Drawn by Josias C. Beare of Newton Abbot. Watercolour. 39 x 88cm. Torre Abbey Art Gallery.

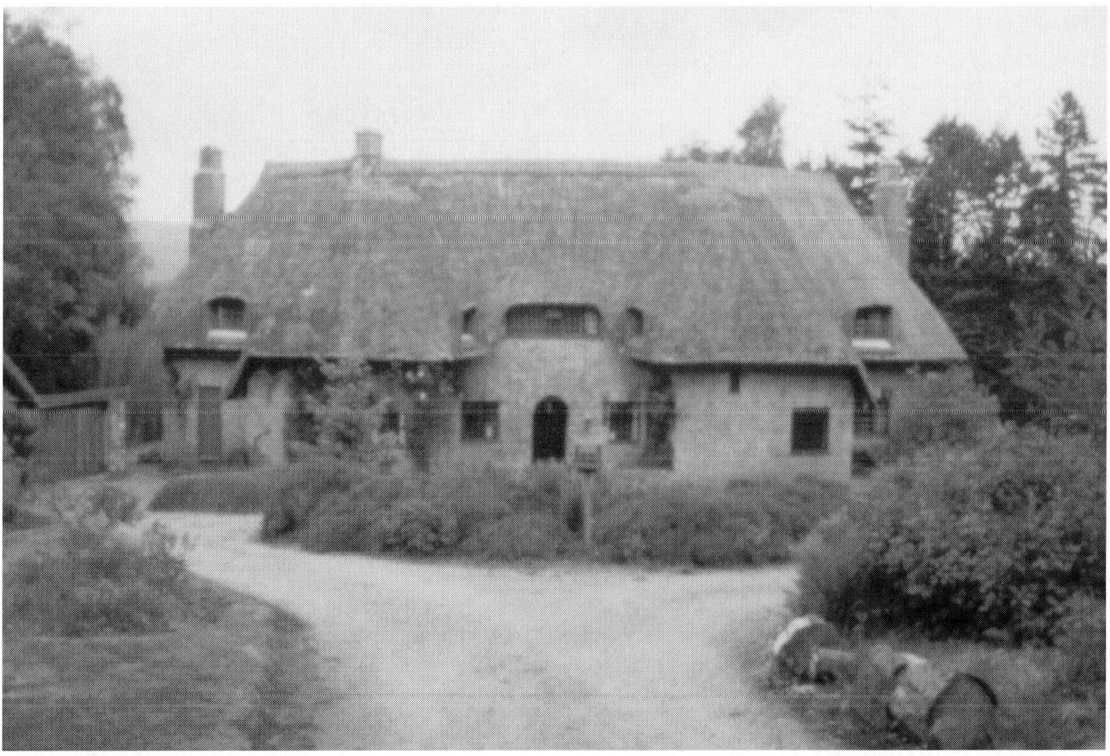

14. Fred Harrild. Pixie's Hill, Holne. Entrance elevation. 1928. Photo: John Schofield.

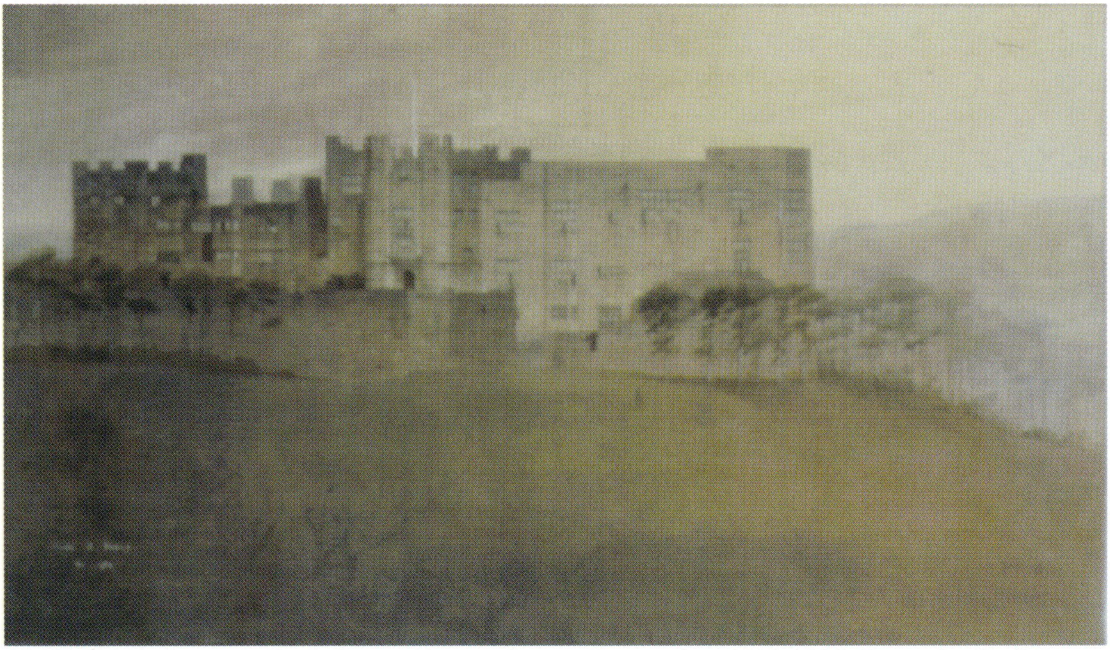

15. Sir Edwin Lutyens. Castle Drogo, Drewsteignton. Perspective. 1910-1930. Drawn by Cyril Farey. Watercolour. 91.4 x 132.1cm. The National Trust.

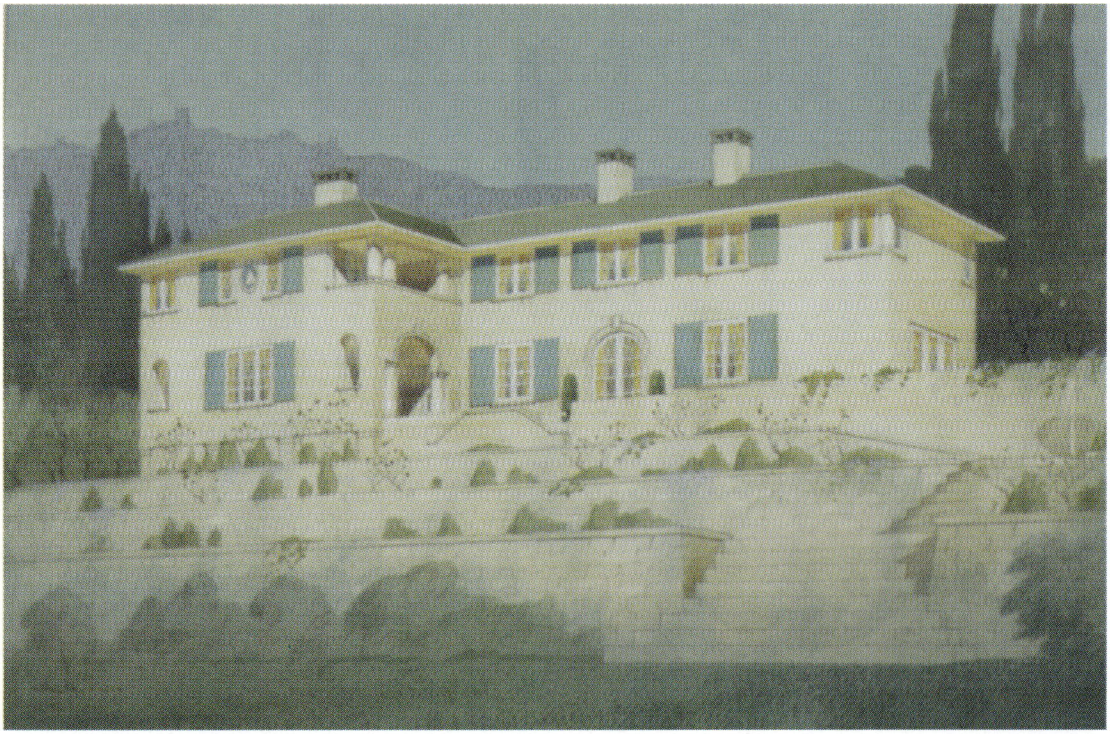

16. Fred Harrild. Casa di Sole. East Portlemouth, Salcombe. Perspective. December 1925. Built 1925-28. Drawn by Cyril Farey. Watercolour on board. 39 x 59cm. Private Collection.

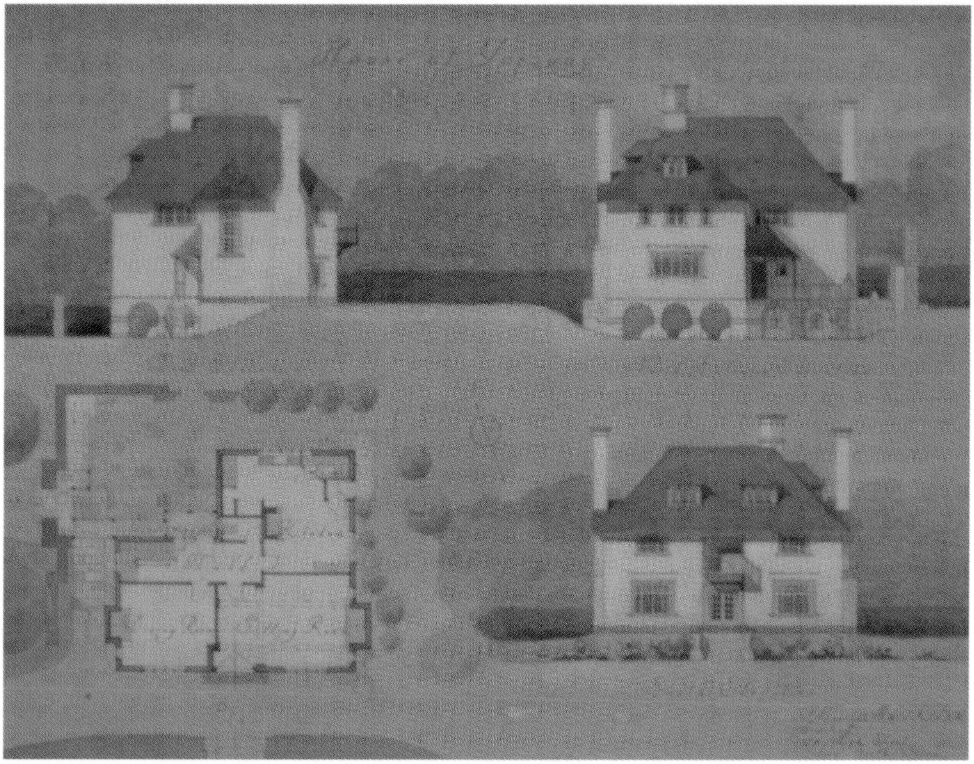

17. Fred Harrild. Little Tor, Torquay. Plan and Elevations. 1932. Drawn by Cyril Farey. Watercolour on board. 42 x 53cm. Private Collection.

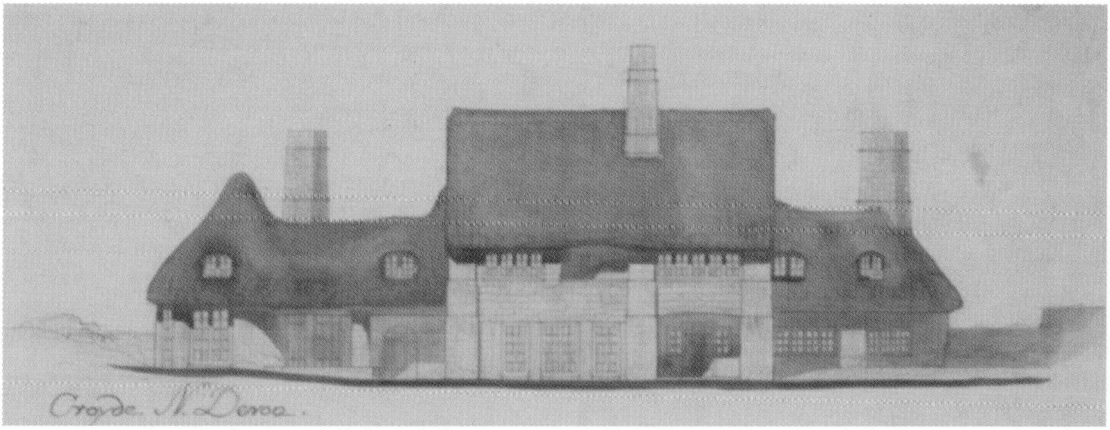

18. Oliver Hill. Cock Rock, Croyde. Elevation drawing. 1925-26. Office of Oliver Hill. Watercolour and pencil on board. 17 x 44cm. Mr and Mrs P.B. Petrides.

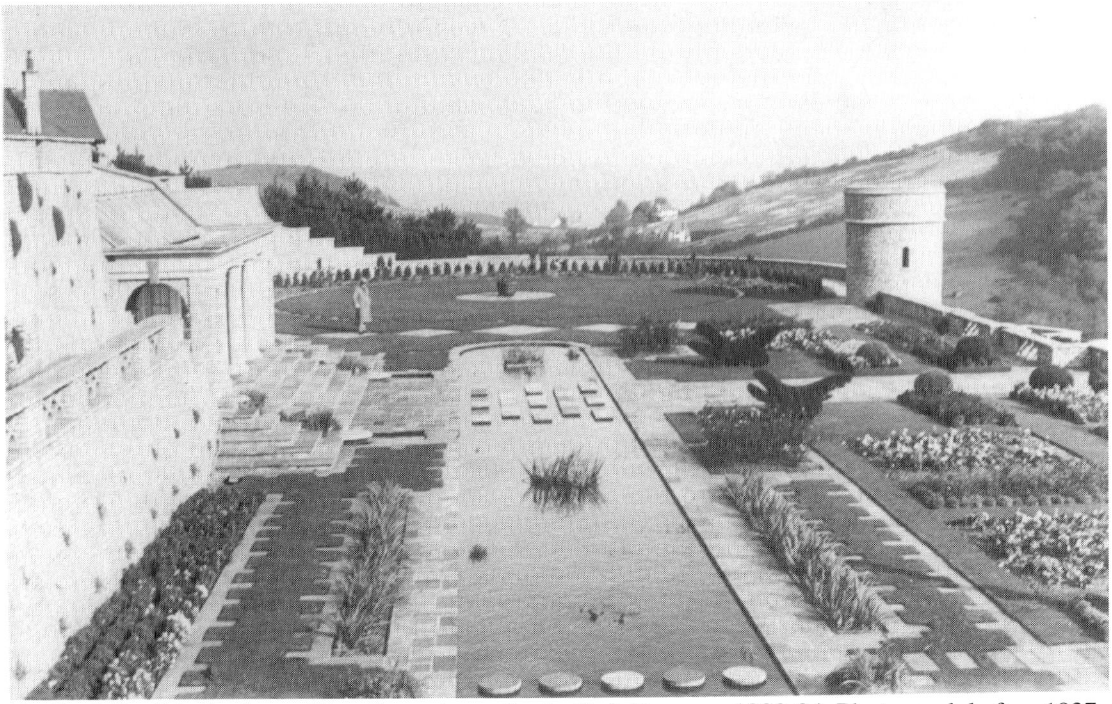

19. Fred Harrild. Garden at Glen Gorse (now Castle Tor), Torquay. 1930-34. Photograph before 1937. Office of Fred Harrild. Private Collection.

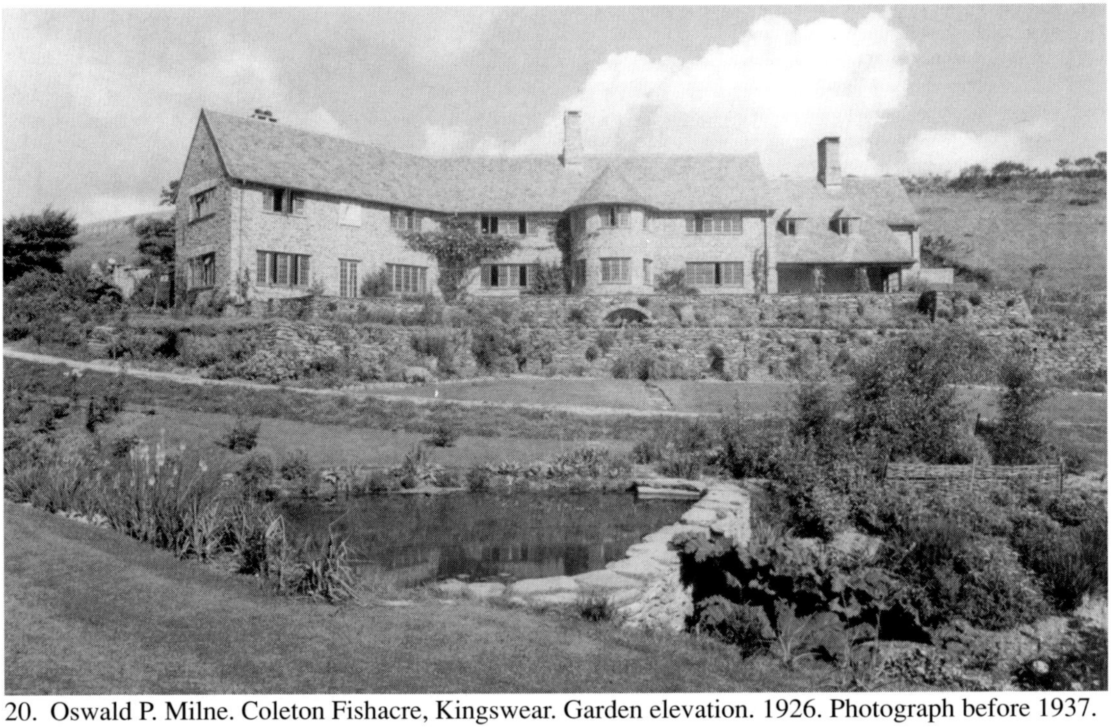

20. Oswald P. Milne. Coleton Fishacre, Kingswear. Garden elevation. 1926. Photograph before 1937. Office of O.P. Milne. The National Trust.

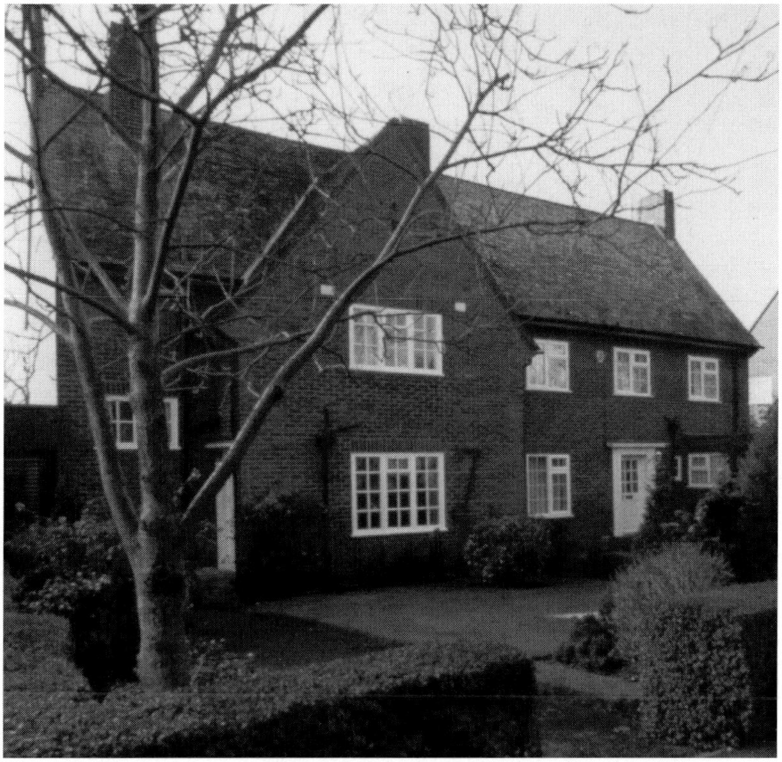

21. Louis de Soissons. Houses at St. James' Priory Estate, Exeter. From 1933. Photo: University of Plymouth.

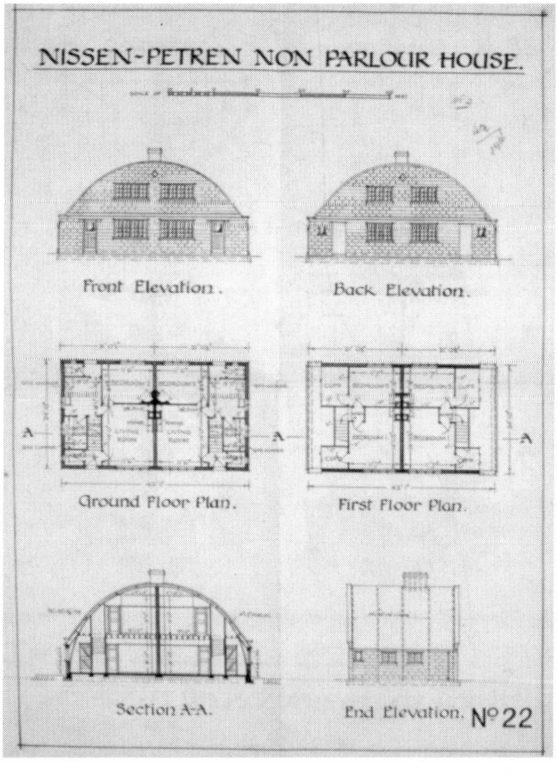

22. Sir Ernest Petter and Lt.Col. Peter N. Nissen with D.J. Dean, Surveyor for Bampton Urban District Council. Houses (Nissen-Petren Non Parlour House), Bampton. Drawing No. 22. Plans and Elevations. 1926. Print. 57 x 41cm. Devon Record Office, Exeter.

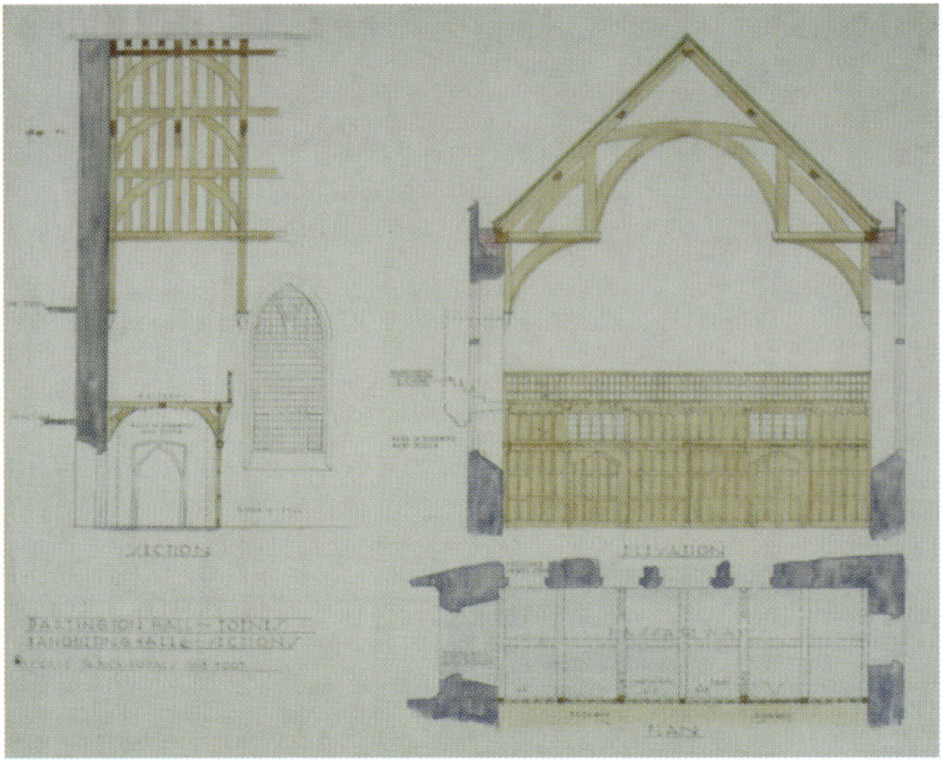

23. William Weir. Reconstruction of Great Hall, Dartington Hall, Dartington. Banqueting Hall - Sections. 1926-38. Watercolour on linen print. 52 x 64cm. The Dartington Hall Trust Collection.

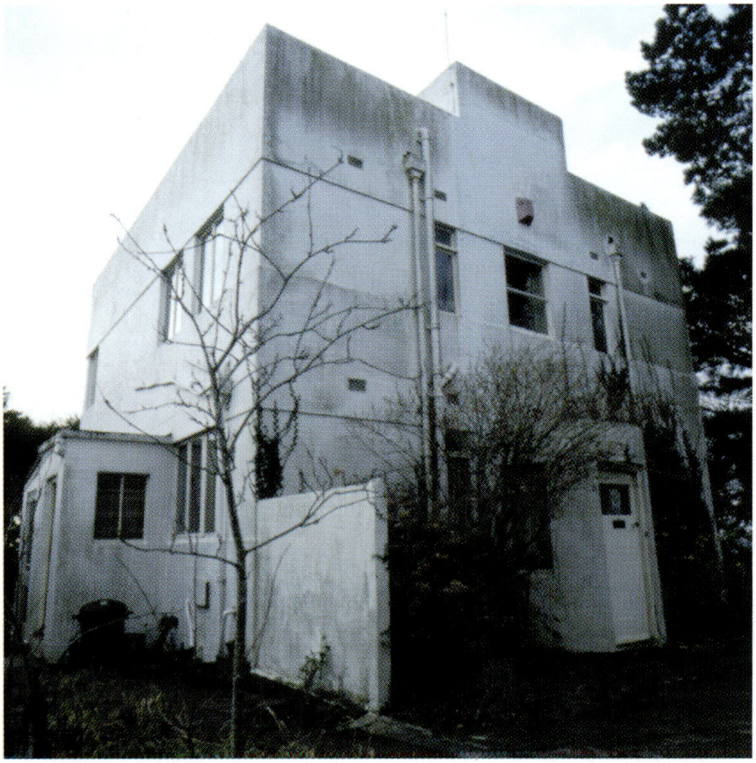

24. William Walter Wood. Oversound House, Down Thomas. 1930. Photo: University of Plymouth.

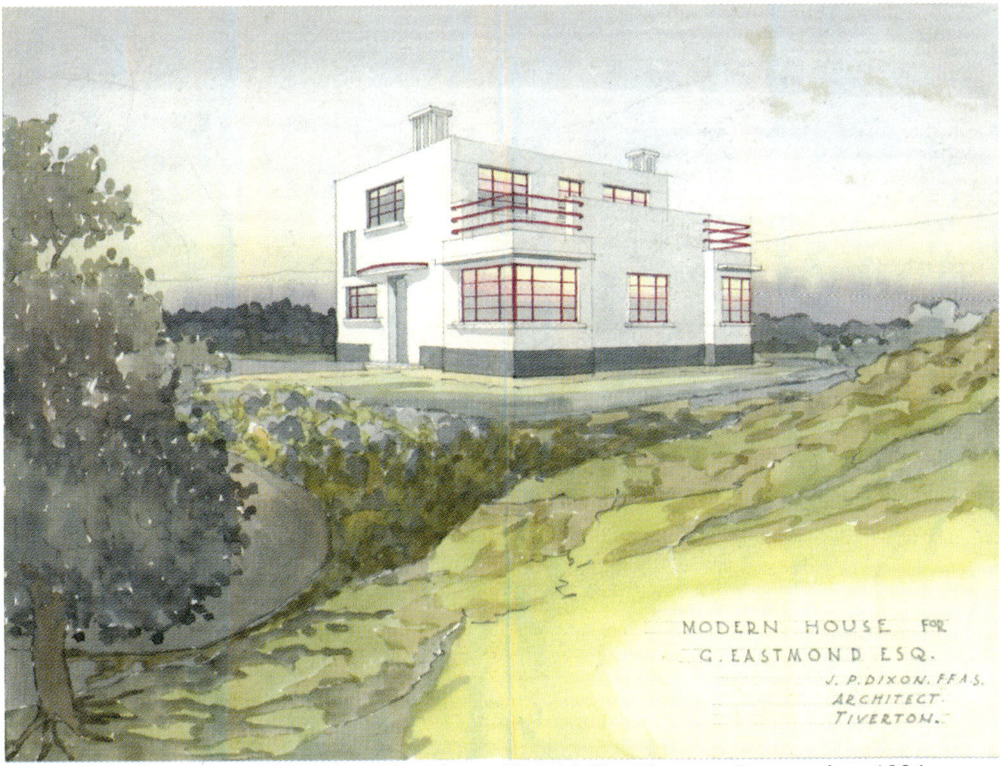

25. G.G.G. Saunders of J.P. Dixon Architect. Shrinkhills, Tiverton. Perspective. 1934. Drawn by G.G.G. Saunders. Watercolour. 17.5 x 23cm. Francis E. Eastmond.

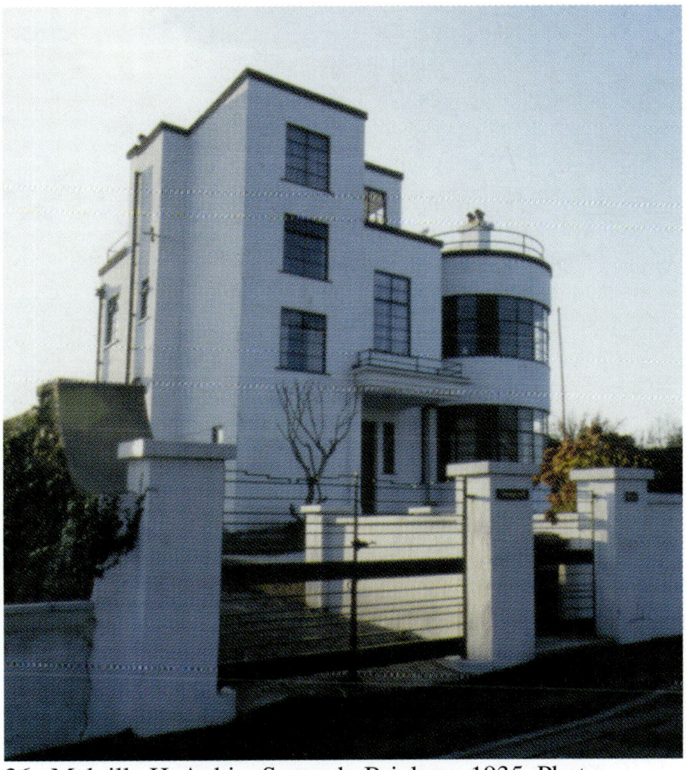

26. Melville H. Aubin. Sunpark, Brixham. 1935. Photo: University of Plymouth.

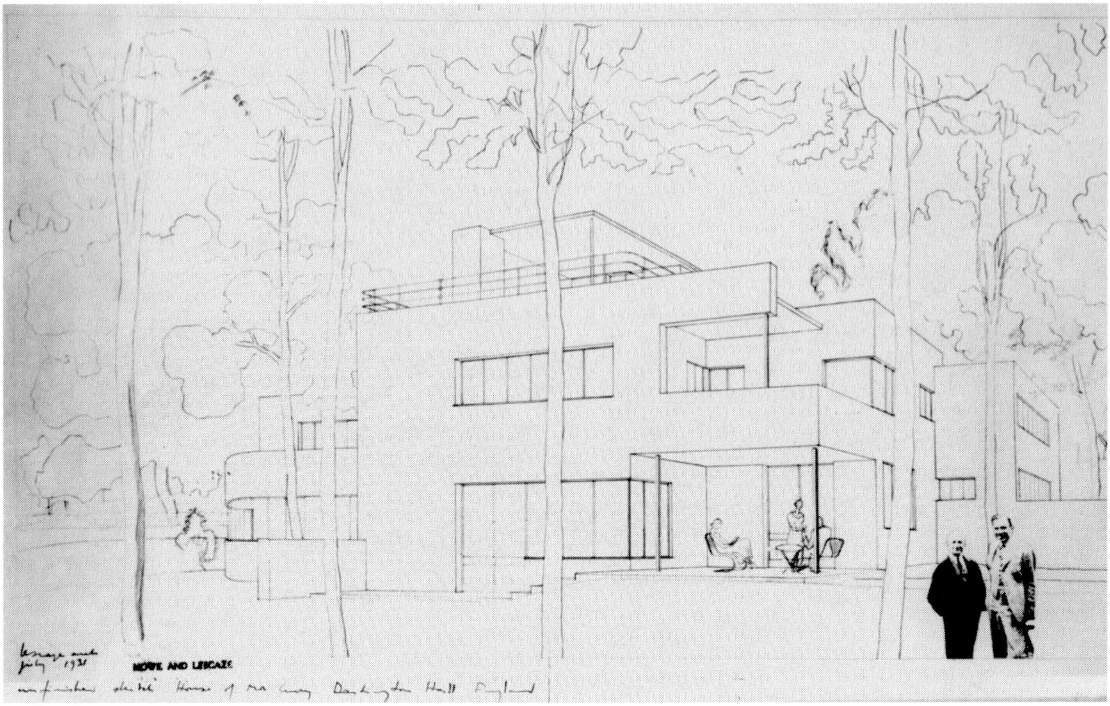

27. William Lescaze of Howe & Lescaze. High Cross House, Dartington Hall, Dartington. 1931 - 32. Office of Howe & Lescaze. Photographic print with photo-montage. 31 x 45cm. The Dartington Hall Trust Collection.

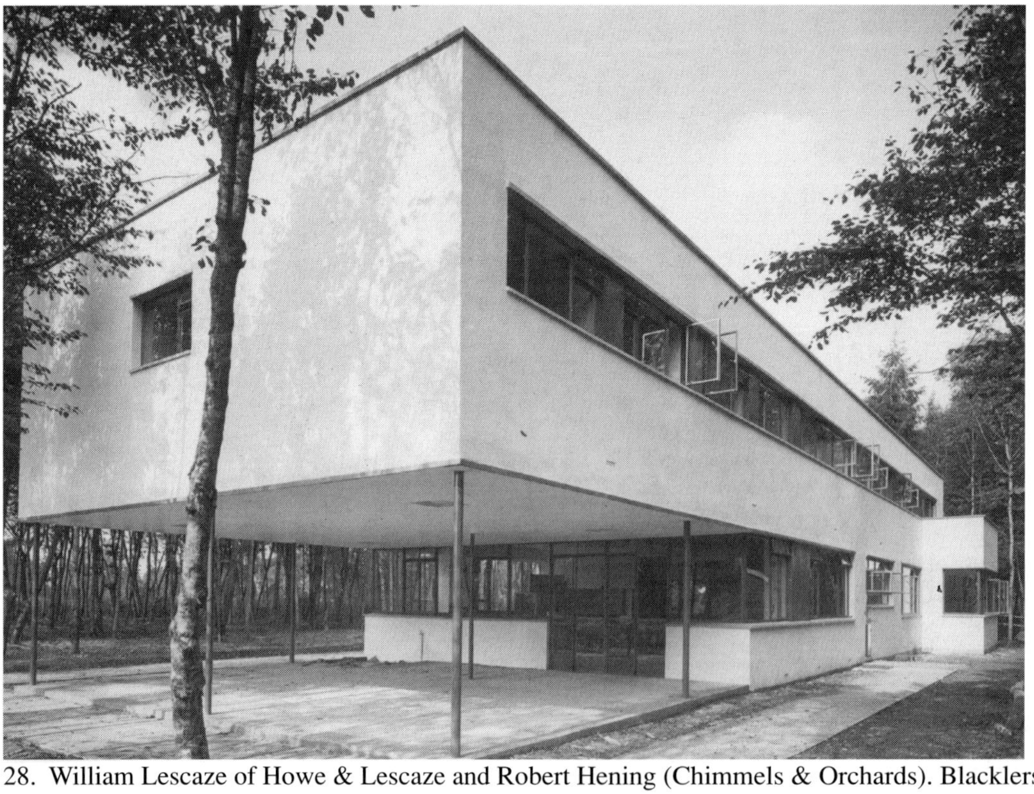

28. William Lescaze of Howe & Lescaze and Robert Hening (Chimmels & Orchards). Blacklers, Chimmels and Orchards, Boarding Houses, Dartington School, Dartington. 1933 (Blacklers), 1934 (Chimmels), 1935 (Orchards). Photo: The Dartington Hall Trust Collection.

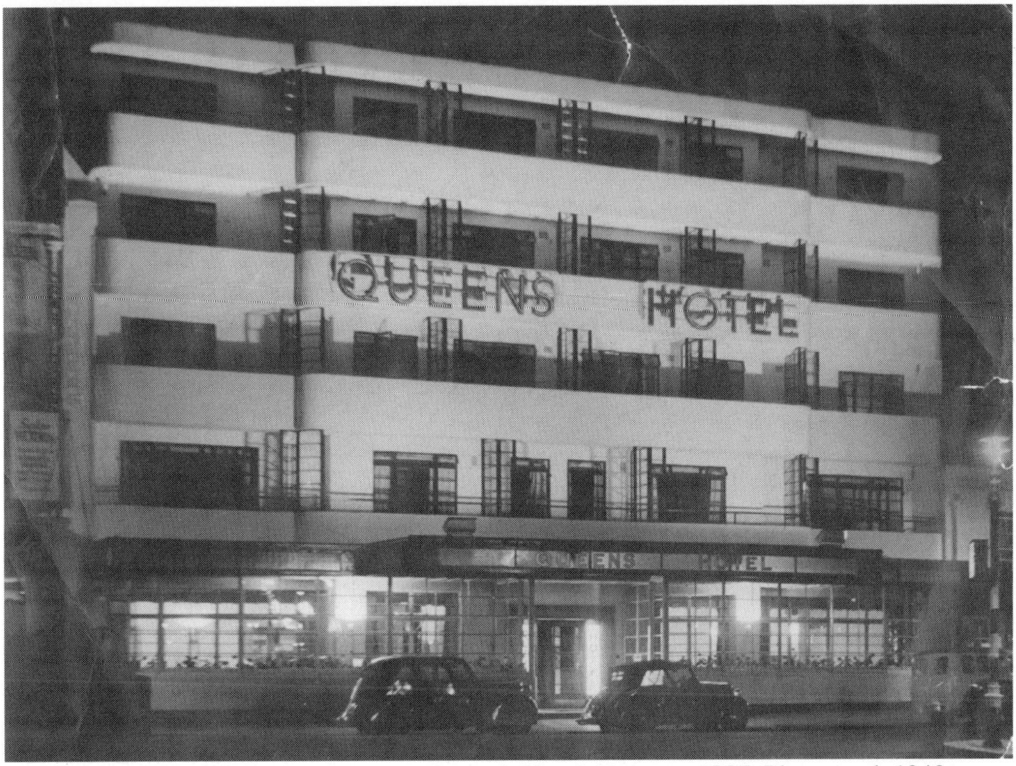

29. Attributed to A.J. Seal & Partners. Queen's Hotel, Torquay. 1937. Photograph 1940s. Photo: Queen's Hotel.

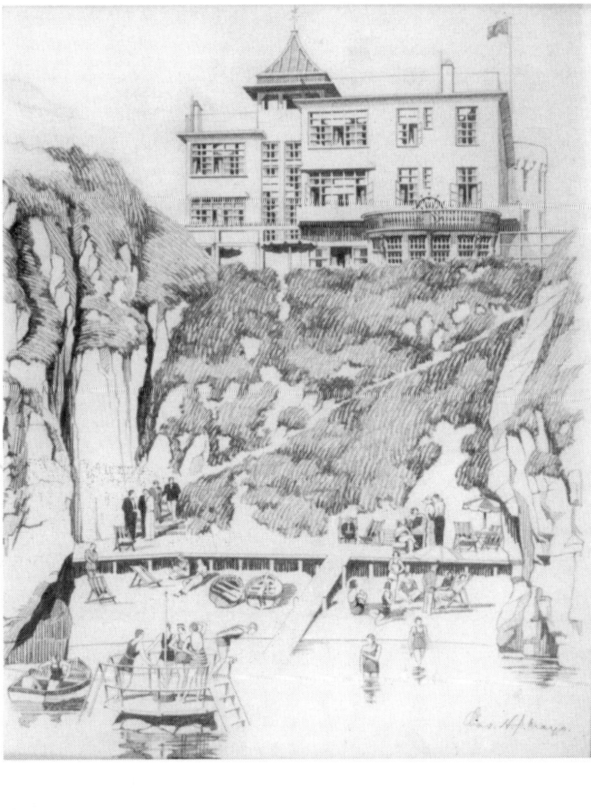

30. Matthew Dawson. Hotel at Burgh Island, Bigbury-on-Sea. 1929 - 34. Drawing early 1930s. Drawn by Chas. H.P. Mayo. Pencil on paper. 33.5 x 26.5. Tony & Beatrice Porter, Burgh Island.

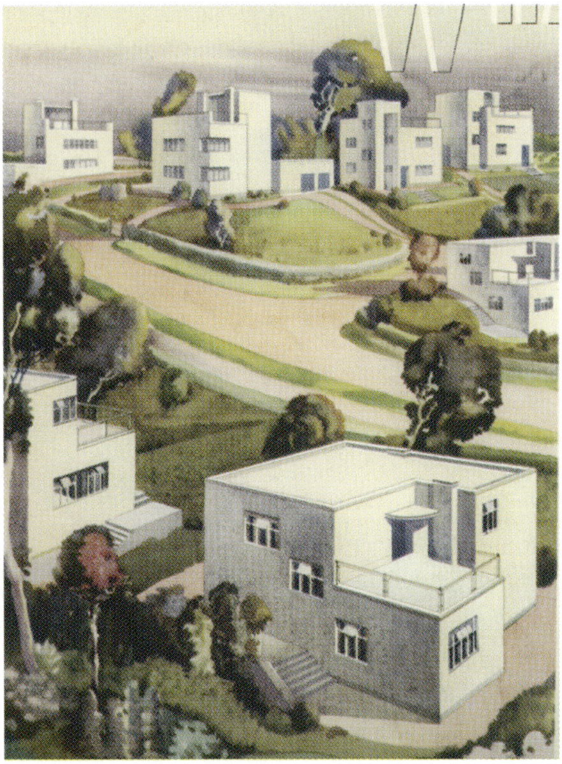

31. William Lescaze with Henry Wright (planning) and Beatrix Farrand (landscape). Housing at Churston Ferrers. Illustration from sales brochure. 1935. Print of watercolour. 27 x 17cm. The Dartington Hall Trust Collection.

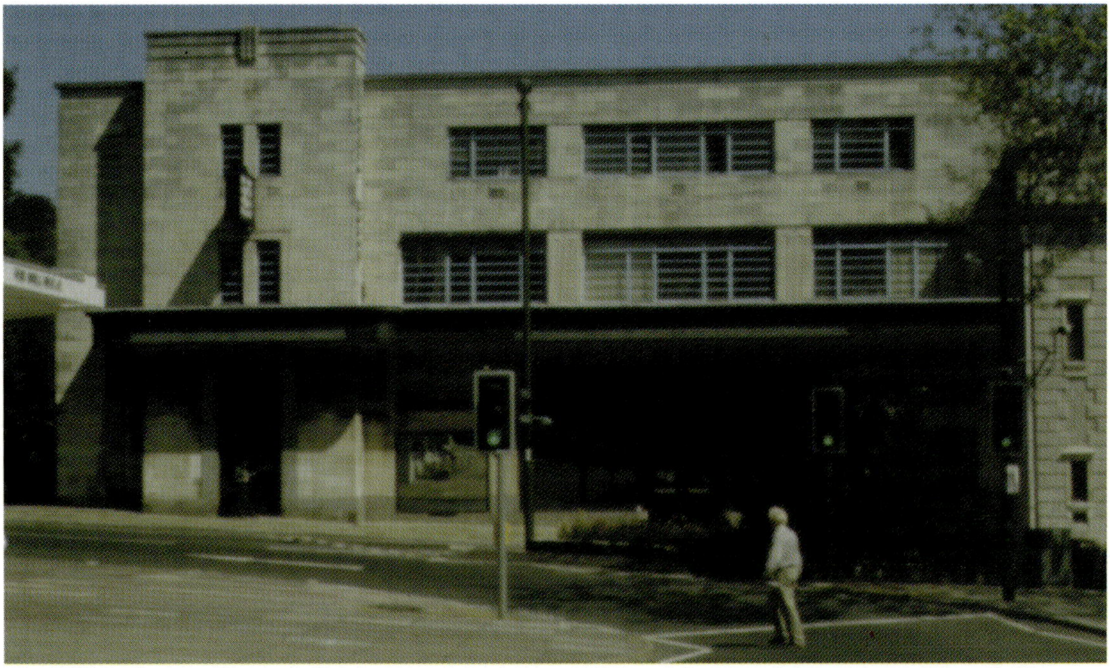

32. P.W. Ladmore, Borough Engineer and Architect. William Marsden, job architect. Electric House, Torquay. 1935. Photo: Jeremy Gould.

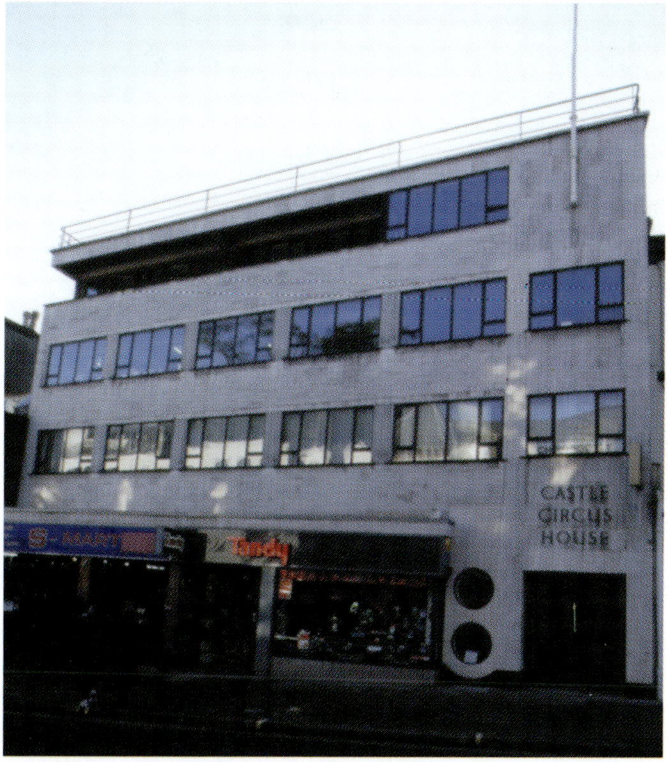

33. Stewart Lloyd Thomson. Castle Circus House, Union Street, Torquay. 1935. Photo: University of Plymouth.

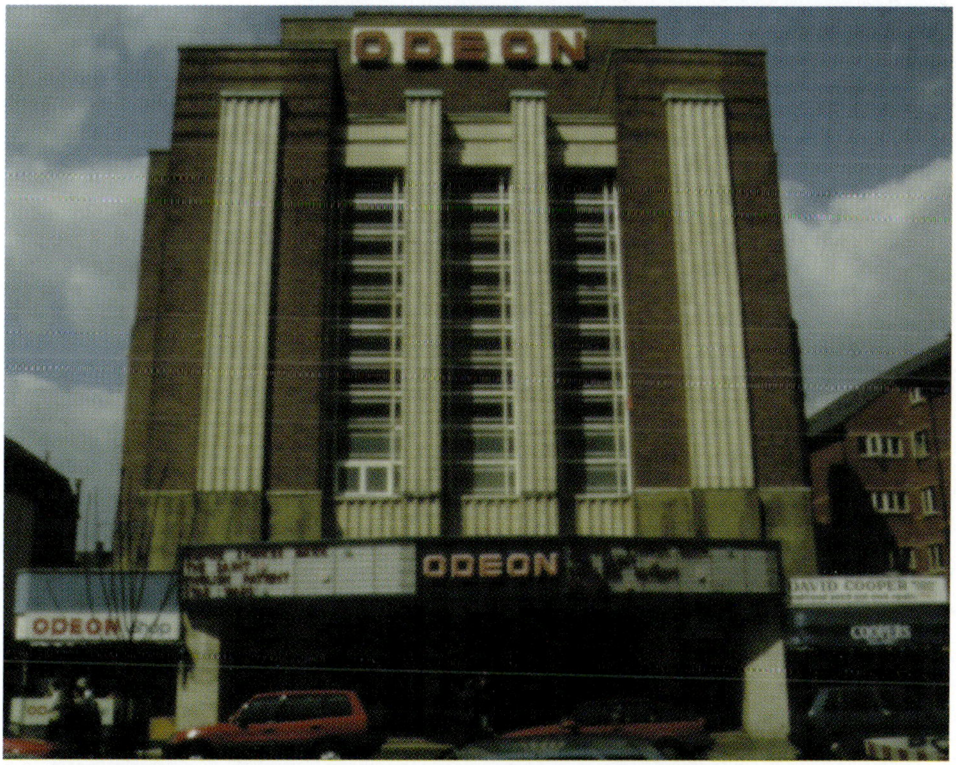

34. Roger Bullivant of Harry Weedon. Odeon Cinema, Sidwell Street, Exeter. 1937. Photo: Jeremy Gould.

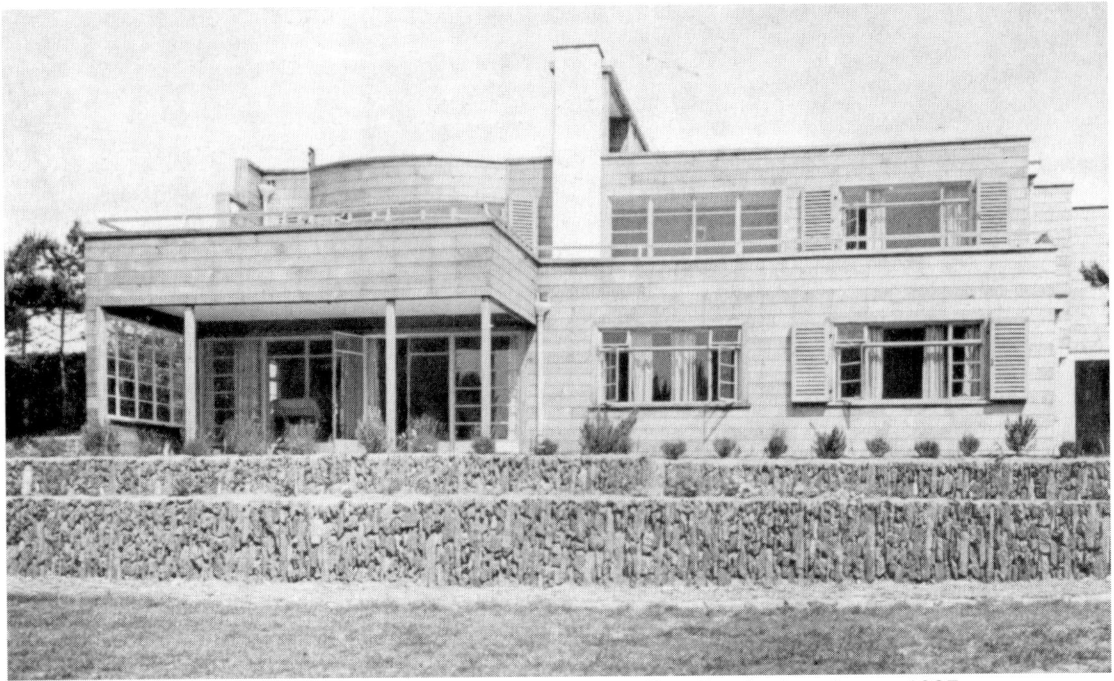

35. Felix Goldsmith of London. Cedar House, Bigbury-on-Sea. South elevation. c. 1937.

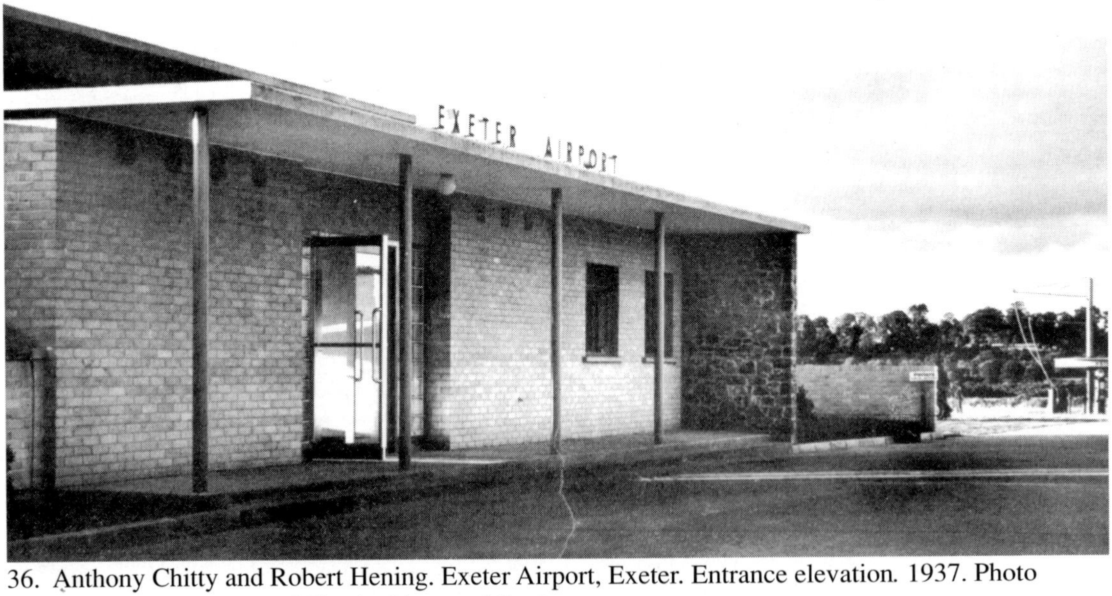

36. Anthony Chitty and Robert Hening. Exeter Airport, Exeter. Entrance elevation. 1937. Photo reproduced courtesy of *The Architectural Review*.

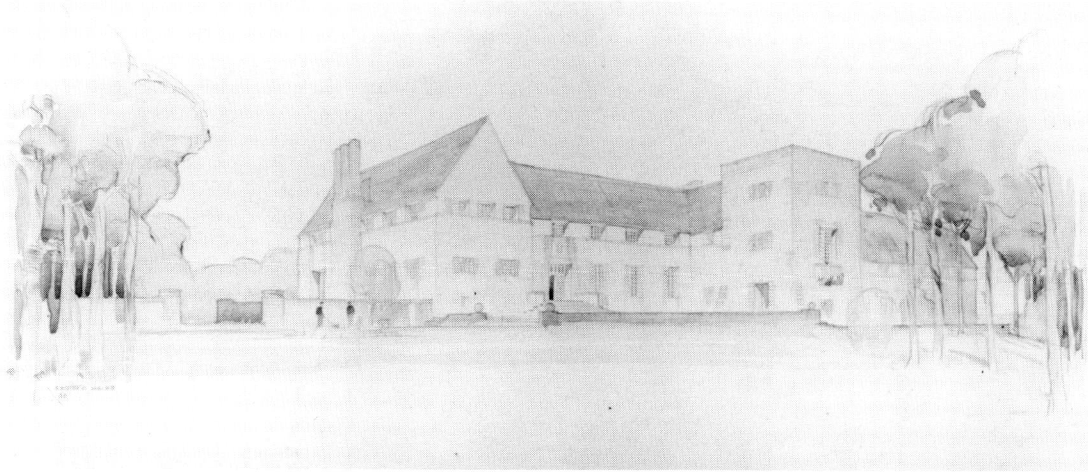

37. Brian O'Rorke. Ashcombe Tower, Dawlish. Perspective of north elevation. 1933, built 1933-35. Drawn by Brian O'Rorke. Watercolour. 38 x 56cm. British Architectural Library Drawings Collection, RIBA, London.

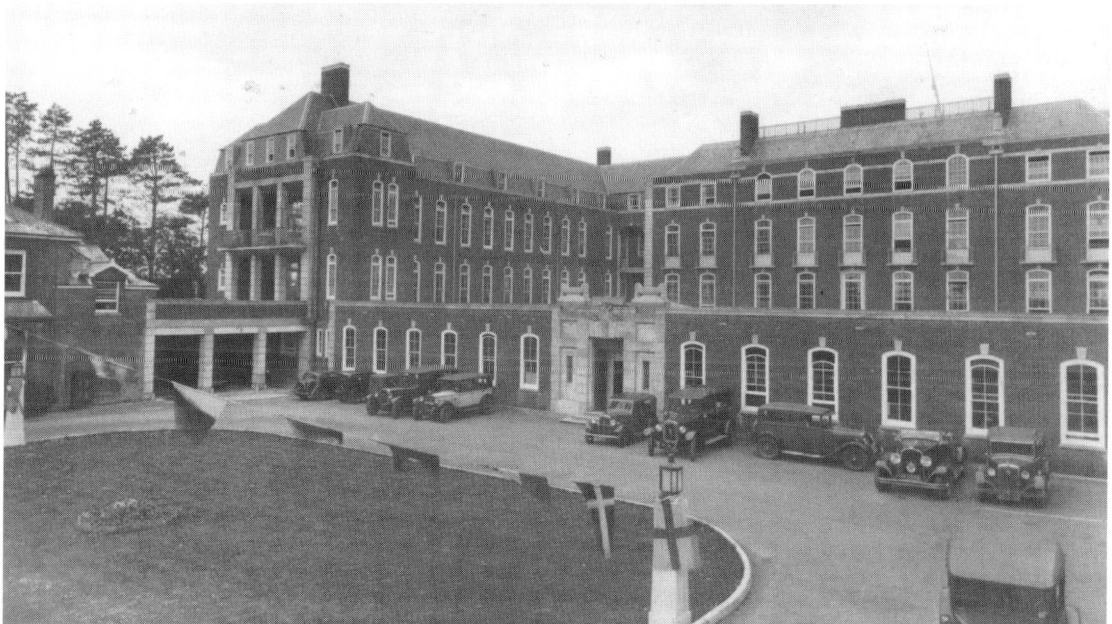

38. Adams Holden & Pearson. Ward Block, Torbay Hospital, Torquay. West wing and Hengrave House. 1925-28. Photo: Fred Payne.

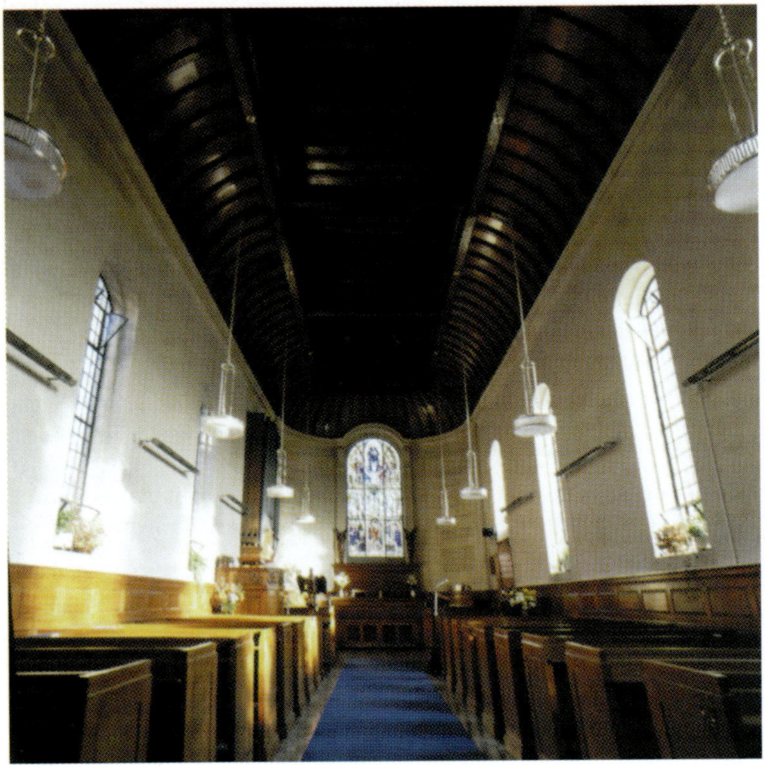

39. Adams Holden & Pearson. Chapel, Torbay Hospital, Torquay. Interior of nave, towards altar. 1925-30. Photo: University of Plymouth.

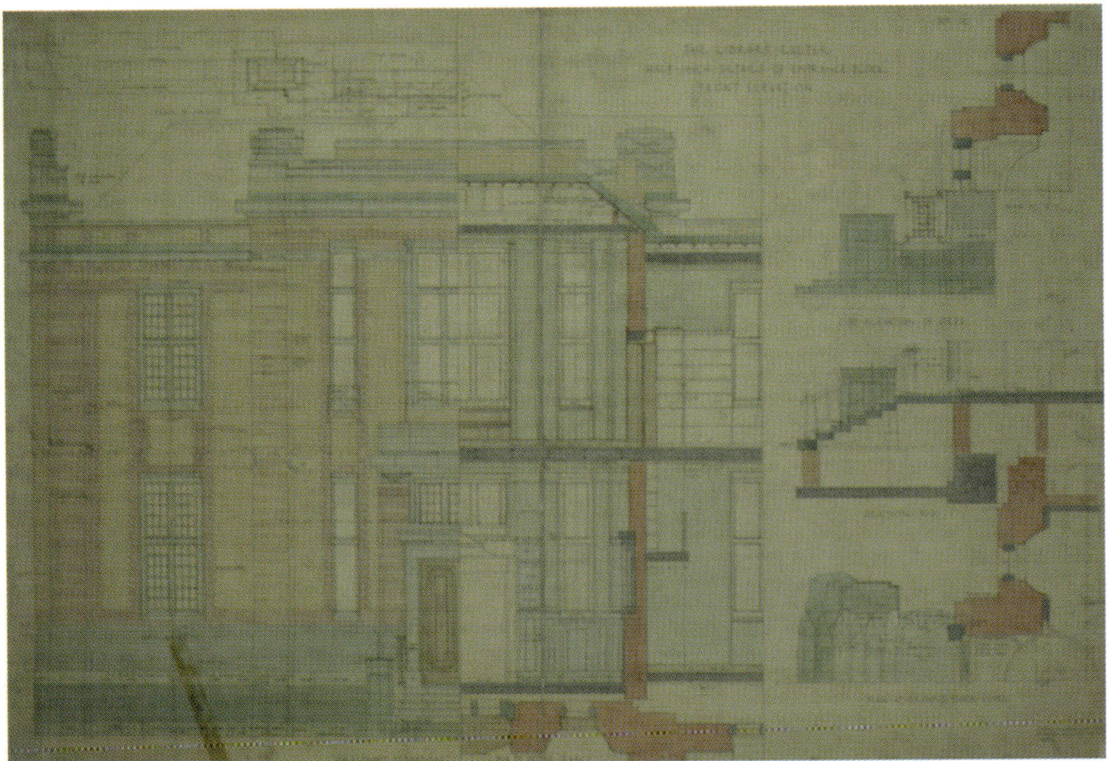

40. Sydney Greenslade. City Public Library, Exeter. Half Inch Details of Entrance Block. Front Elevation/First Floor Plan. Drawing No.16. Drawing October 1926, built 1925-26. Office of Sydney Greenslade. Watercolour on linen print, 66 x 100cm. Devon Record Office, Exeter.

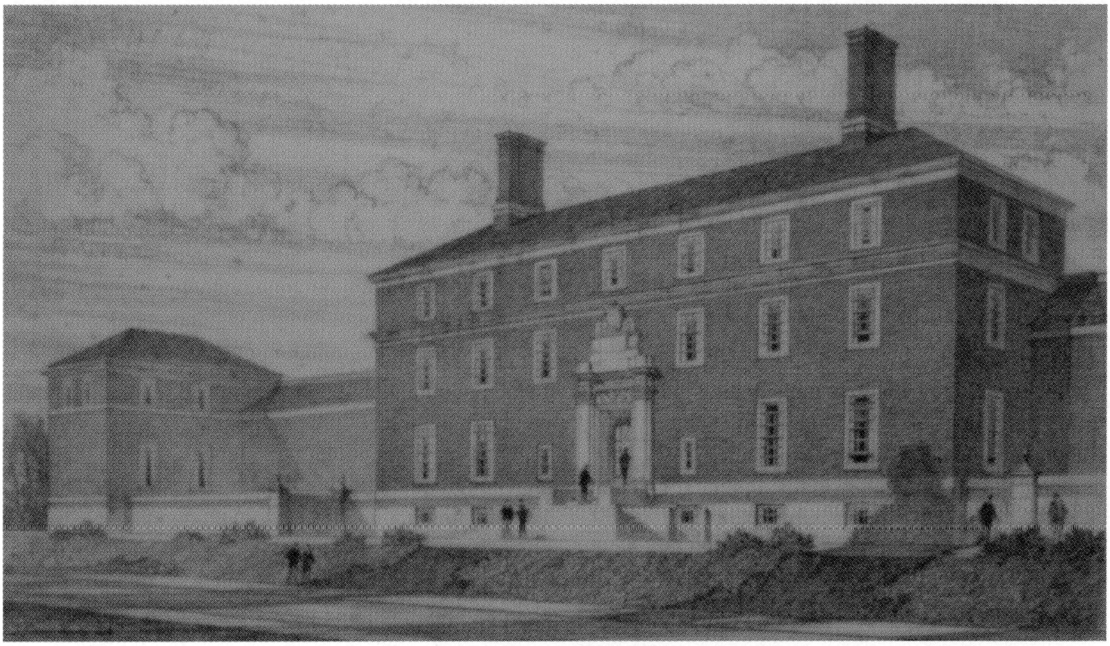

41. E. Vincent Harris. Hatherly Laboratories, Exeter University. Perspective drawing 1948-52. Drawn by P.D. Hepworth. Pencil on paper. 66 x 96cm. University of Exeter.

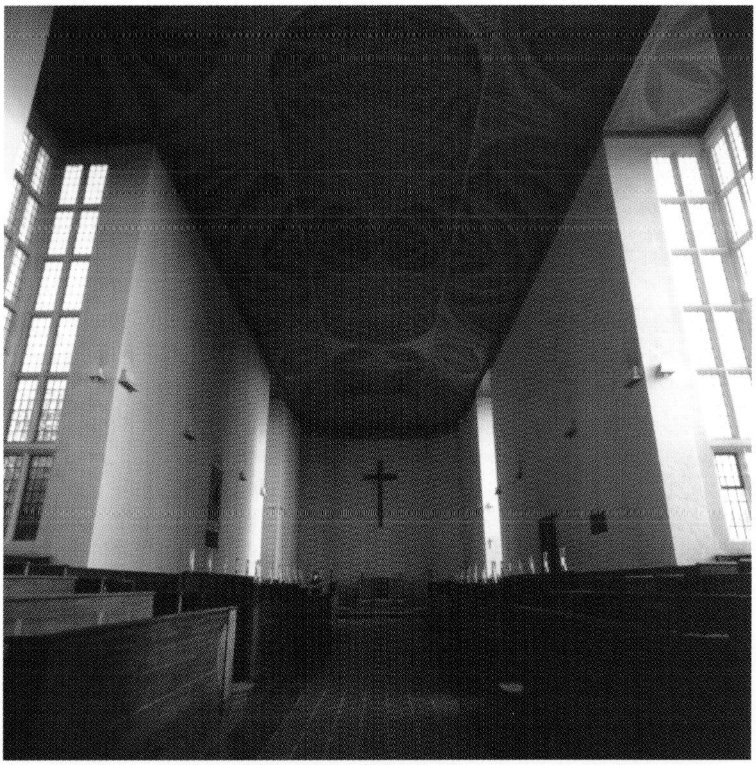

42. E. Vincent Harris. The Mary Harris Memorial Chapel, Exeter University. Nave. 1958. Photo: University of Plymouth.

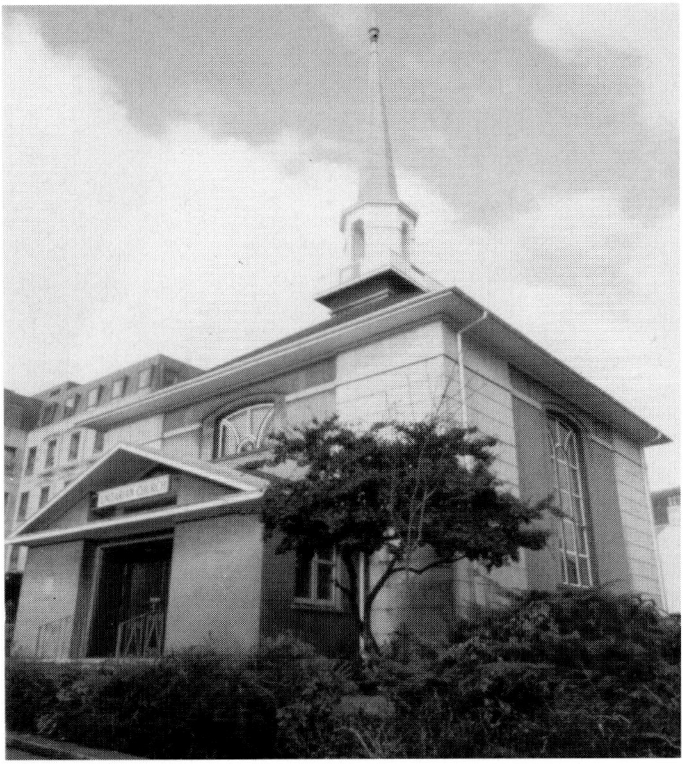

43. Louis de Soissons RA & Partners. Plymouth Unitarian Church, Notte Street, Plymouth. 1955-58. Photo: University of Plymouth.

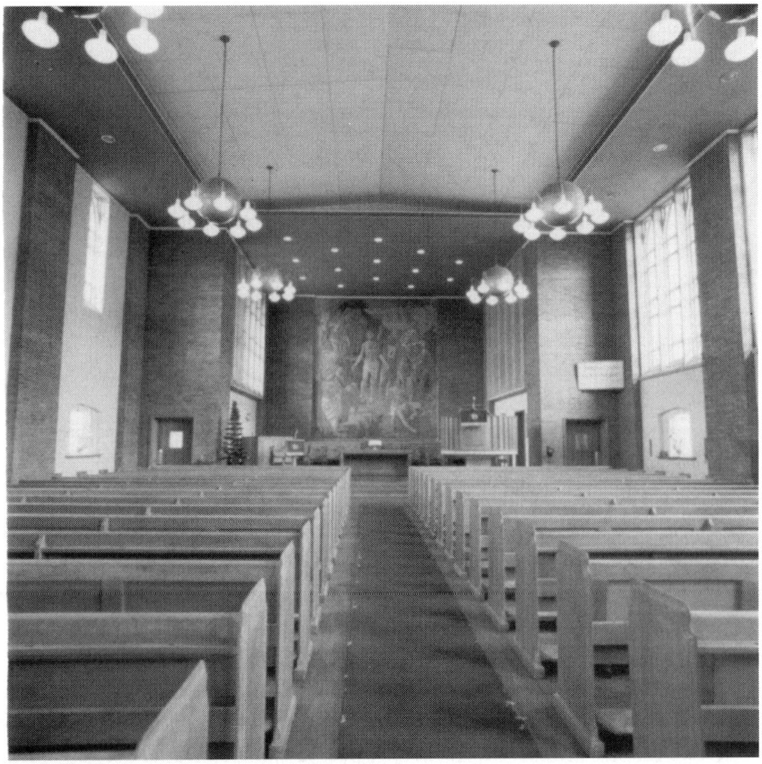

44. Louis de Soissons RA & Partners. George Street Baptist Church, Catherine Street, Plymouth. Nave with 'Baptism of Christ' mural by Hans Feibusch. 1956-58. Photo: University of Plymouth.

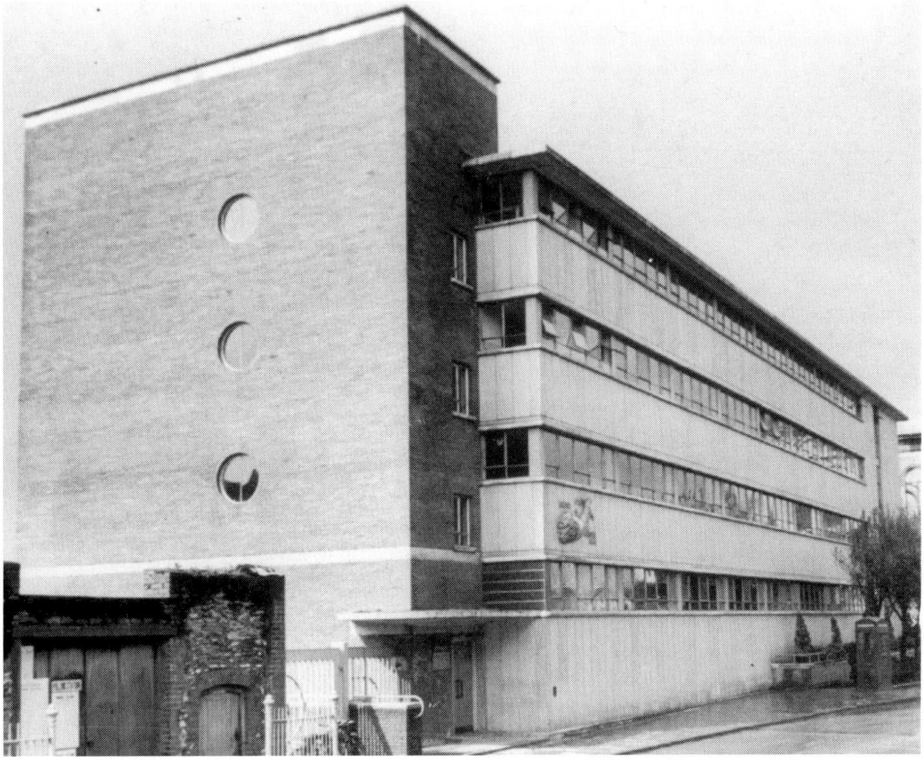

45. Sir John Burnet Tait & Lorne. Dingles Bakery and Store, Beaumont Street, Plymouth. 1946-50. Photo: Devon Record Office, Plymouth.

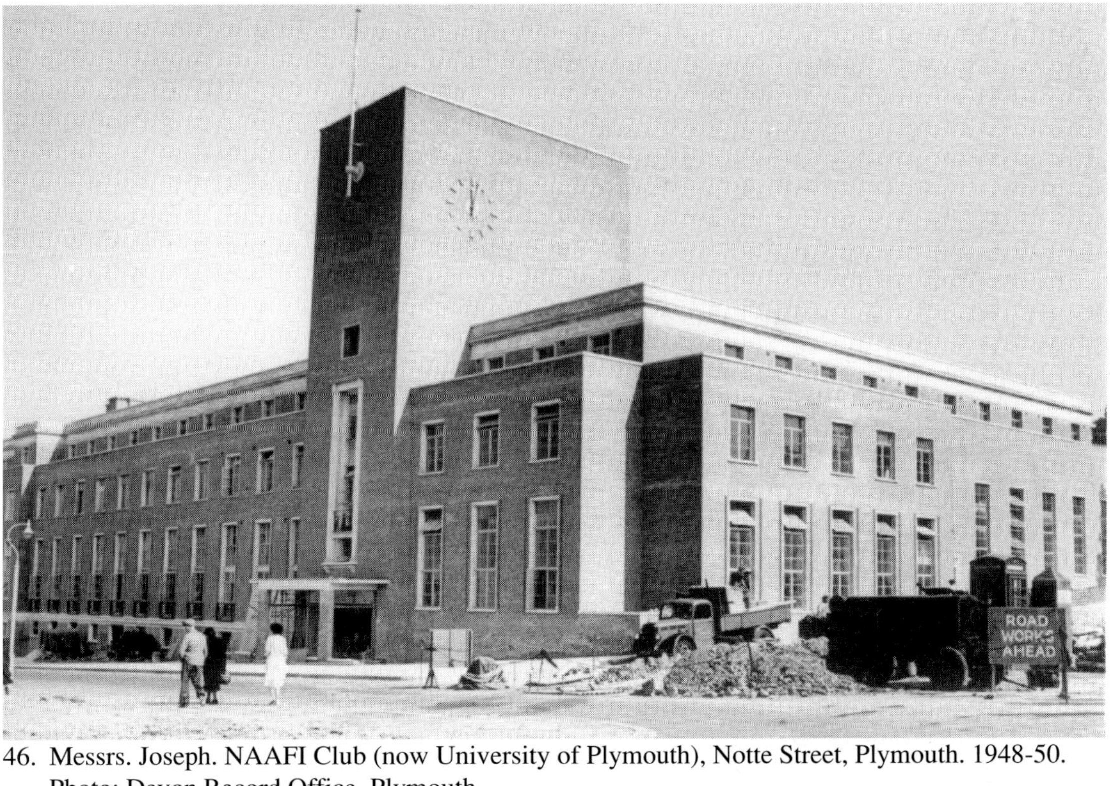

46. Messrs. Joseph. NAAFI Club (now University of Plymouth), Notte Street, Plymouth. 1948-50. Photo: Devon Record Office, Plymouth.

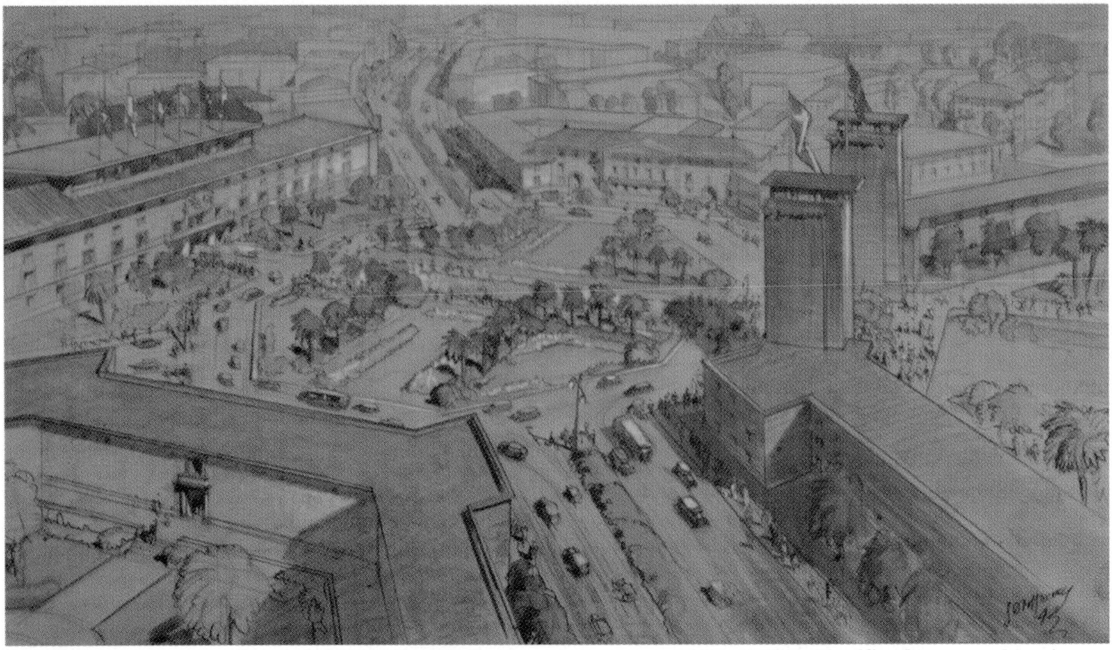

47. Patrick Abercrombie and J. Paton Watson. The Plan for Plymouth. The Traffic Centre at North Road and Cobourg Street. 1943. Drawn by J.D.M. Harvey. 58 x 86cm. Plymouth City Museum and Art Gallery.

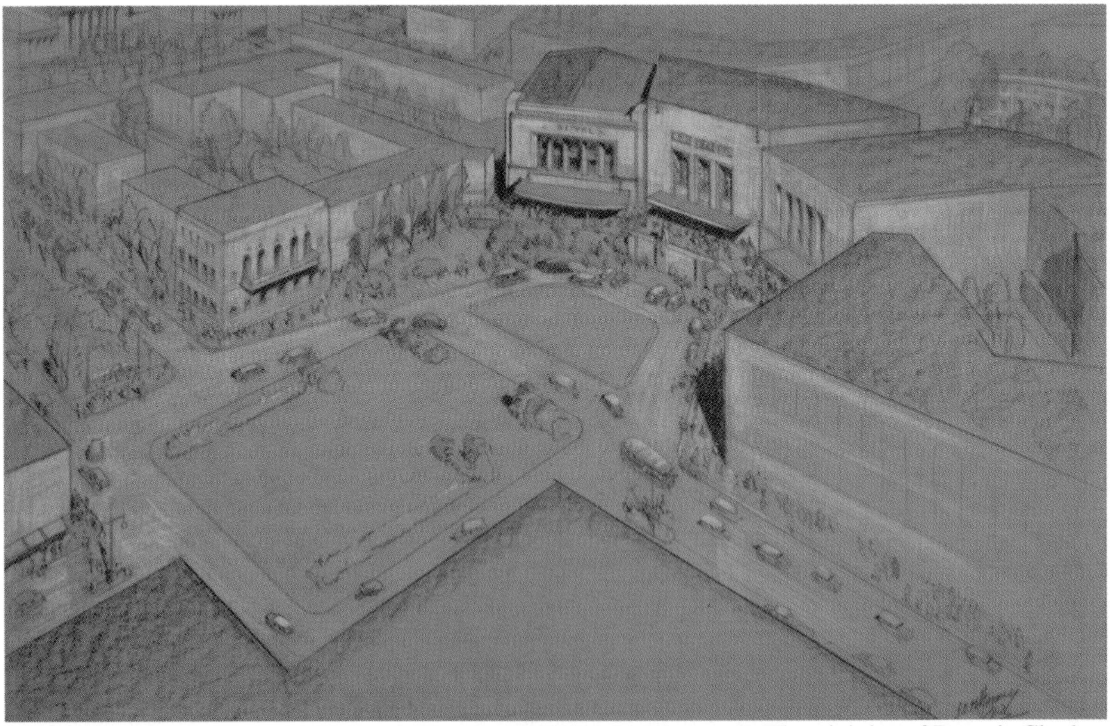

48. Patrick Abercrombie and J. Paton Watson. The Plan for Plymouth. The vicinity of Derry's Clock showing the Civic and Theatre Precincts viewed from Roof Level. 1943. Drawn by J.D.M. Harvey. 64 x 89cm. Plymouth City Musuem and Art Gallery.

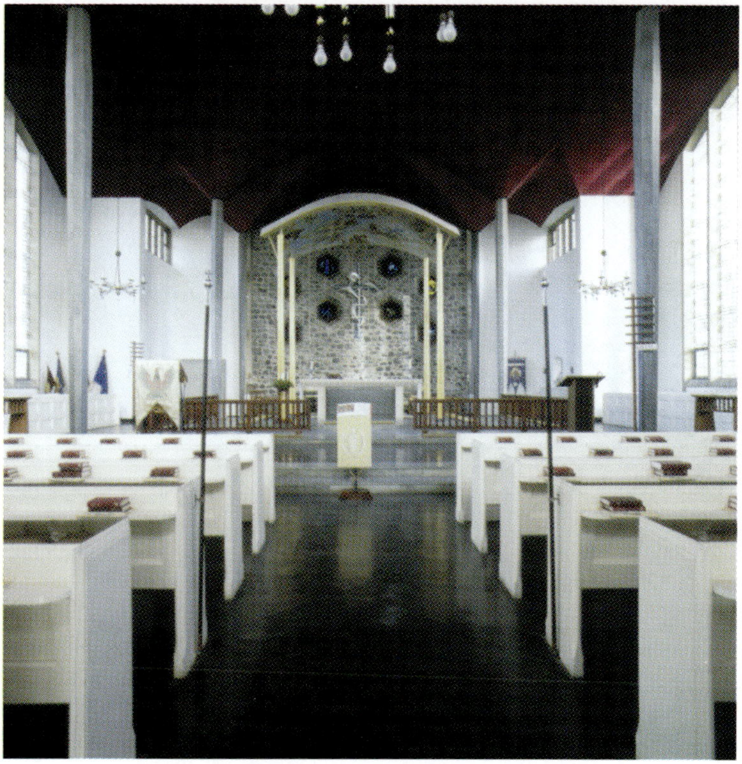

49. Robert Potter and Richard Hare. Church of the Ascension, Crownhill, Plymouth. Nave. 1956. Photo: University of Plymouth.

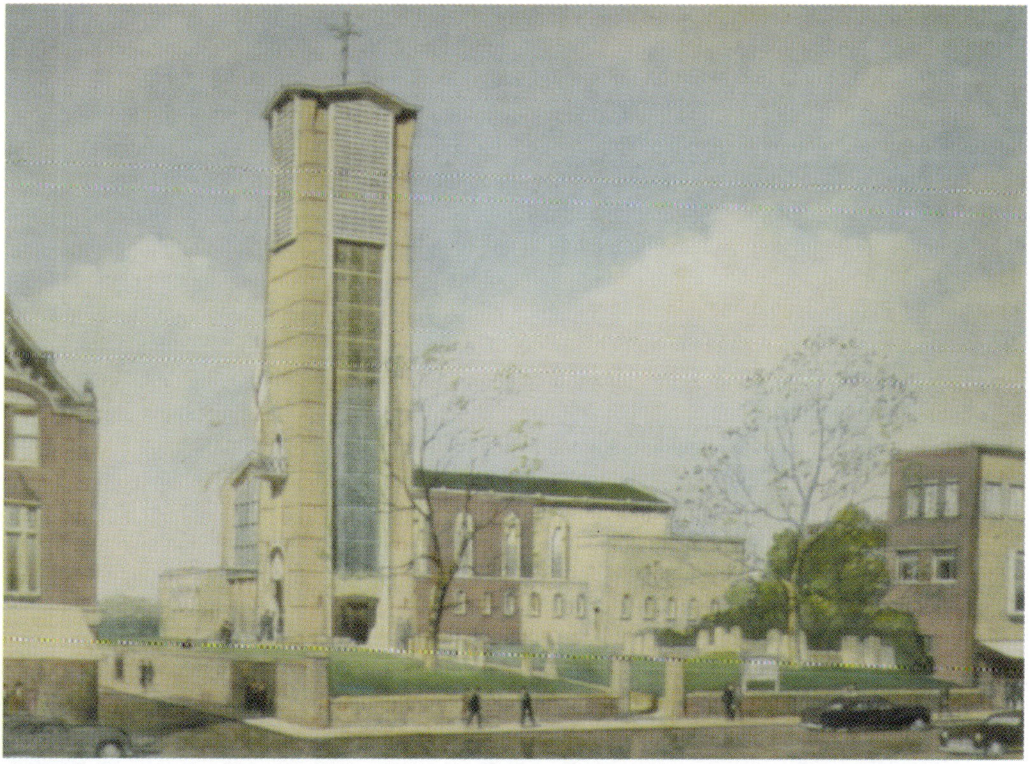

50. Lucas Roberts & Brown. St. Sidwell, Sidwell Street, Exeter. Perspective drawing of exterior with tower. Drawing 1956, built 1957. Drawn by John Adams. Watercolour on board. 45 x 59cm. Lucas Roberts & Brown.

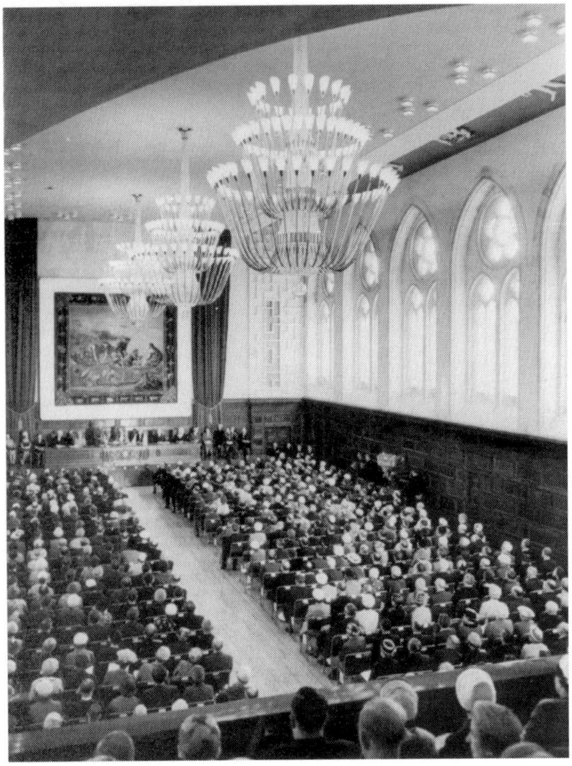

51. H.J.W. Stirling, City Architect. Reconstruction of The Guildhall, Armada Way, Plymouth. Opening Ceremony - interior of Hall. 1951 - 59, photograph 24 September 1959. Photo: Devon Record Office, Plymouth.

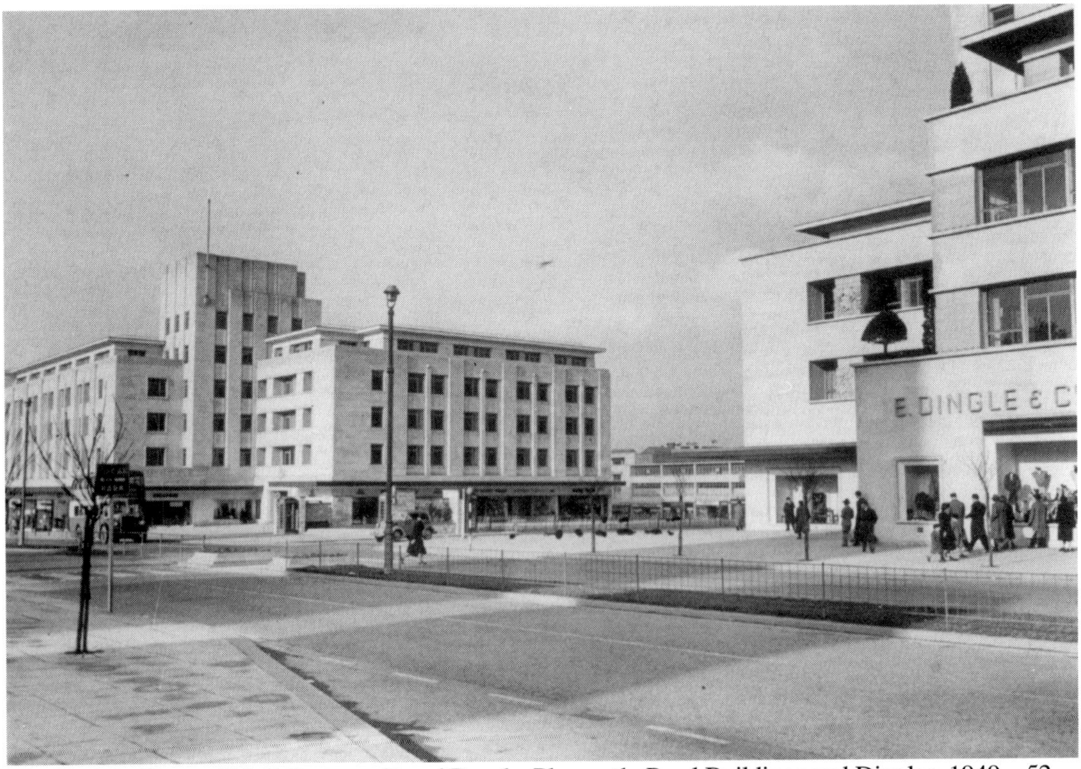

52. Sir John Burnet Tait & Partners. Royal Parade, Plymouth. Pearl Buildings and Dingles. 1949 – 52. Photo: Devon Record Office, Plymouth.

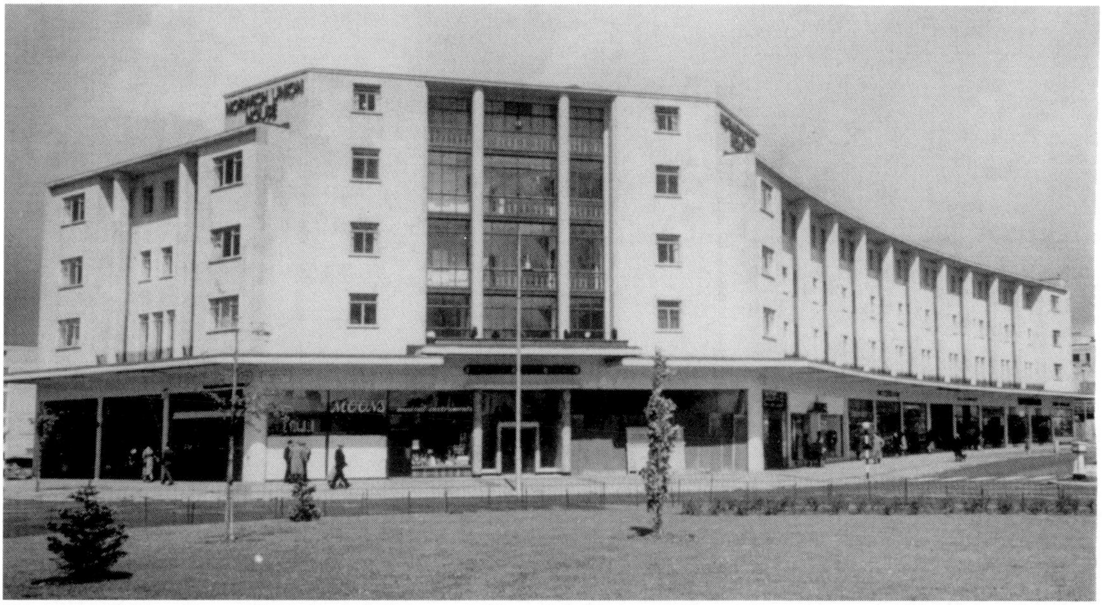

53. Donald Hamilton, Wakeford & Partners. Norwich Union Offices, Royal Parade/Old Town Street, Plymouth. 1950-52. Photo: Devon Record Office, Plymouth.

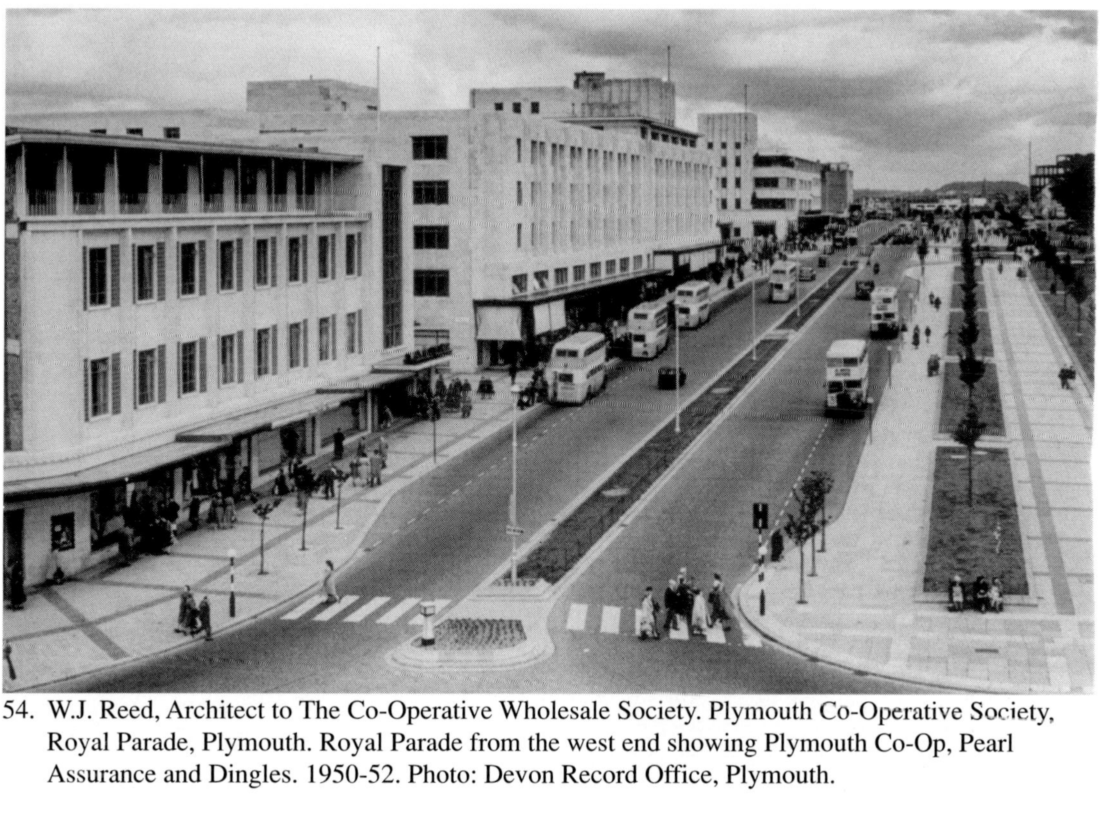

54. W.J. Reed, Architect to The Co-Operative Wholesale Society. Plymouth Co-Operative Society, Royal Parade, Plymouth. Royal Parade from the west end showing Plymouth Co-Op, Pearl Assurance and Dingles. 1950-52. Photo: Devon Record Office, Plymouth.

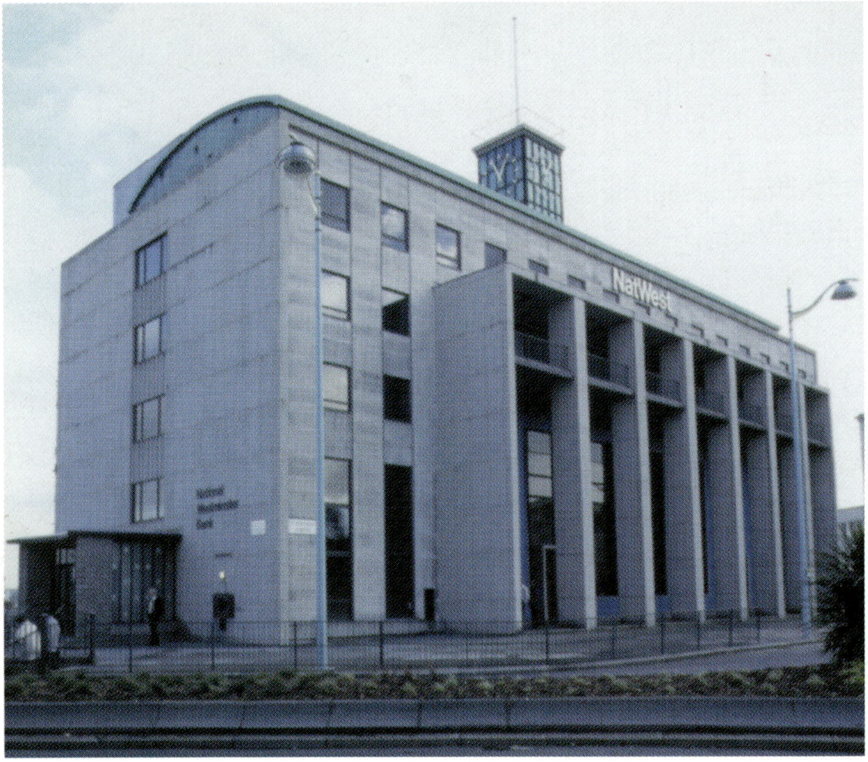

55. B.C. Sherren, Architect to The National Provincial Bank. F. Norman James, Deputy Architect. A.E. Souter, job architect. G.F. Miles, assistant architect. National Provincial Bank (now Nat West), St. Andrews Cross, Plymouth. 1955. Photo: University of Plymouth.

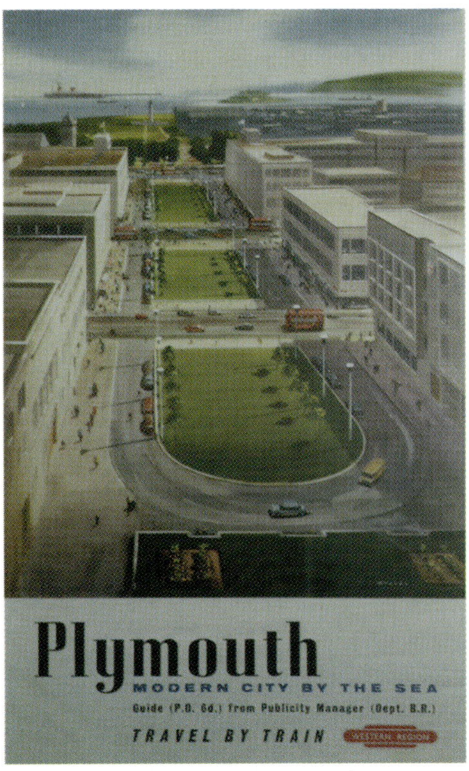

56. Bagley. Plymouth - Modern City by the Sea. British Railways Poster. Early 1950s. 102 x 63cm. Plymouth City Museum & Art Gallery.

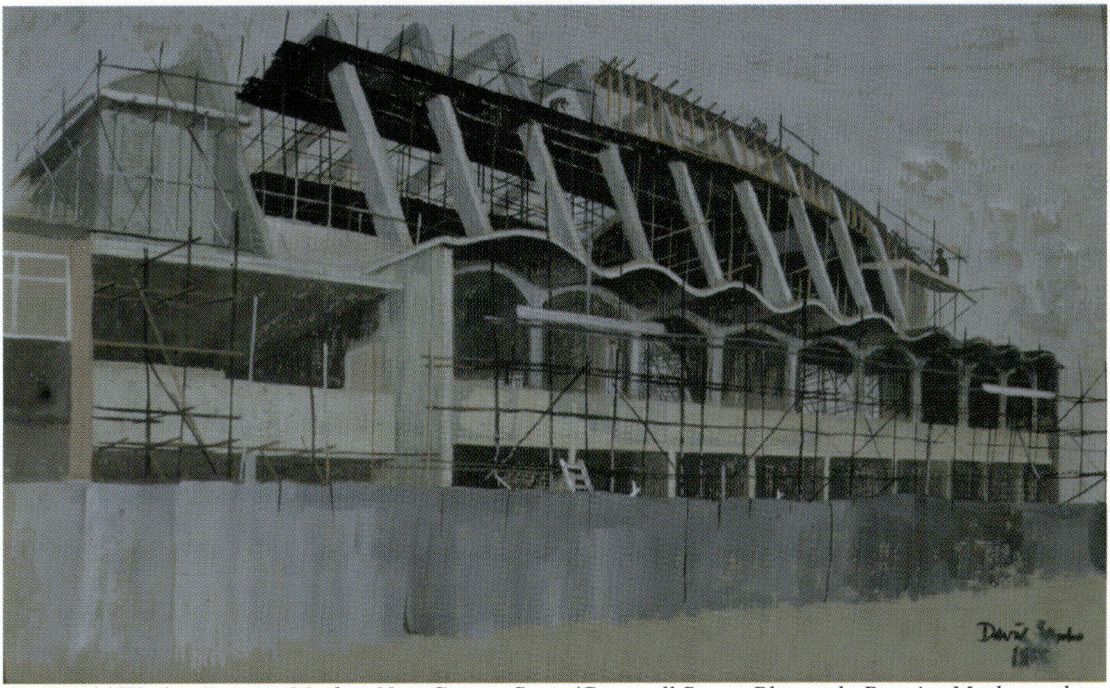

57. David Weeks. *Pannier Market, New George Street/Cornwall Street, Plymouth. Pannier Market under construction*. 1955. Gouache on grey/buff paper. 38 x 53cm. Plymouth City Museum & Art Gallery.

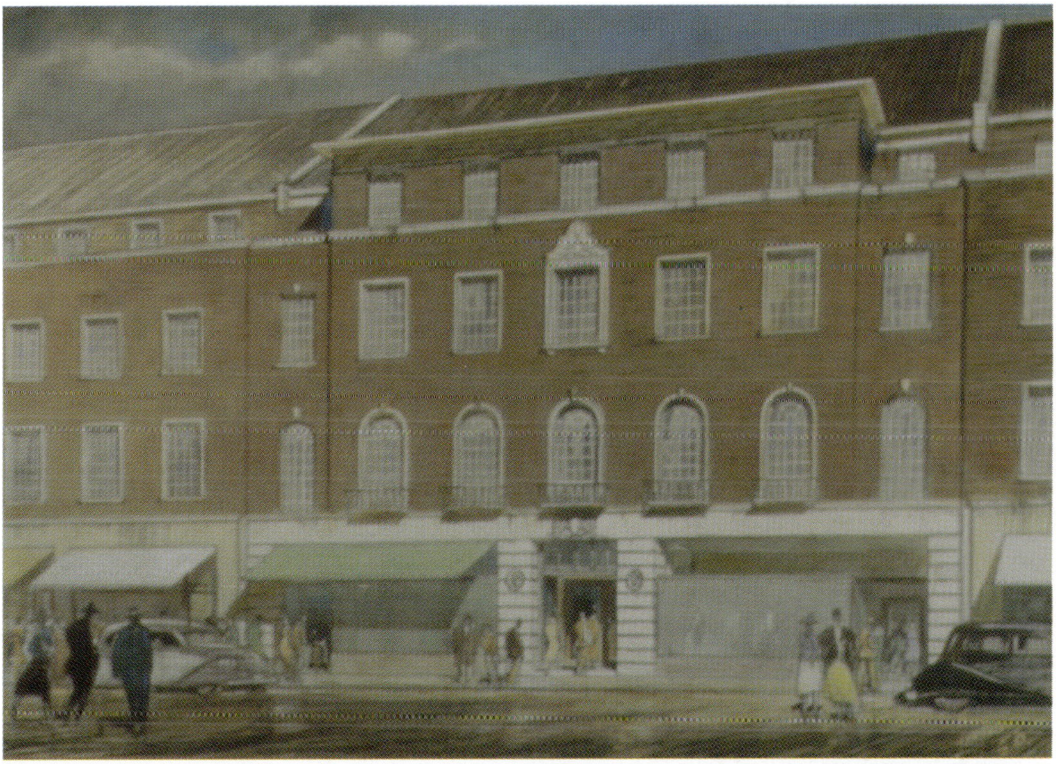

58. Lucas Roberts & Brown. Commercial Union Offices (now Co-op Bank), High Street, Exeter. Perspective. 1950. Drawn by J.D.M. Harvey. Watercolour. 36 x 49cm. Lucas Roberts & Brown.

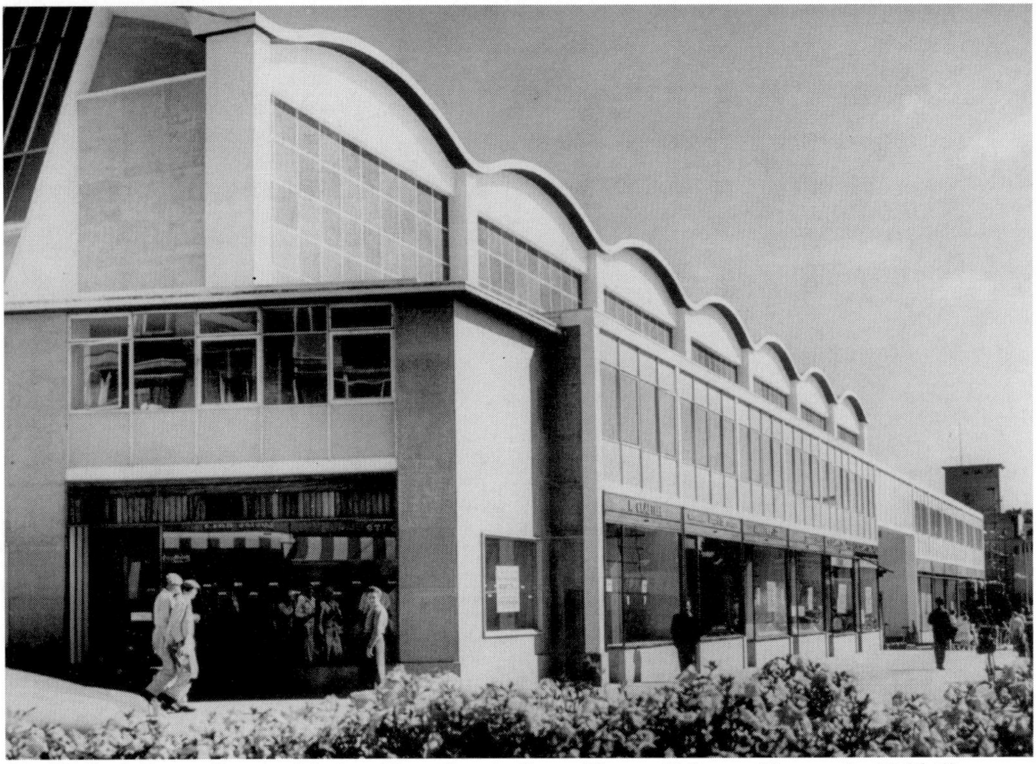

59. Walls & Pearn. Pannier Market, New George Street/Cornwall Street, Plymouth. 1956-59, photograph 26 August 1959. Photo: Devon Record Office, Plymouth.

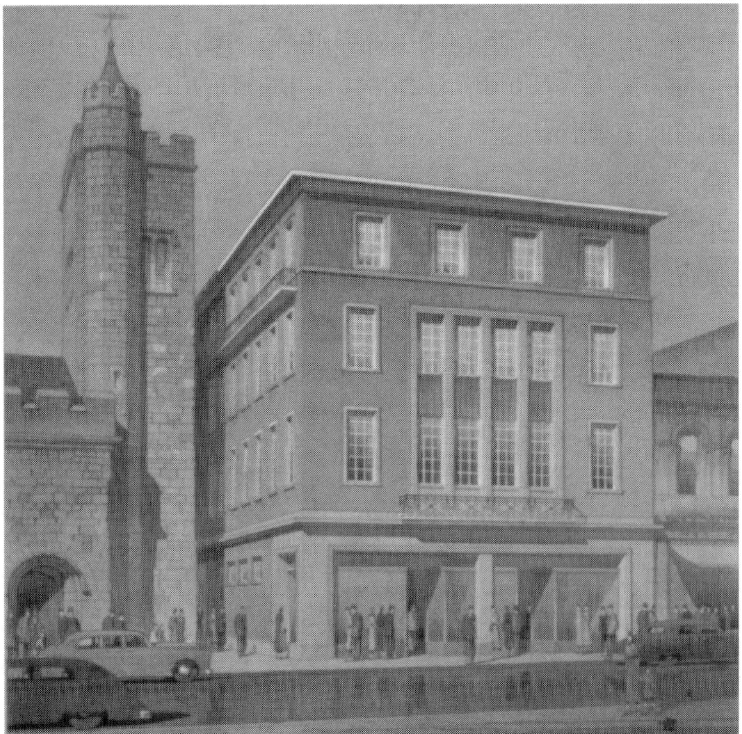

60. Lucas Roberts & Brown. Willsons & Wymans (now Dingles), High Street, Exeter. Perspective. 1949, built 1949-53. Drawn by Cyril A. Farey & Adams. Watercolour. 55 x 52cm. Lucas Roberts & Brown.

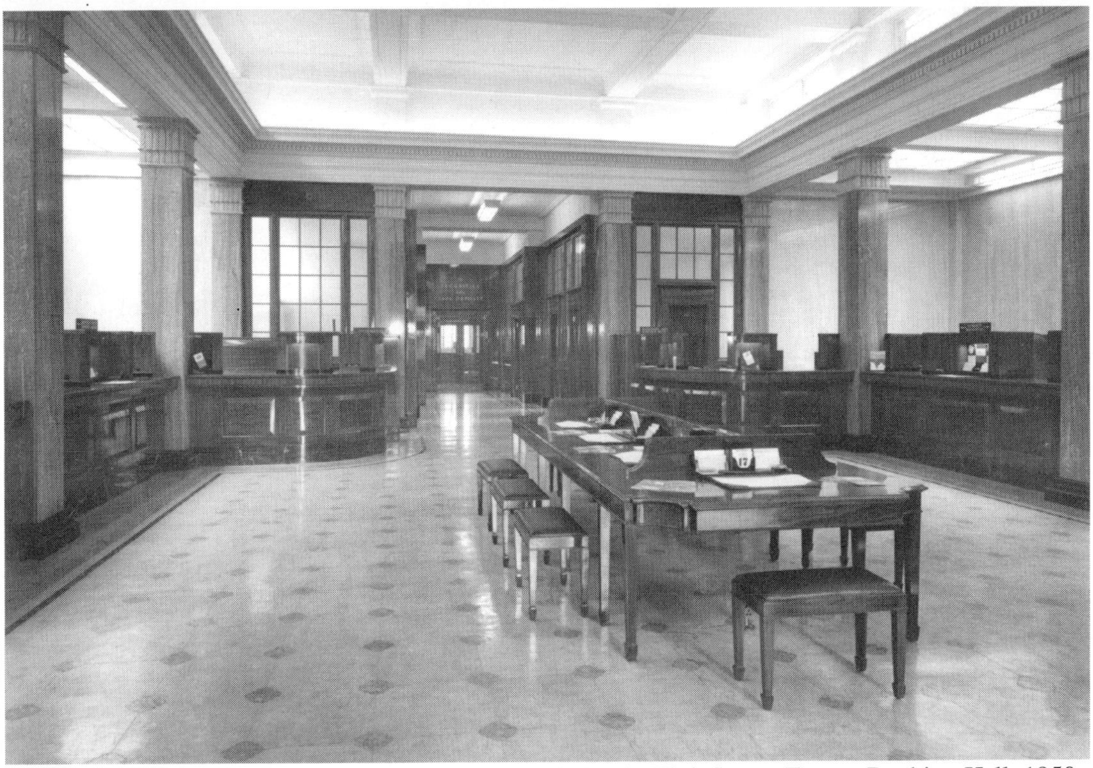

61. E. Victor Beer of Charles E. Ware & Son. Lloyds Bank, High Street, Exeter. Banking Hall. 1950-53. Photo: Charles E. Ware & Son.

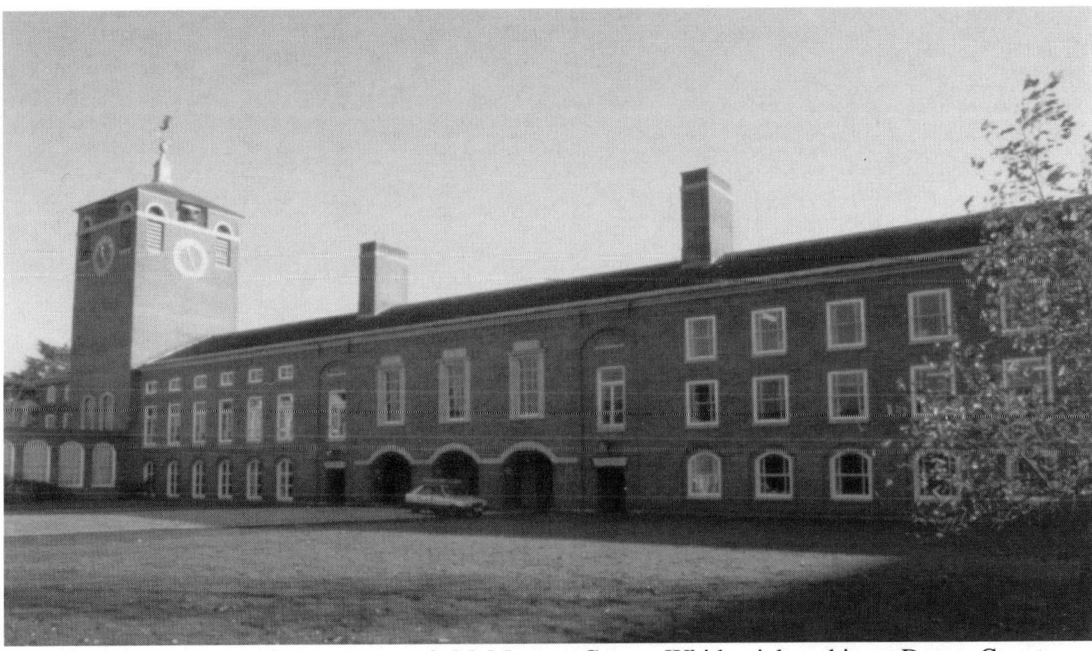

62. Donald McMorran of Farquharson & McMorran. George Whitby, job architect. Devon County Hall, Exeter. 1957 - 64. Photo: University of Plymouth.

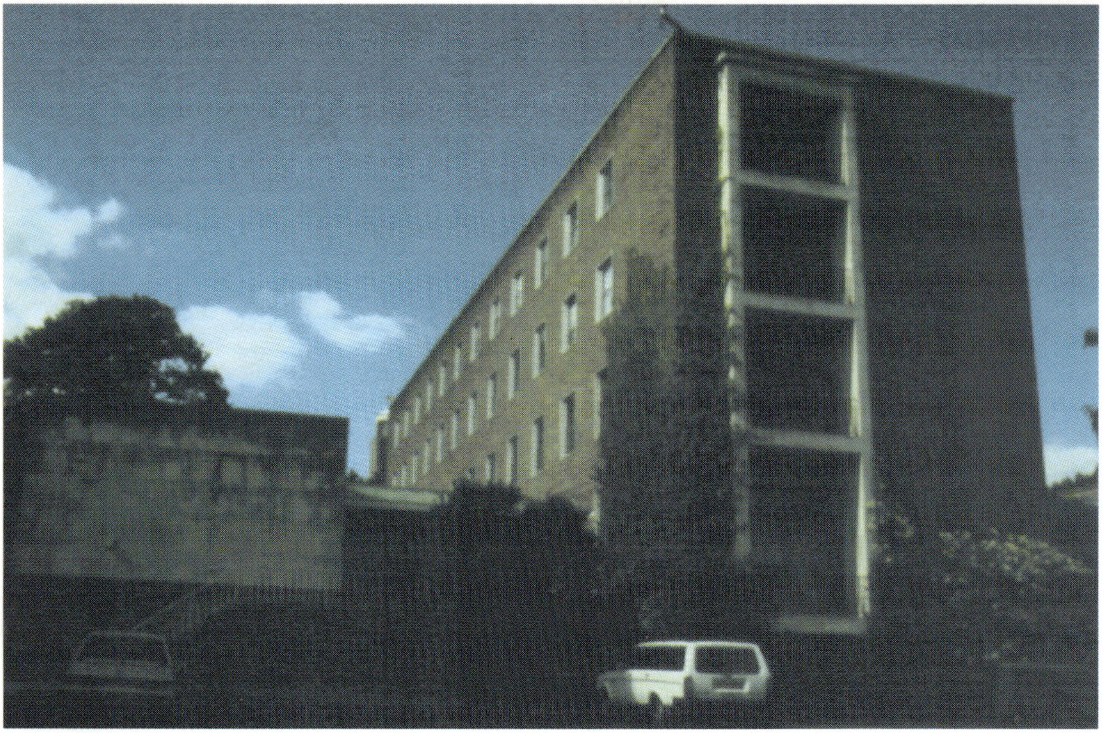

63. Sir William Holford. Bernard Cadd, job architect. Queen's Building, Exeter University.1956 - 58.
Photo: Jeremy Gould.

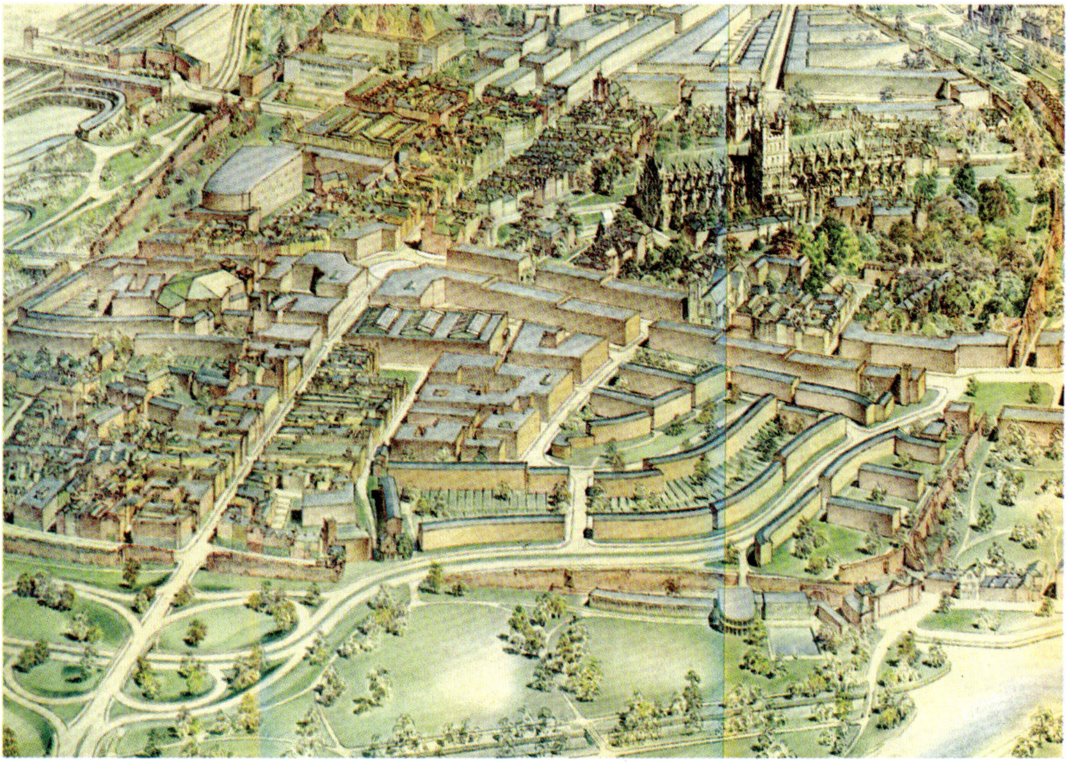

64. Thomas Sharp. *Exeter Phoenix*. A view of the redeveloped city from the south. 1946.

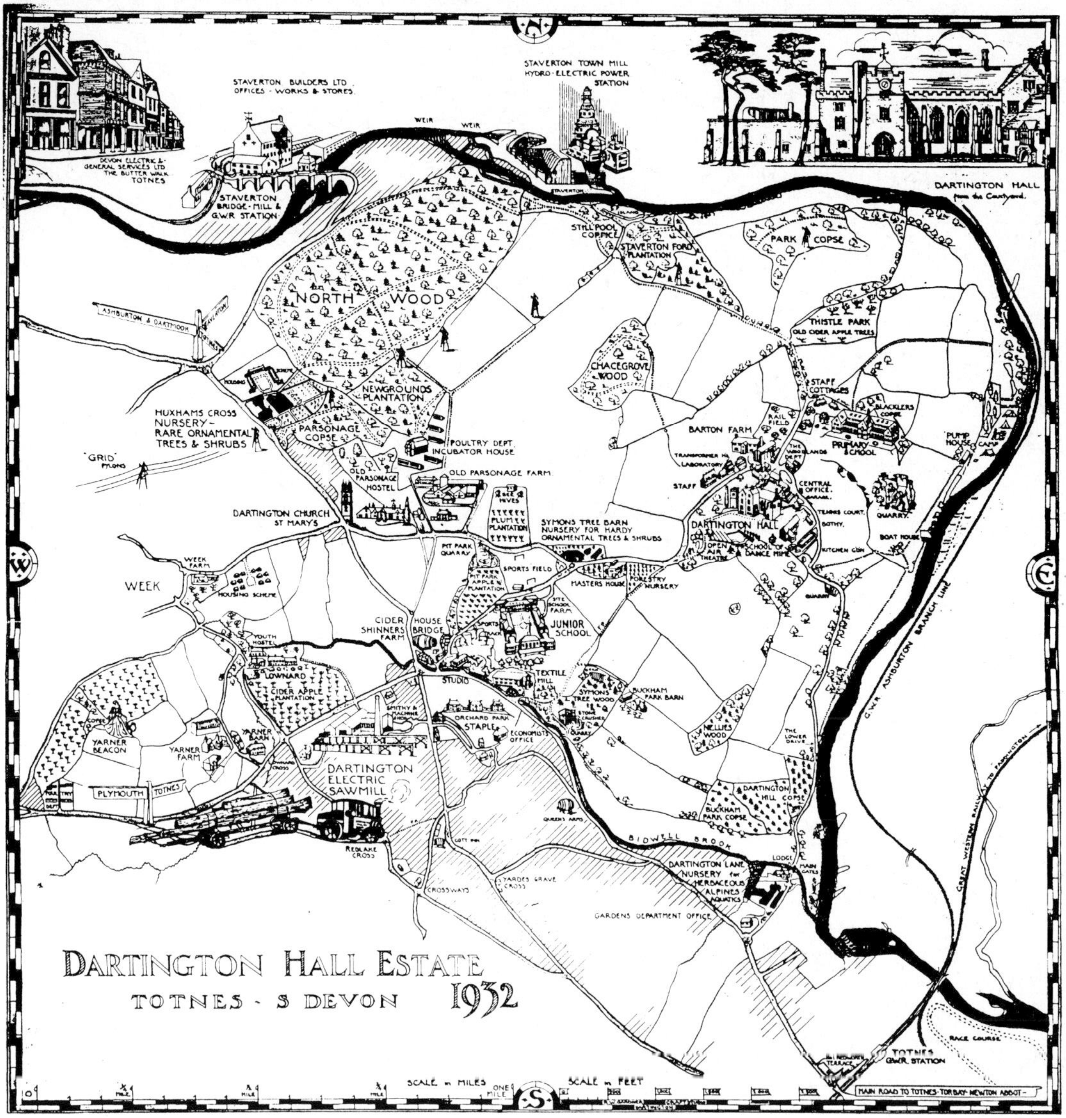

65. Rex Gardner. Dartington Estate. Illustrated Map. 1932.

Figs. 65-95: The Dartington Hall Trust Collection.

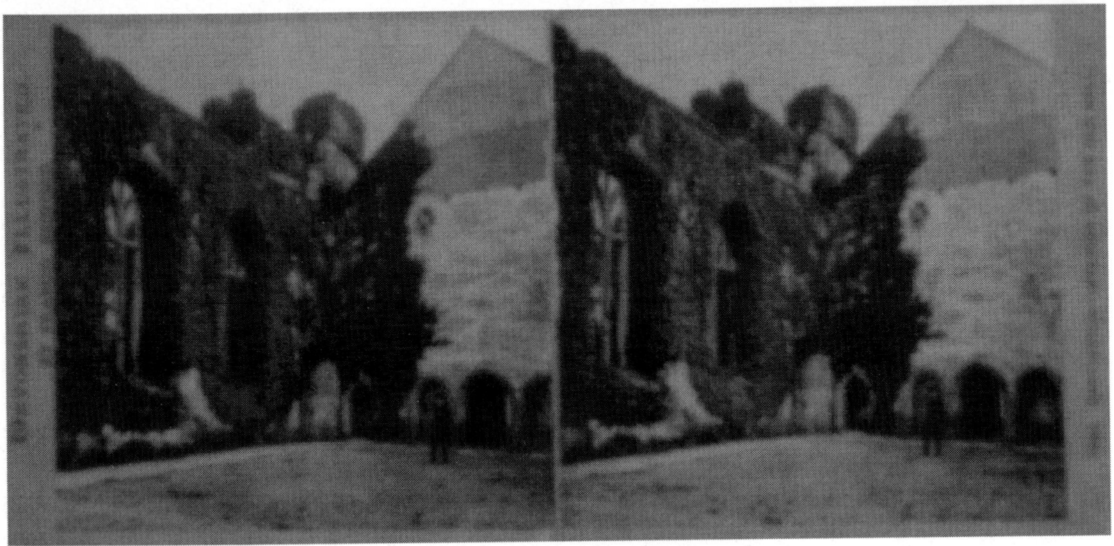

66. Francis Bedford. Dartington Great Hall in *Devonshire Illustrated.*

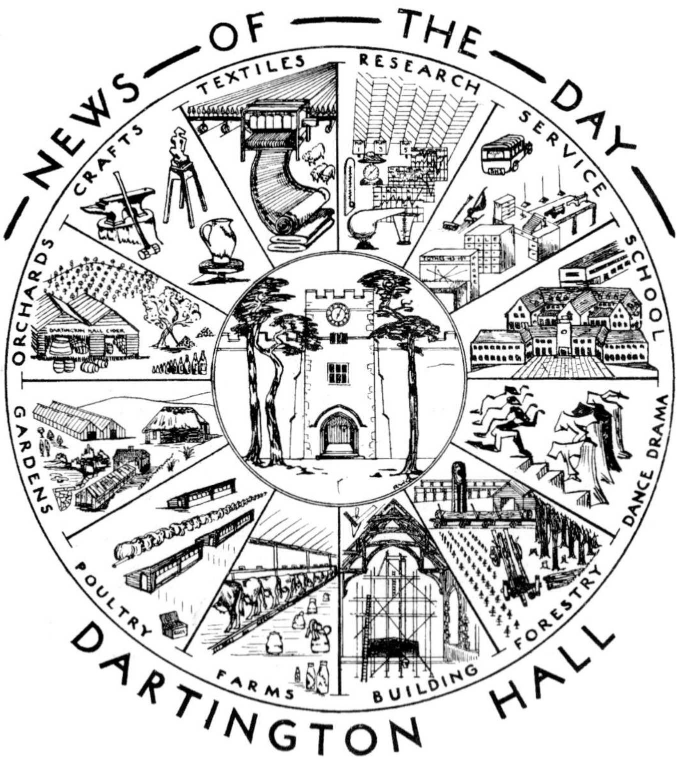

67. Front cover, 500th edition Special Issue, *News of the Day*. 13 March 1934.

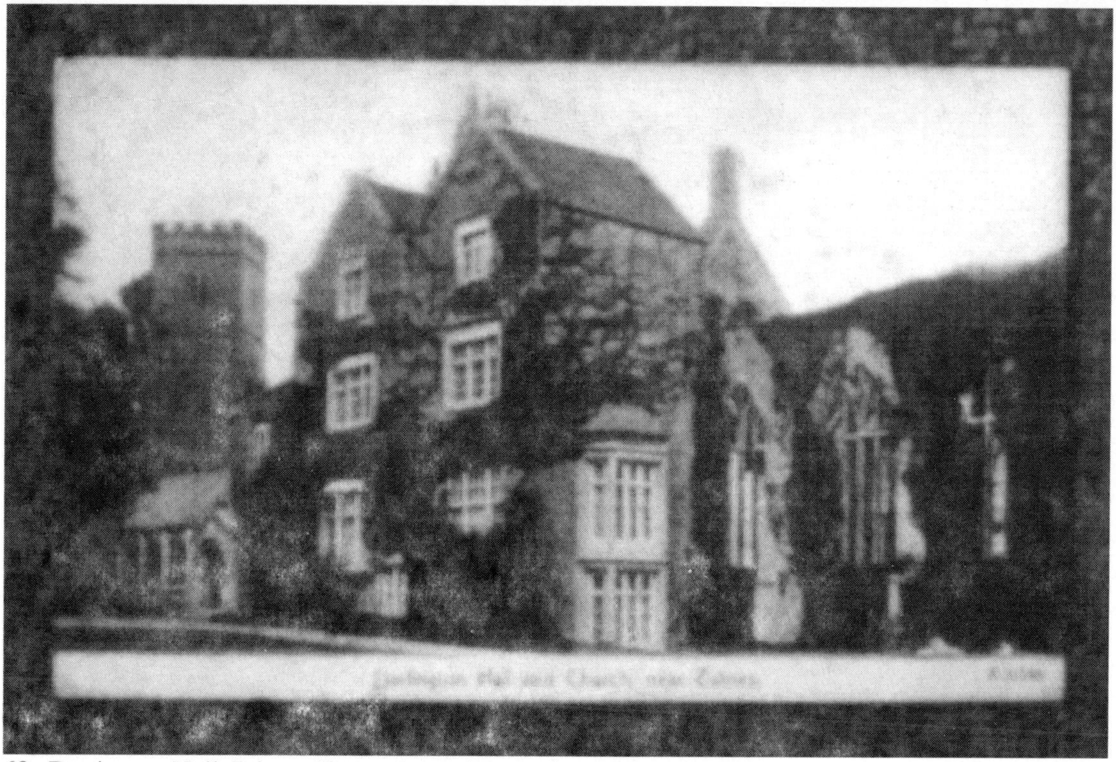

68. Dartington Hall, Private House. Late nineteenth century postcard.

69. Tanner & Weir. Restructuring of Dartington Hall, Private House. Late 1920s.

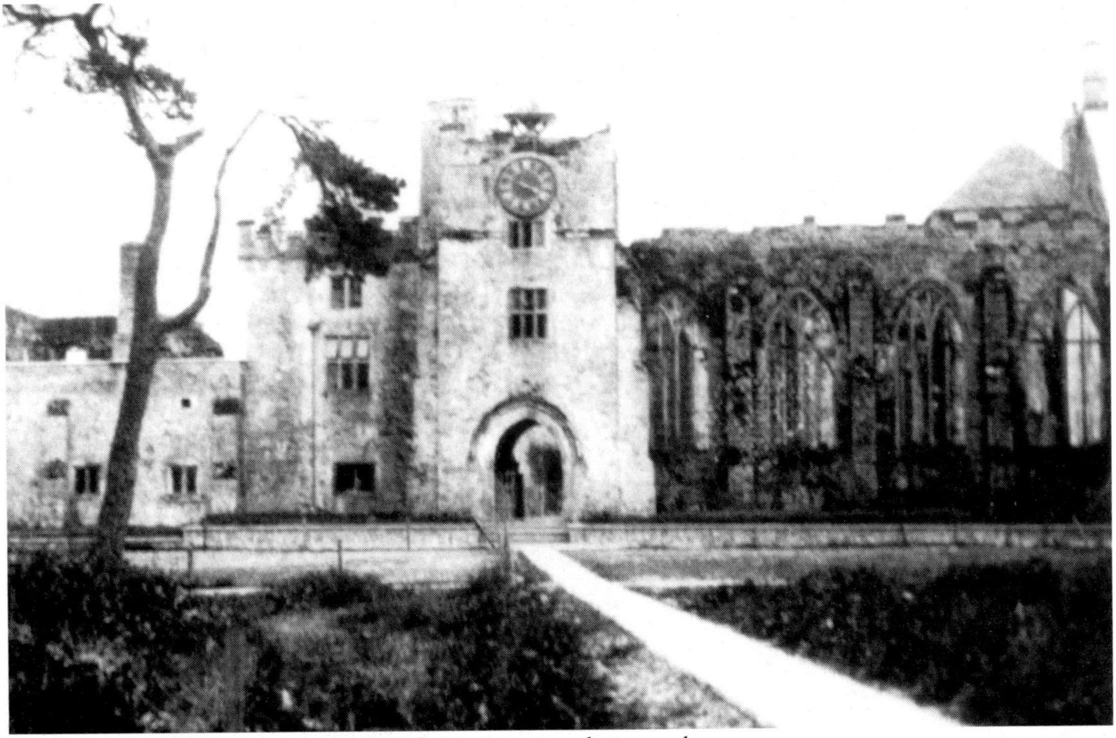

70. Dartington Hall Courtyard 1925. Contemporary photograph.

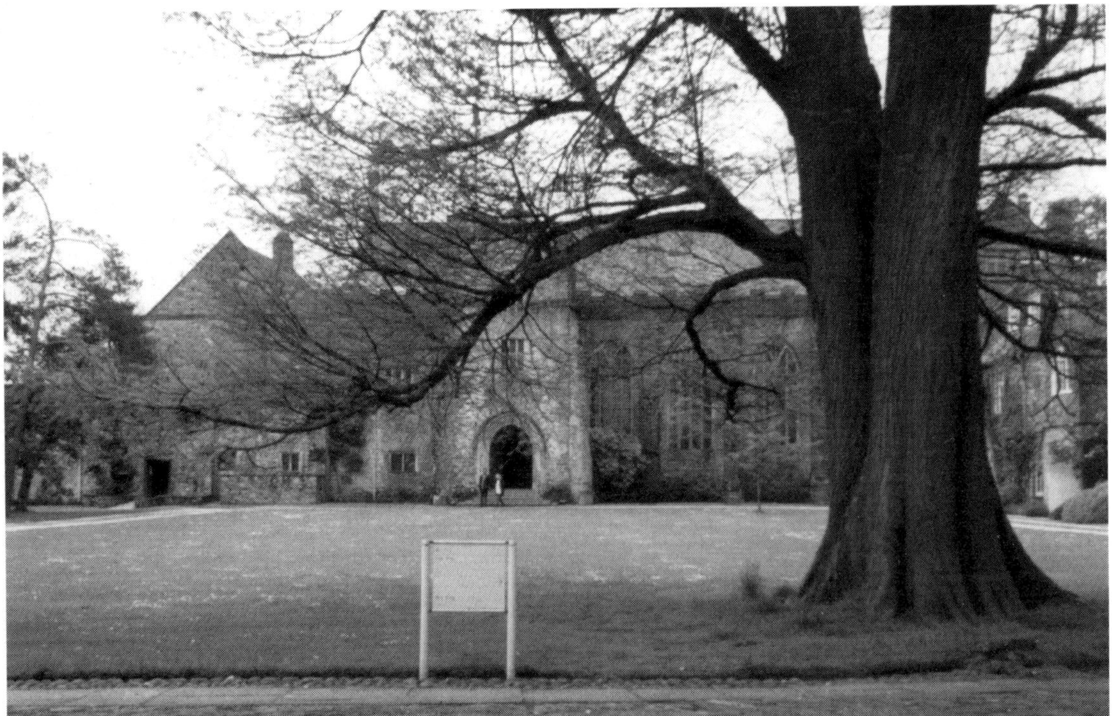

71. Beatrix Farrand. Restoration of Dartington Hall Courtyard.1930s.

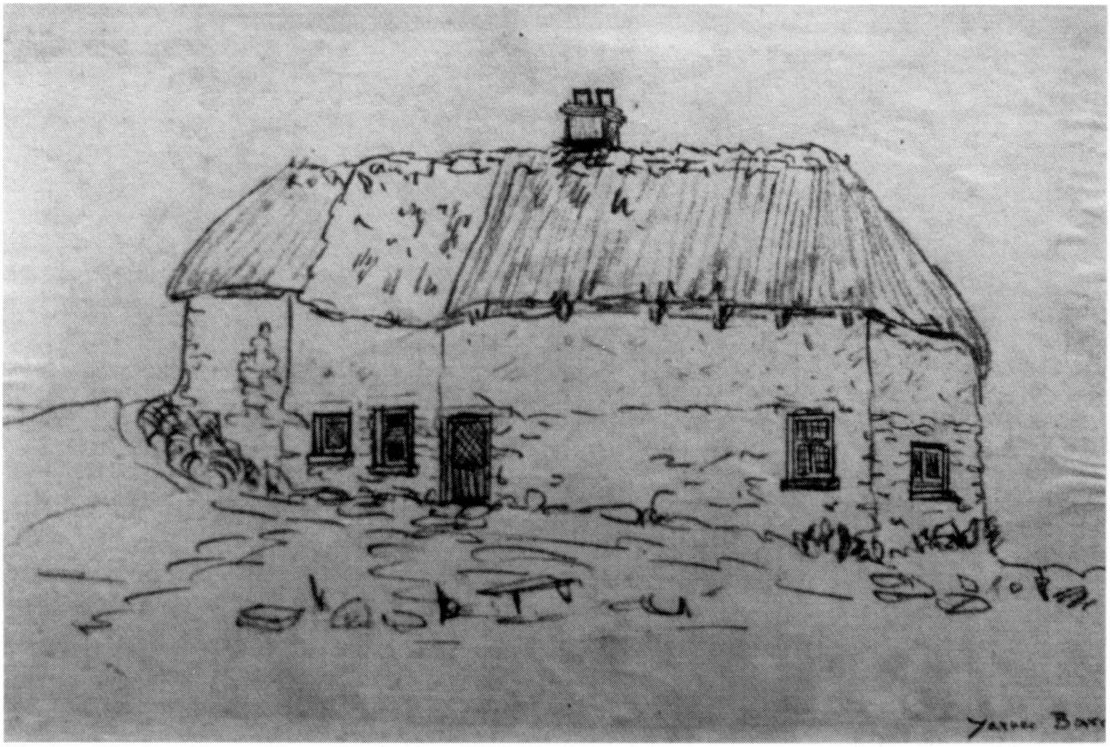

72. Rex Gardner. Yarner Barn, Dartington. 1931. Drawing.

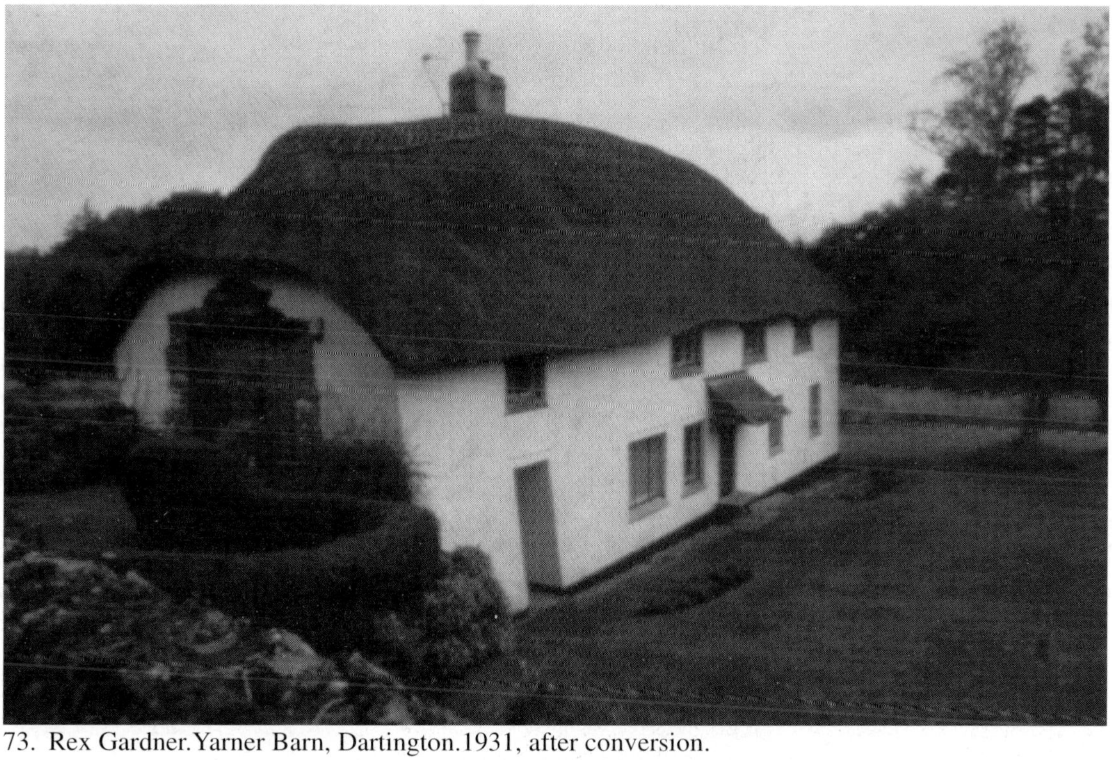

73. Rex Gardner. Yarner Barn, Dartington. 1931, after conversion.

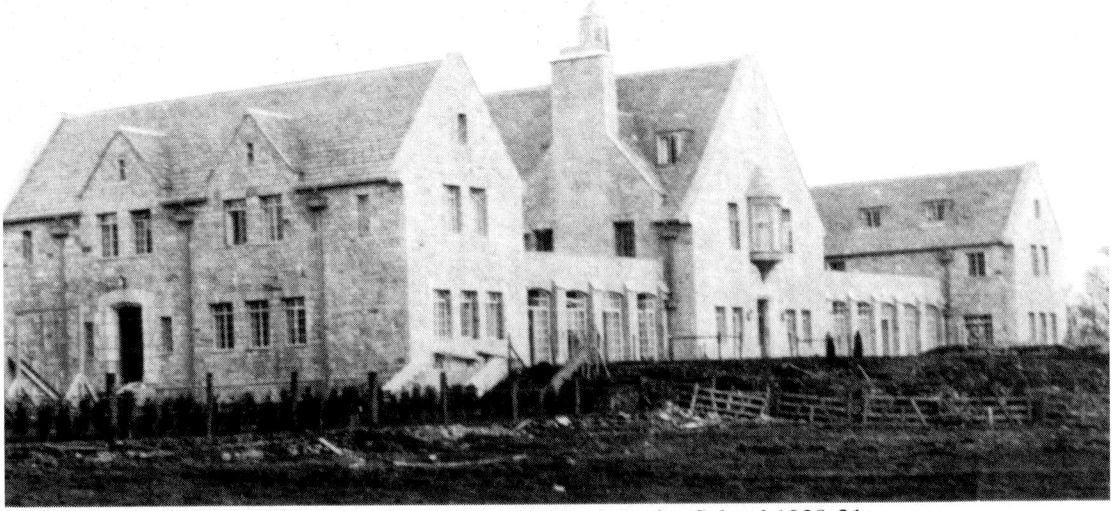
74. Ides van der Gracht of Delano & Aldrich. Aller Park Junior School.1929-31.

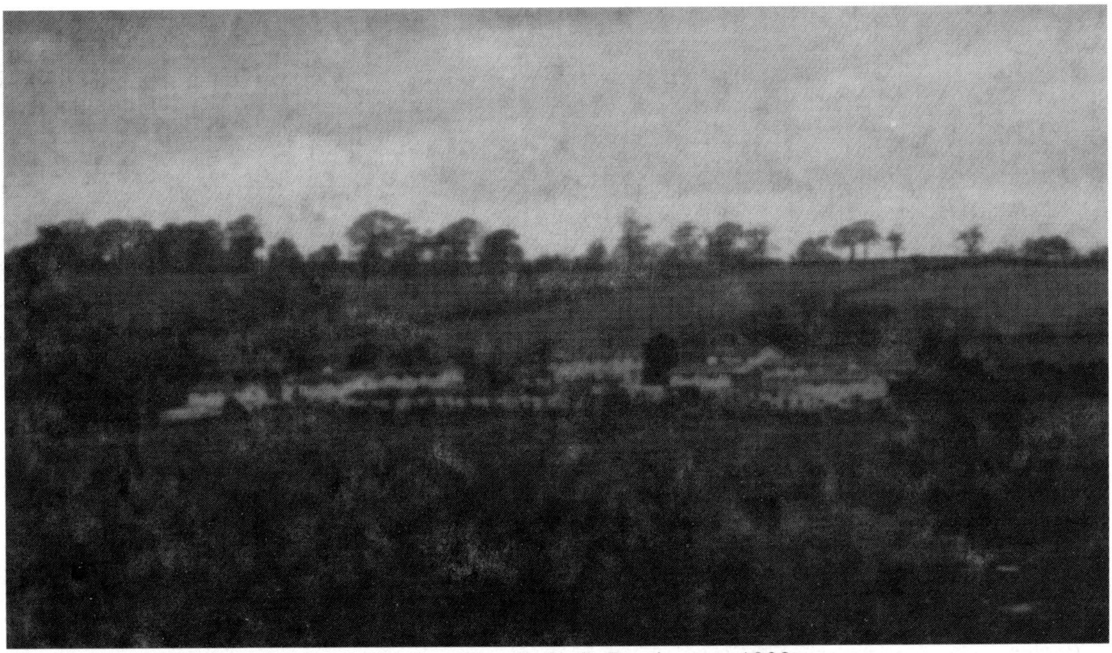
75. Louis de Soissons. Workers' Housing, Broom Park, Dartington. 1932.

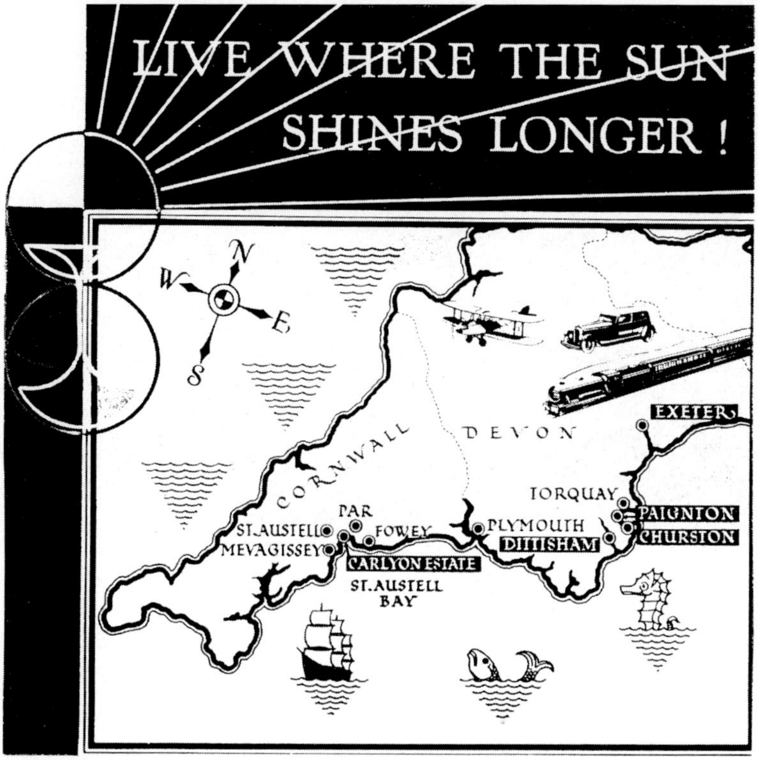

76. Staverton Builders. Brochure, mid-1930s. 'Thc Joy of a Home down in Devon'.

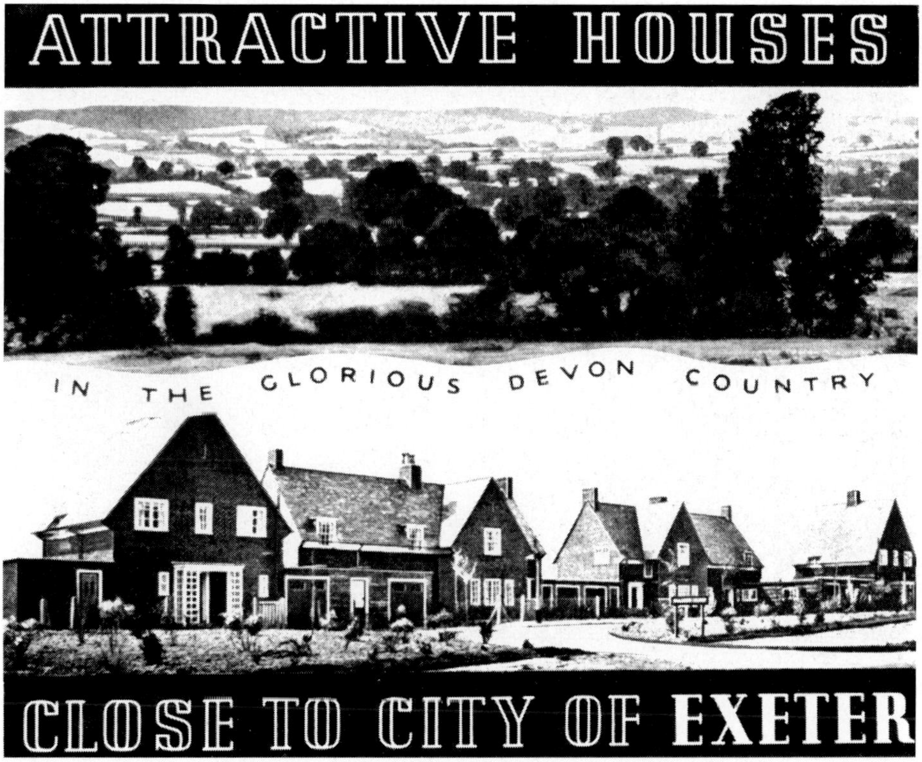

77. Staverton Builders. Brochure, St. James' Priory Estate, Exeter. Architect Louis de Soissons. Mid-1930s.

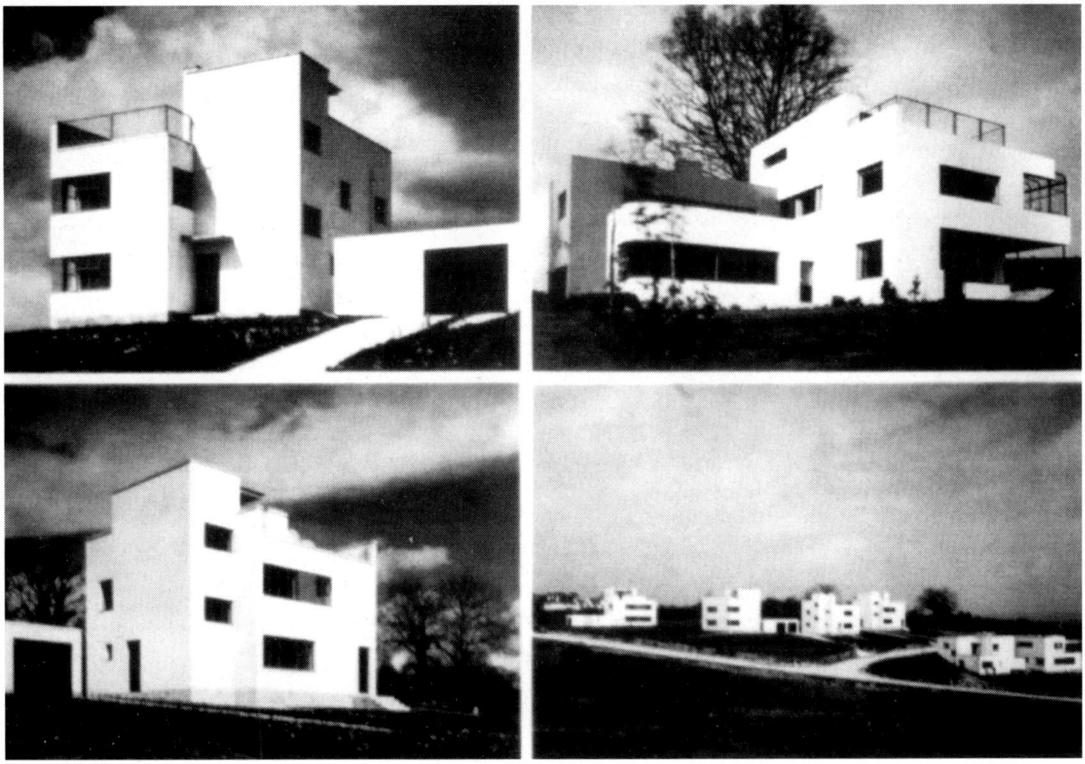

78. William Lescaze et al. Housing at Churston Ferrers. Illustration from sales brochure. 1935. Photo-montage.

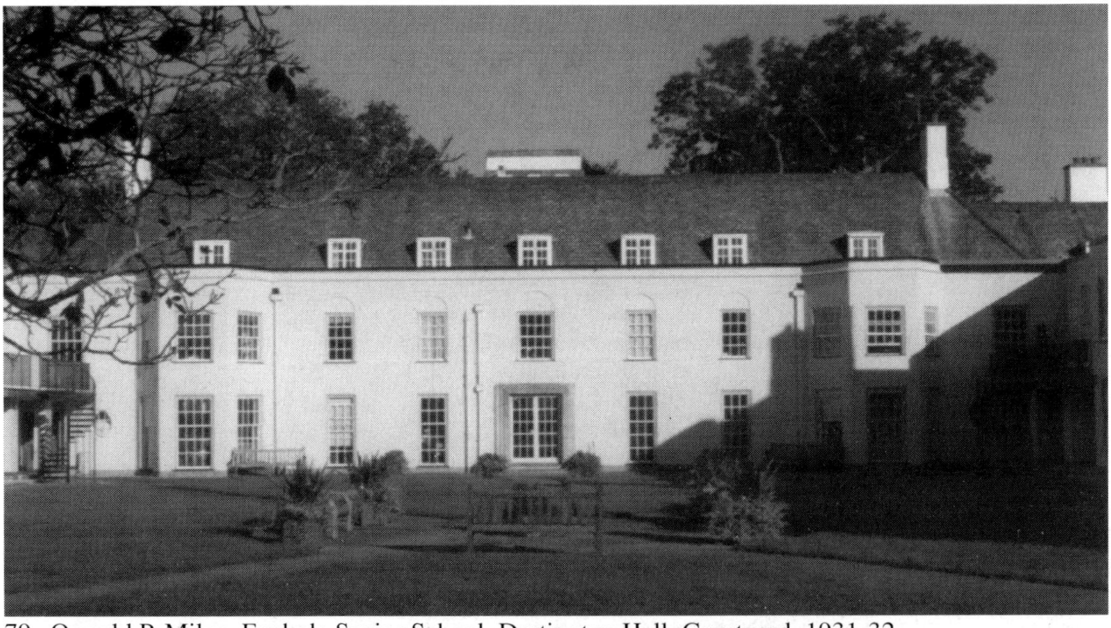

79. Oswald P. Milne. Foxhole Senior School, Dartington Hall. Courtyard. 1931-32.

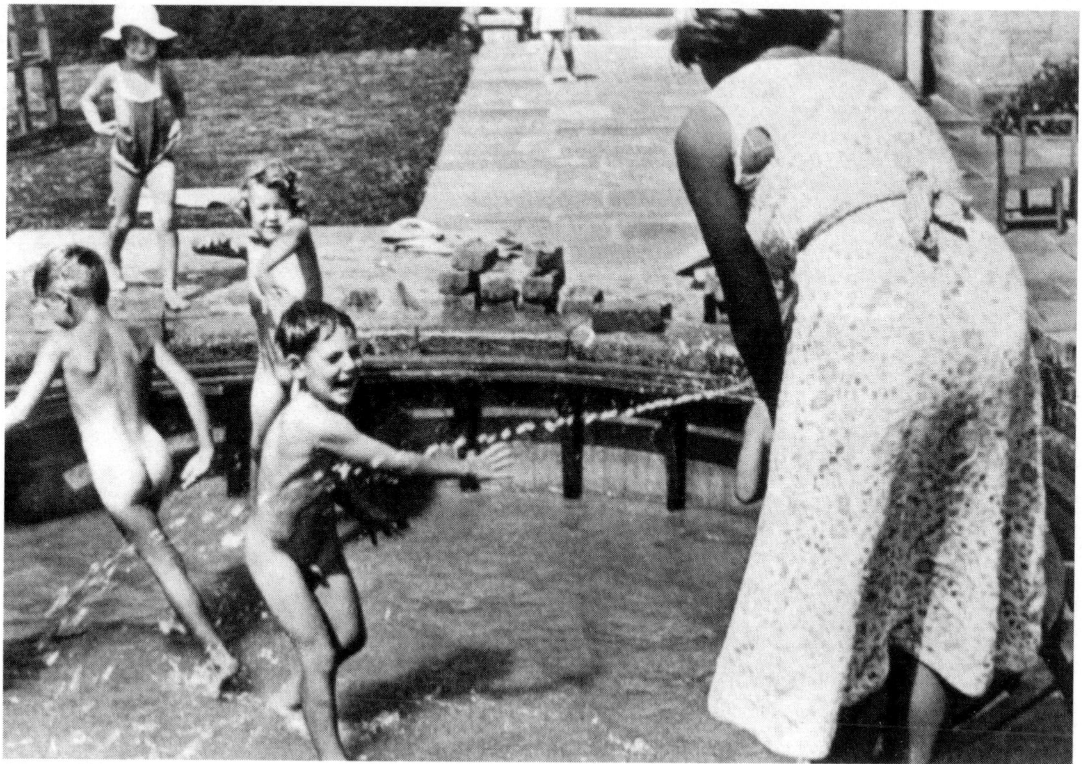

80. 'Children are what you make them'. *Weekly Illustrated* 18 August 1934. Children at Aller Park Junior School, Dartington Hall.

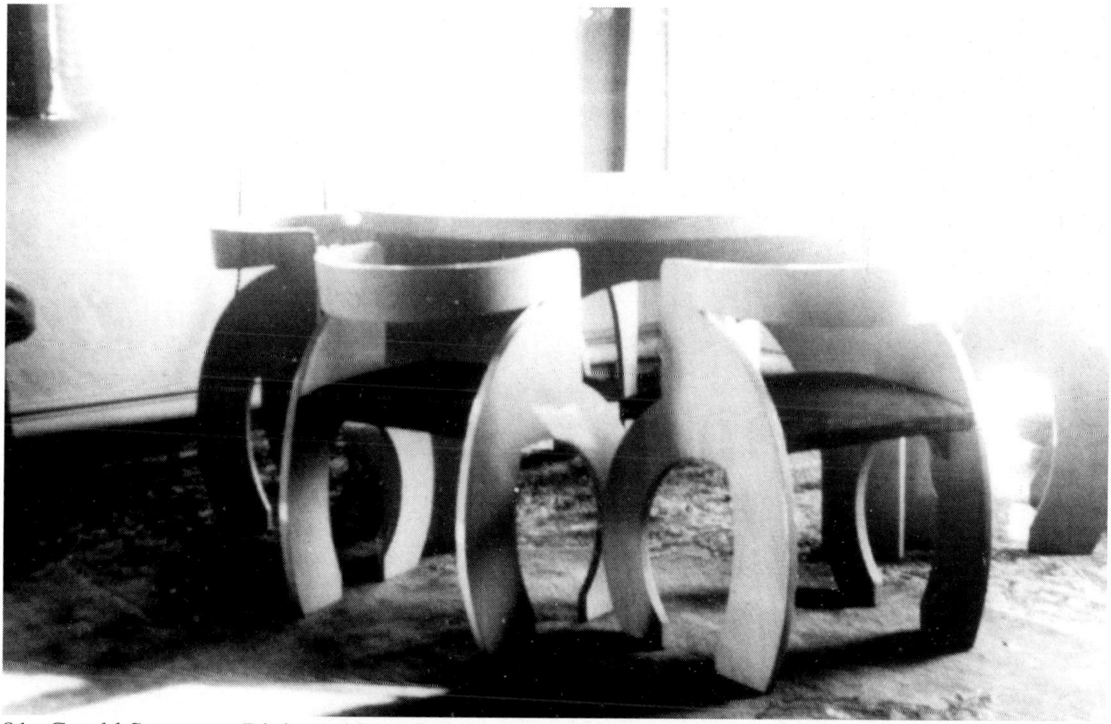

81. Gerald Summers. Dining table and chairs, Chekhov Theatre Studio. 1936. Contemporary photograph.

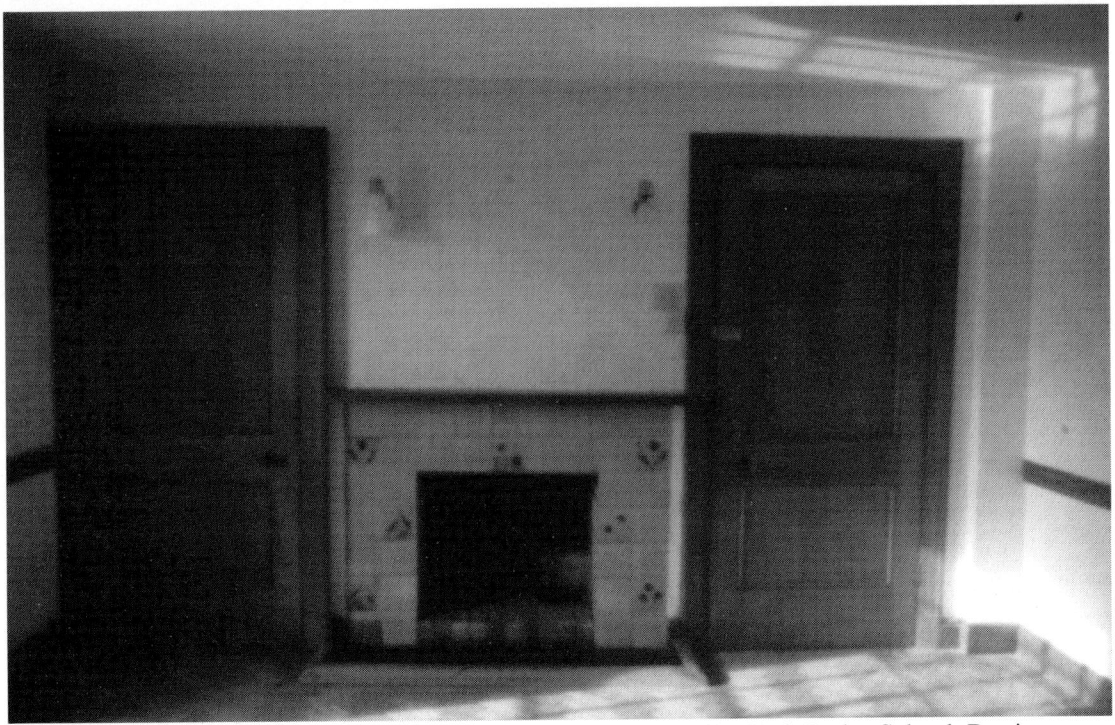

82. Jane Fox-Strangways. Tiles in Childrens' Common Room, Aller Park Junior School, Dartington Hall. c.1930.

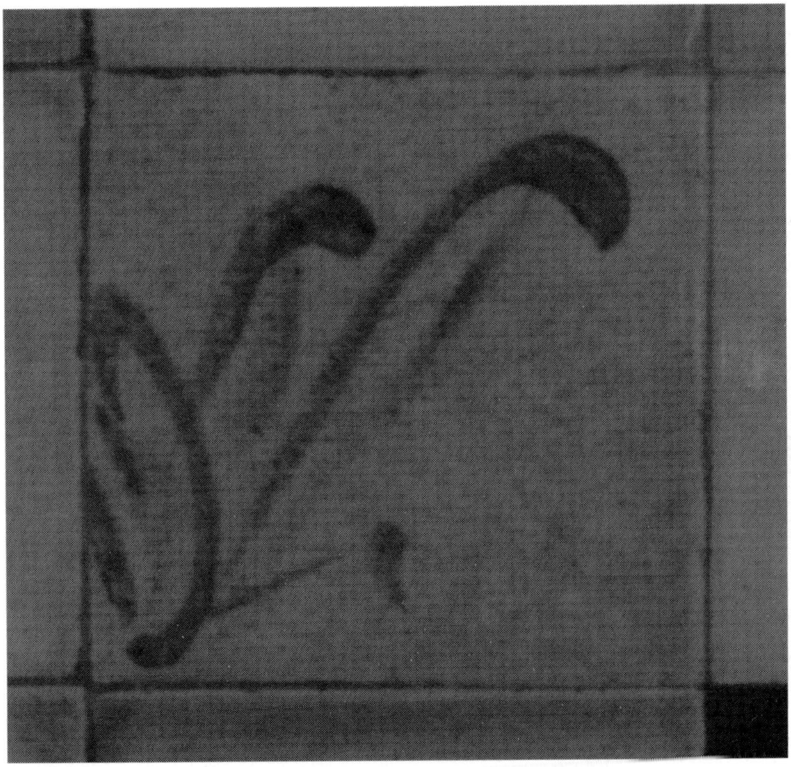

83. Jane Fox-Strangways. Tile, Library fireplace, Aller Park Junior School, Dartington Hall. c.1930

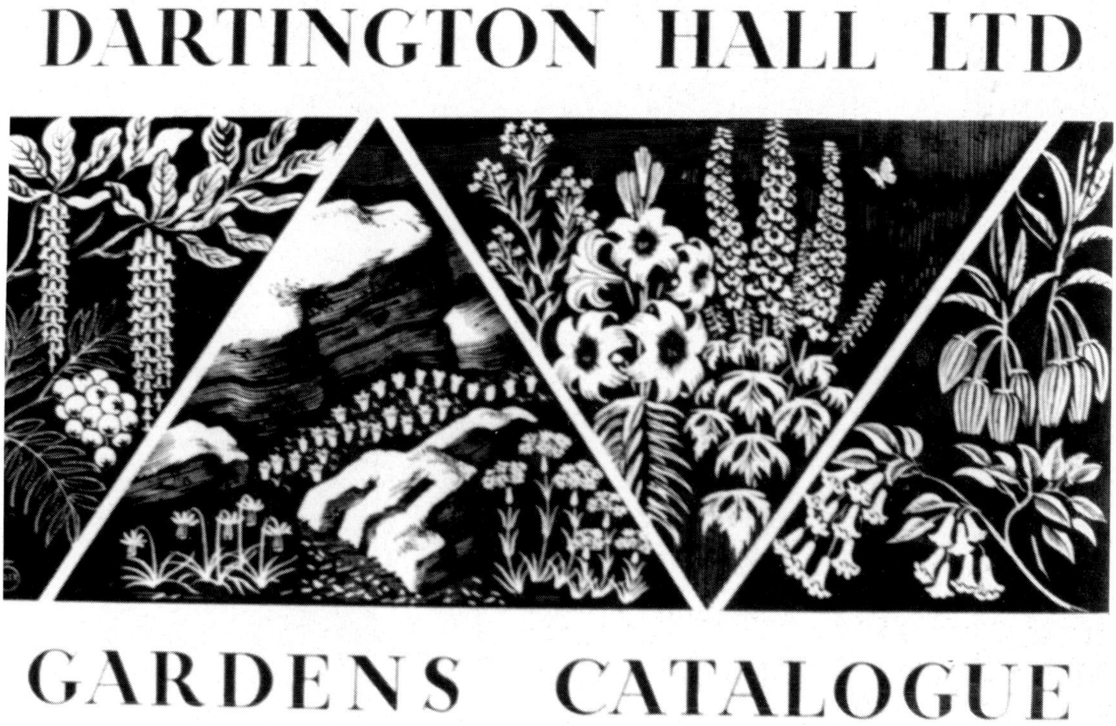

84. Dartington Hall Gardens' Department Nurseries mail order catalogue. Prints by Claire Leighton. Mid-1930s.

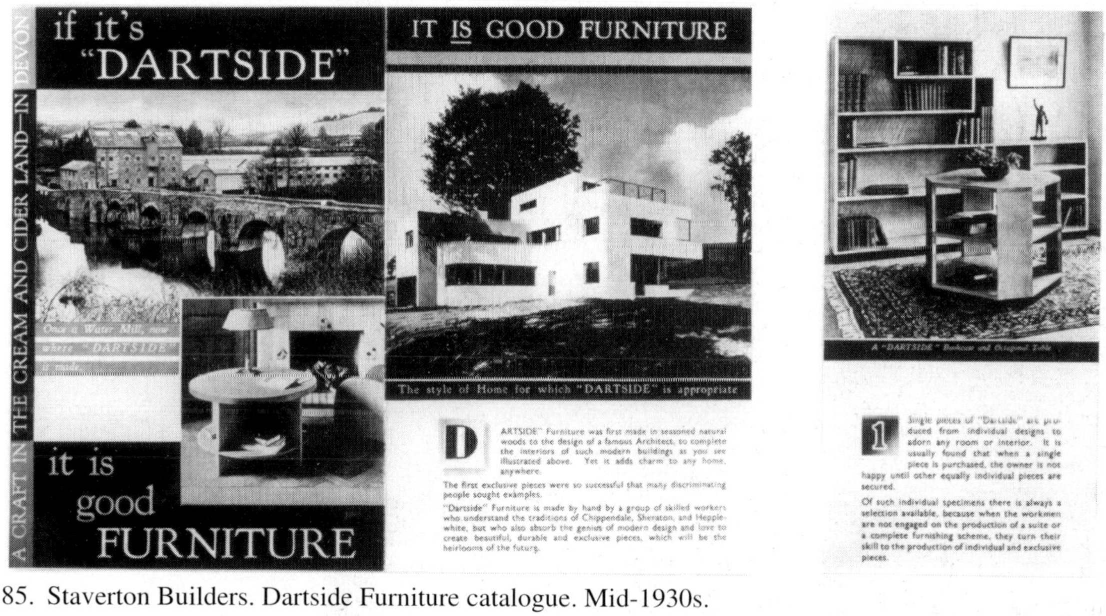

85. Staverton Builders. Dartside Furniture catalogue. Mid-1930s.

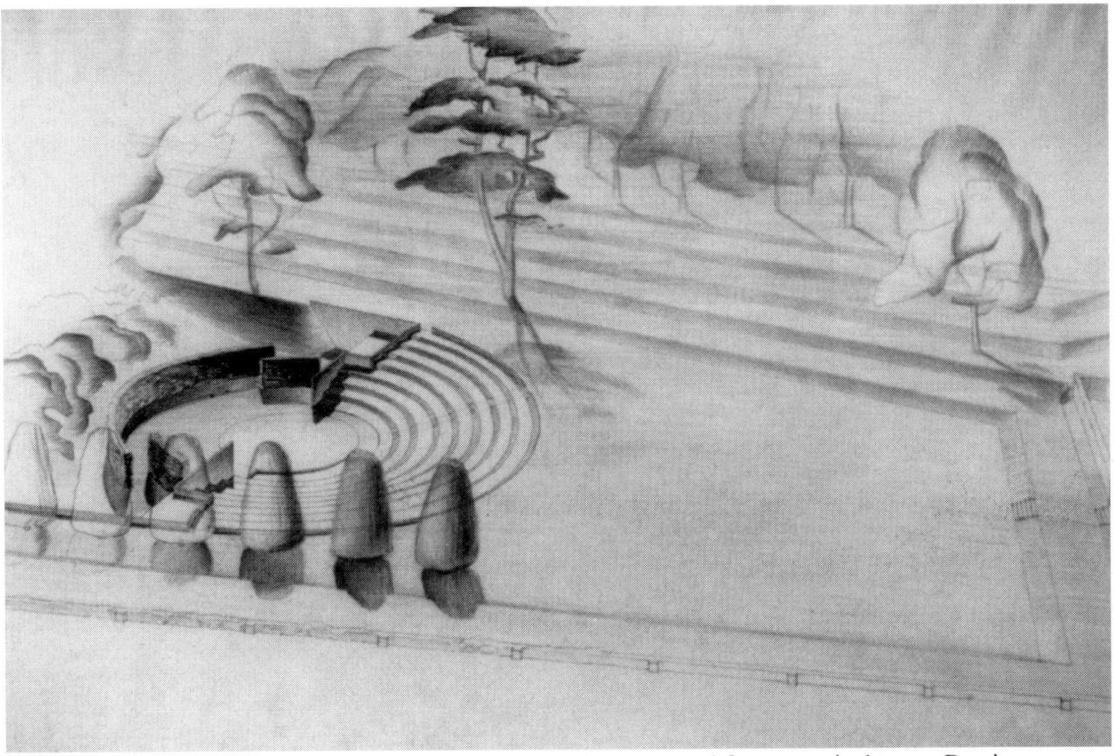

86. Walter Gropius with Adams Thomson & Fry. Design proposal for open air theatre, Dartington. October 1935. Pencil on paper. 35 x 65cm. Dartington Hall.

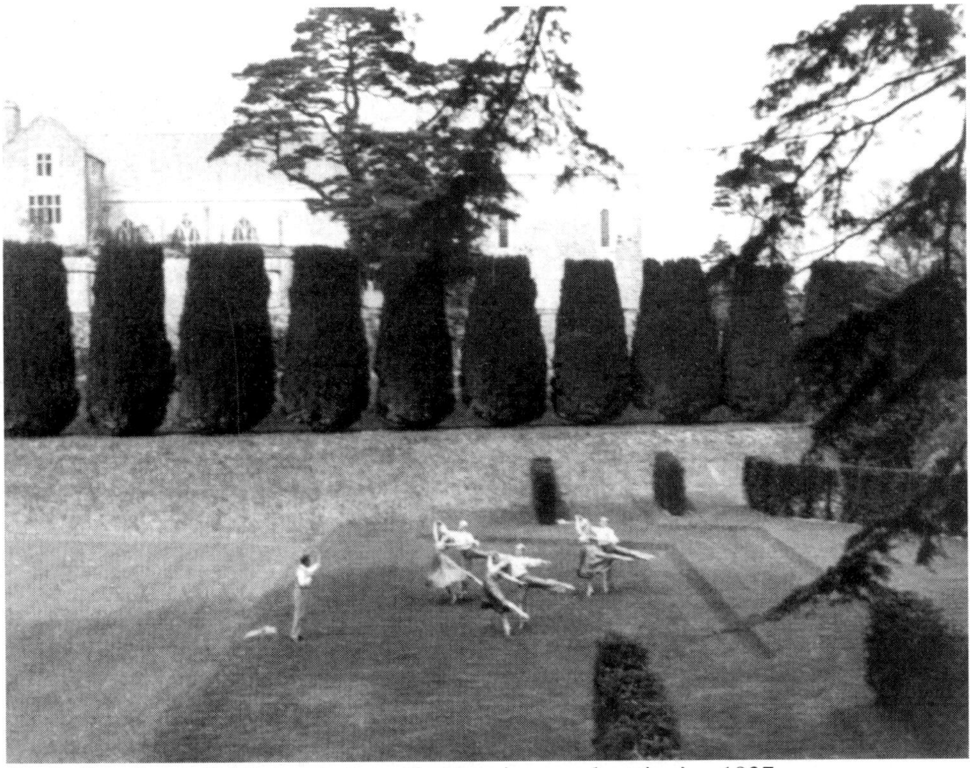

87. Ballets Jooss. Publicity photograph, 'Arts in a rural setting', c.1937.

88. Hein Heckroth. Lamda Furniture. Dartington Hall catalogue. Photographs by Hein Heckroth. 1938.

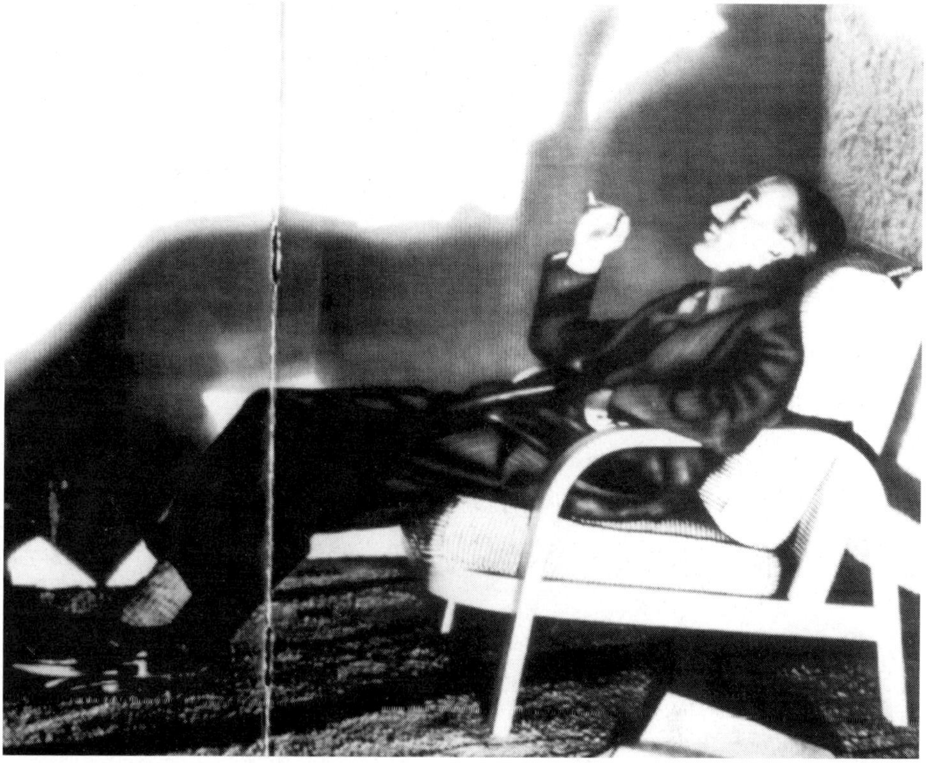

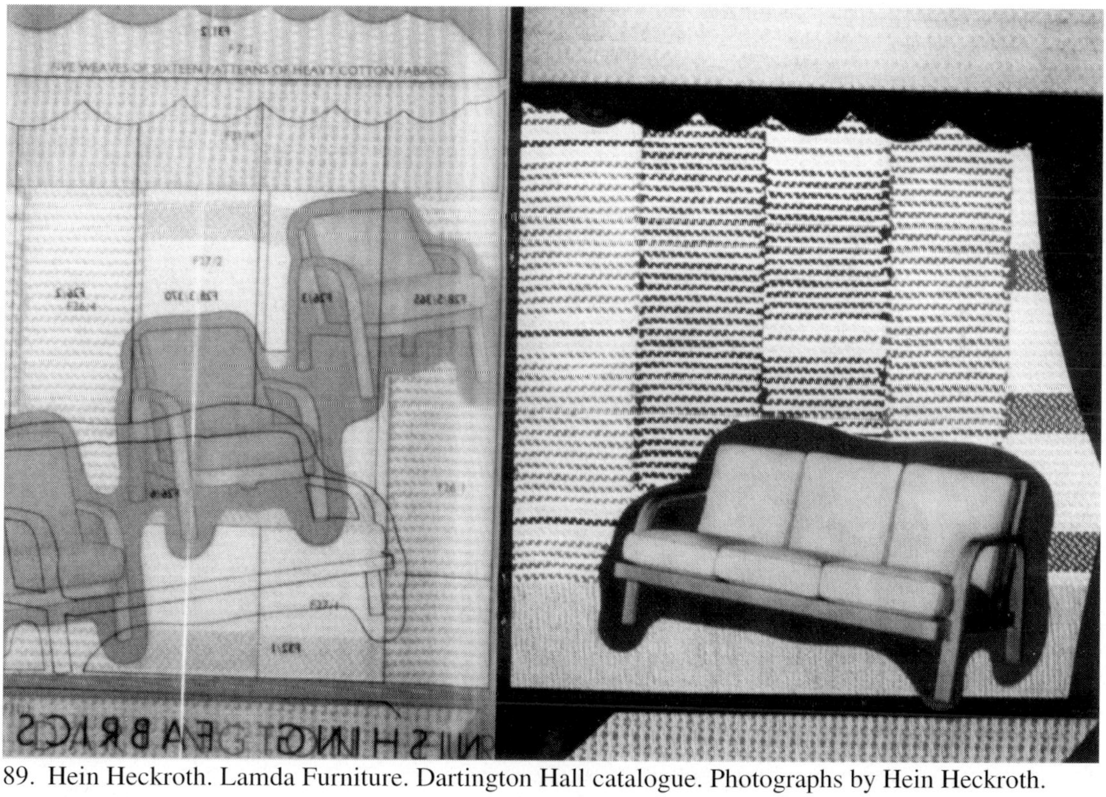

89. Hein Heckroth. Lamda Furniture. Dartington Hall catalogue. Photographs by Hein Heckroth. 1938.

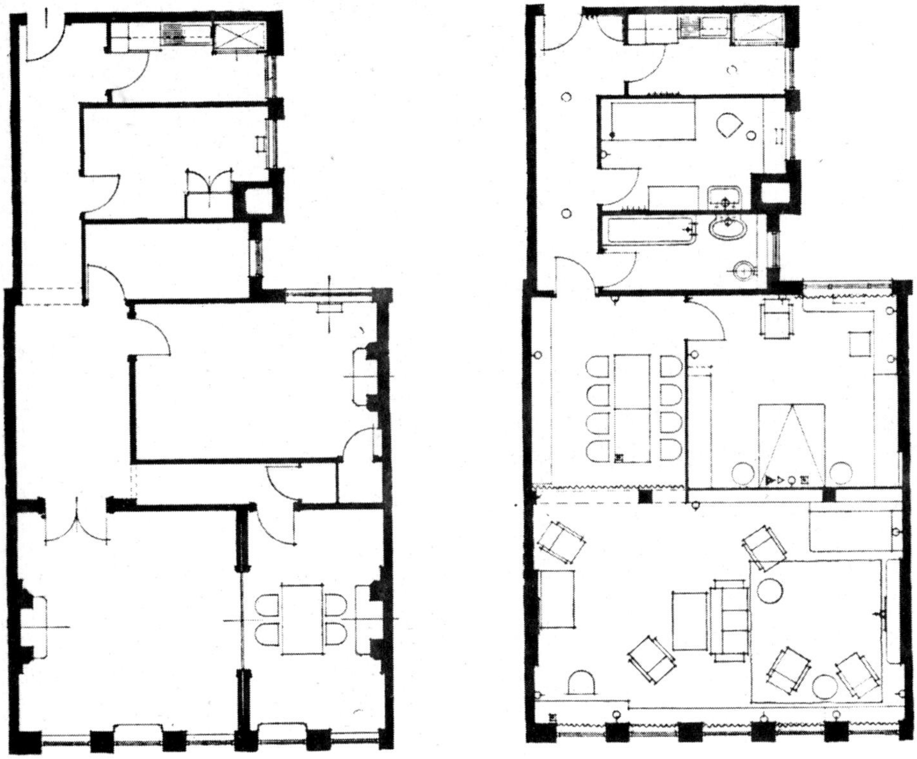

90. Serge Chermayeff. Flat, Upper Brook Street, London. Before and after conversion. 1933.

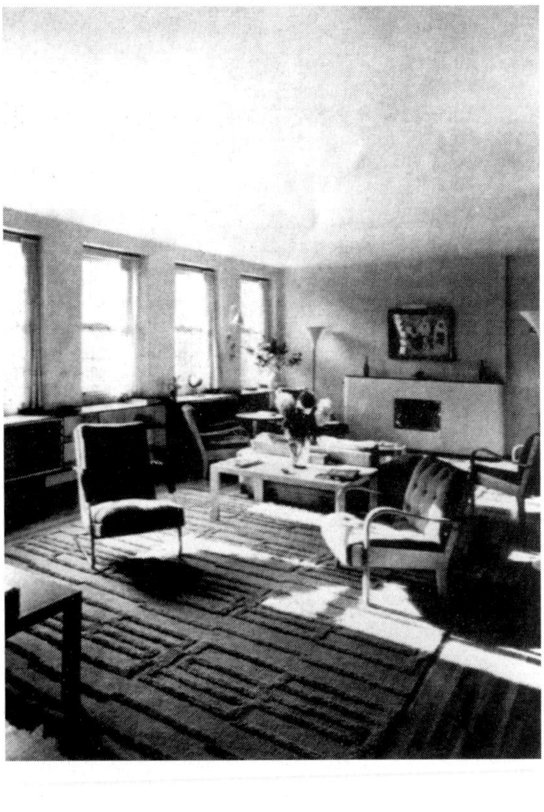

91. Serge Chermayeff. Flat, Upper Brook Street, London. Contemporary photograph showing Christopher Wood's *Dancing Sailors* over the electric fire. 1934.

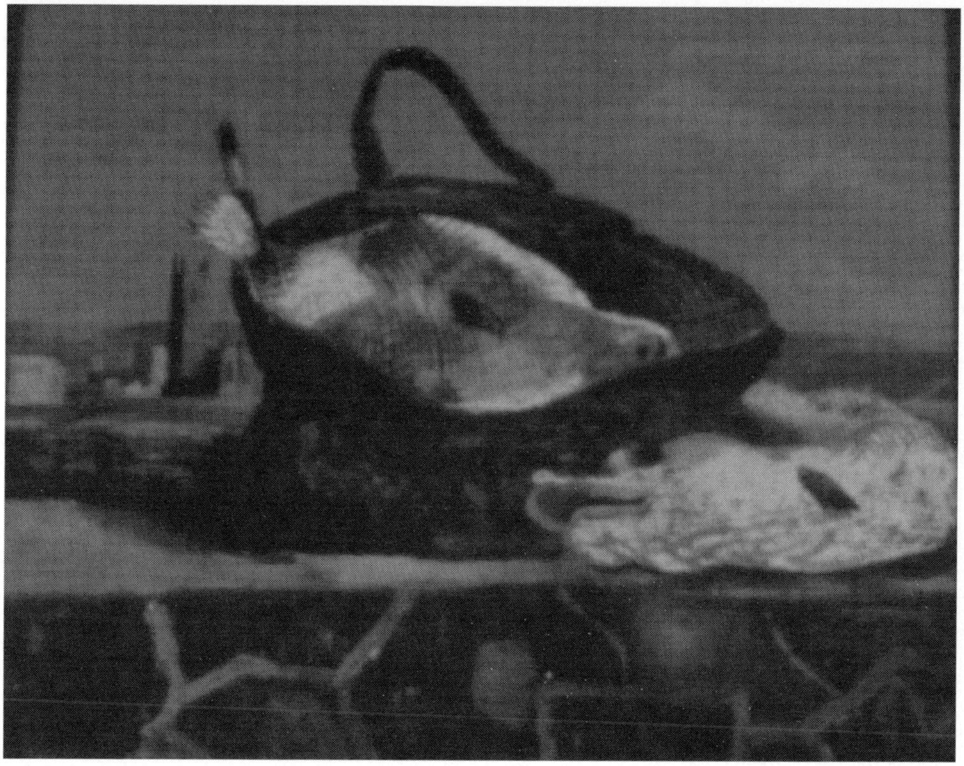

92. Christopher Wood. *Fish in a Basket.* 1930. Oil on board. 39 x 49.5cm. Dartington Hall.

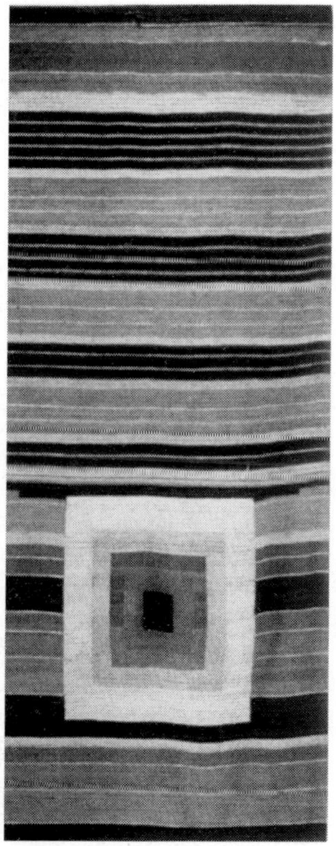

93. Elizabeth Peacock. *Gardens.* Banner for Great Hall, Dartington. 255 x 105cm. 1936-38. Dartington Hall.

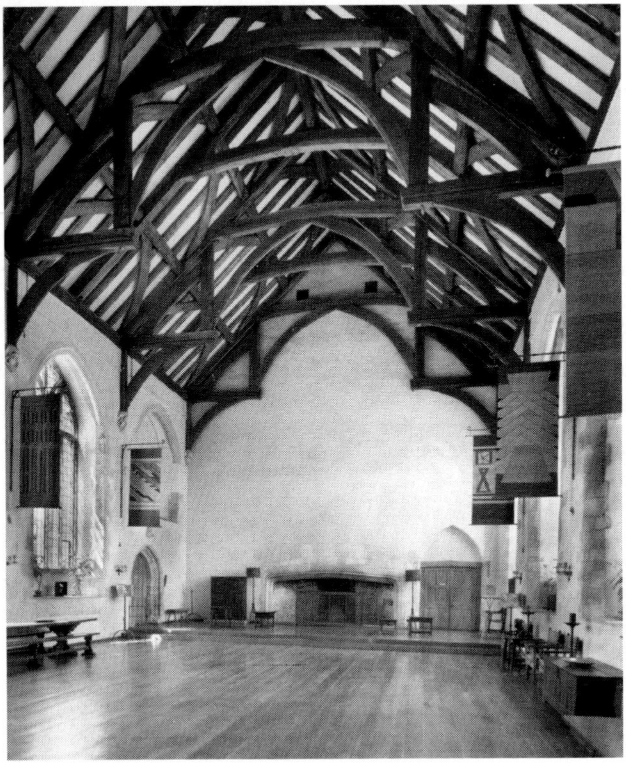

94. William Weir architect, Elizabeth Peacock designer. Interior of Great Hall, Dartington. Medieval furniture and twentieth century adaptations, such as iron standard lamps. Photograph: A. F. Kersting.

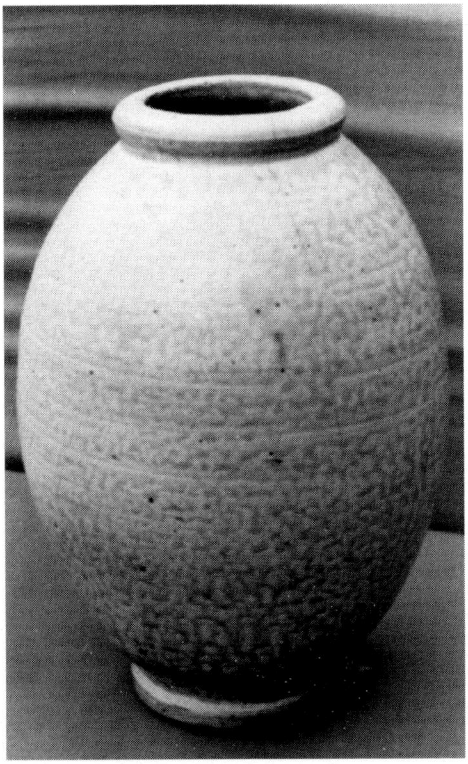

95. Bernard Leach. Ovoid vase. c.1941/42. Stoneware. 21.5 cm high.

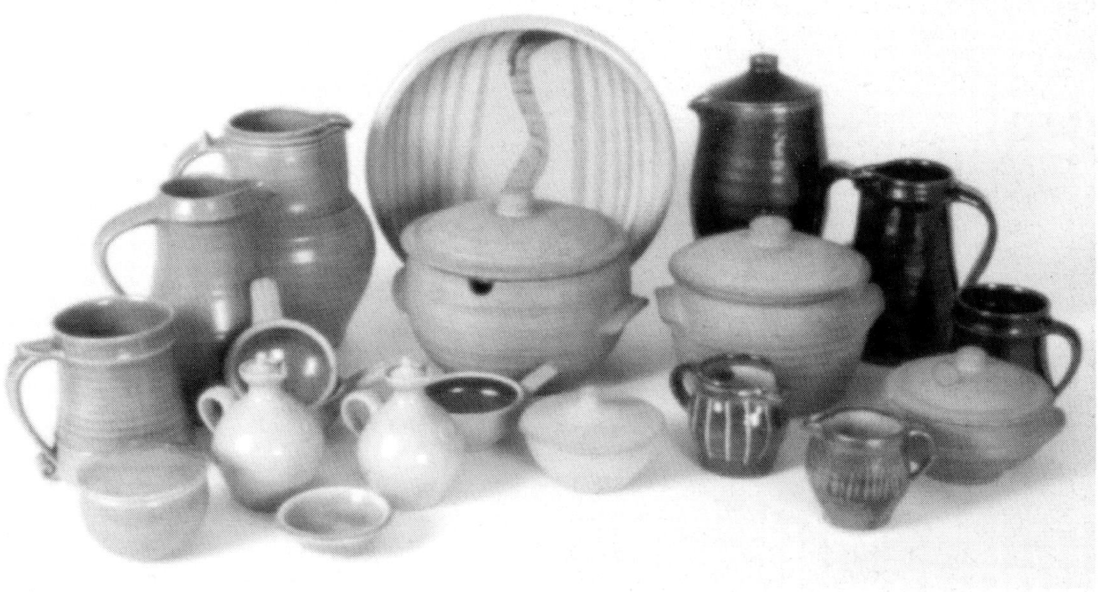

96. Leach Pottery Standardware. Made in St Ives between 1940 and 1983. Stoneware. Diameter of plate 28cm. Collection: D. Fitch, S. Woodruff, A. Barclay. Photo: Jonathan Thompson.

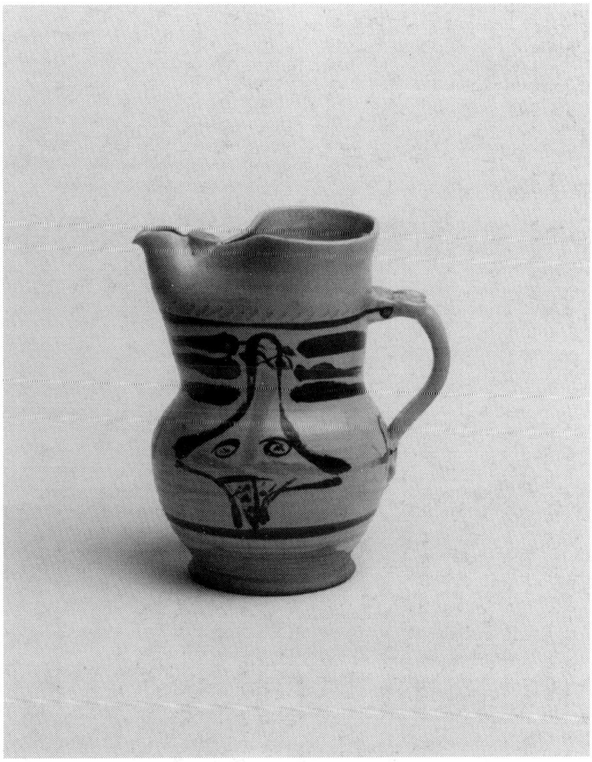

97. T.S. Haile. Jug. Made at Dartington, 1948. Tin glazed earthernware. Height 19.7cm, diameter 17cm. The Board of Trustees of The Victoria and Albert Museum.

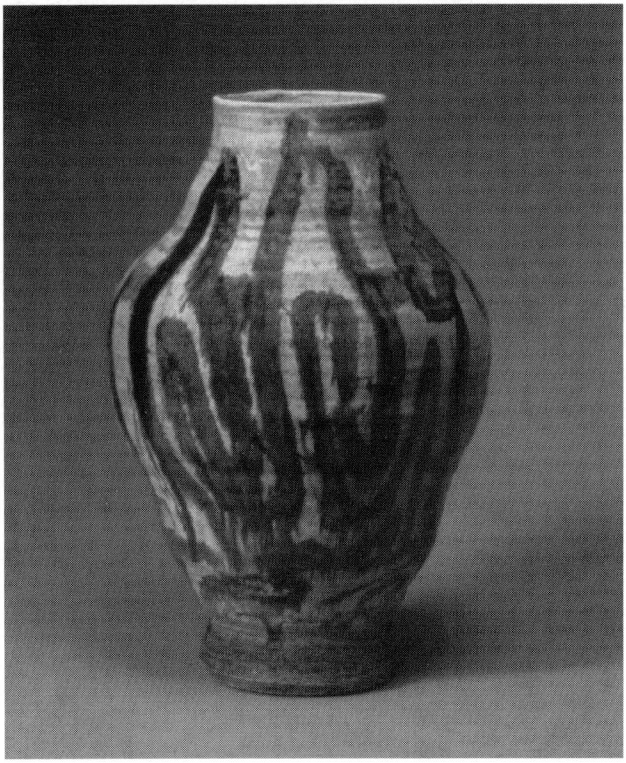

98. T.S. Haile. Vessel. Date and provenence unknown. Stoneware with oxide brushwork. Height 38cm, diameter 24cm. Royal Albert Memorial Museum, Exeter.

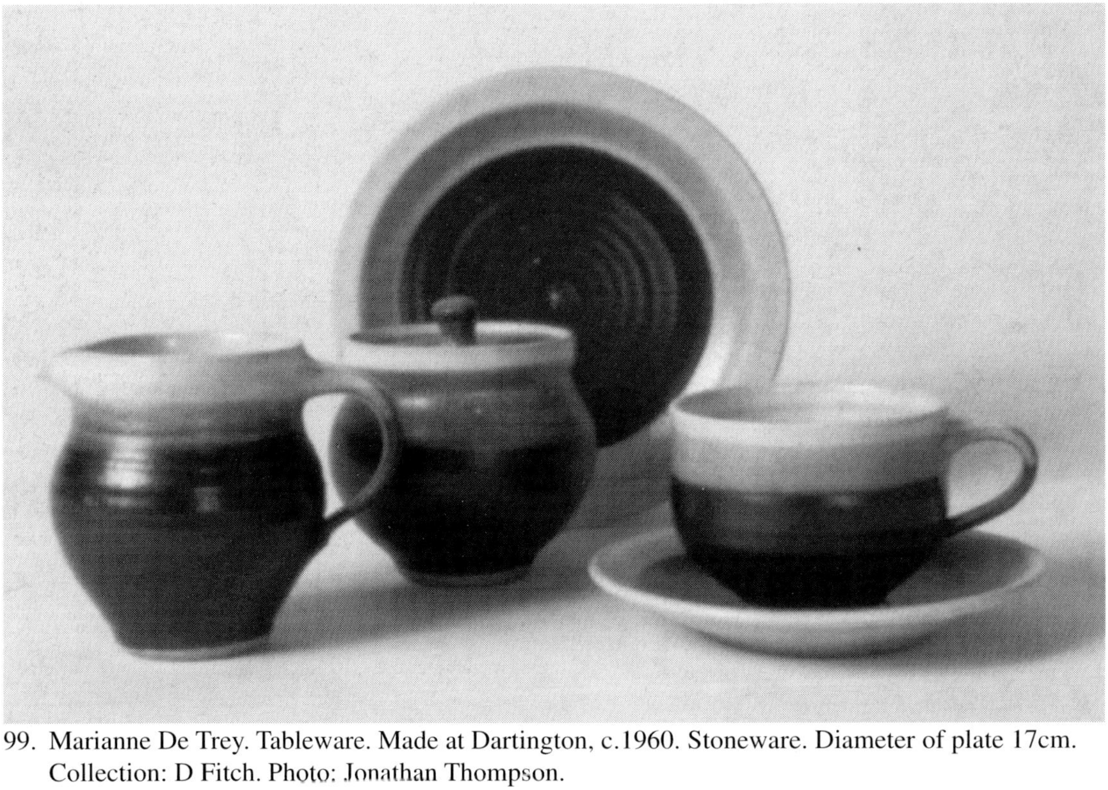

99. Marianne De Trey. Tableware. Made at Dartington, c.1960. Stoneware. Diameter of plate 17cm. Collection: D Fitch. Photo: Jonathan Thompson.

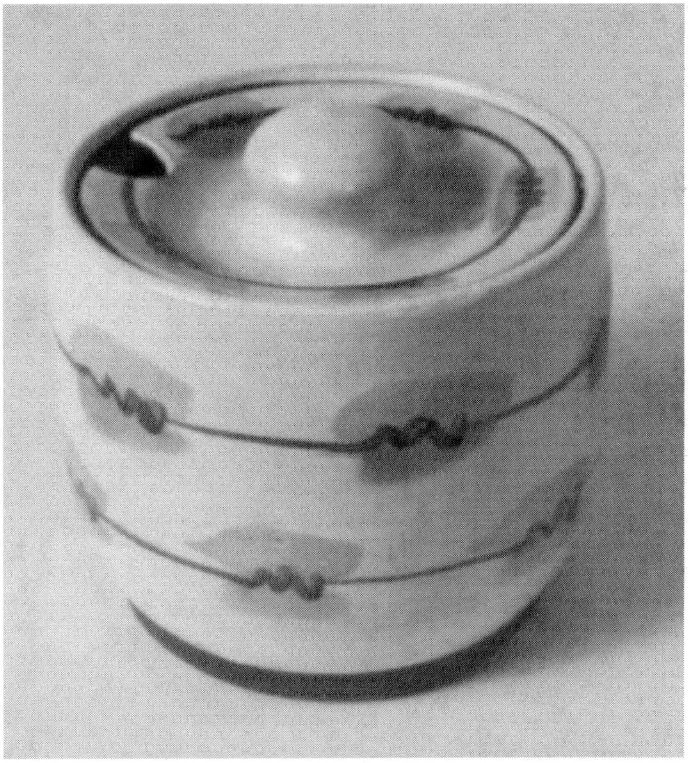

100. Marianne De Trey. Jam pot. Made at Dartington, c. 1955. Tin glazed earthernware. Height 8cm, diameter 8cm. Collection: D. Fitch. Photo: Jonathan Thompson.

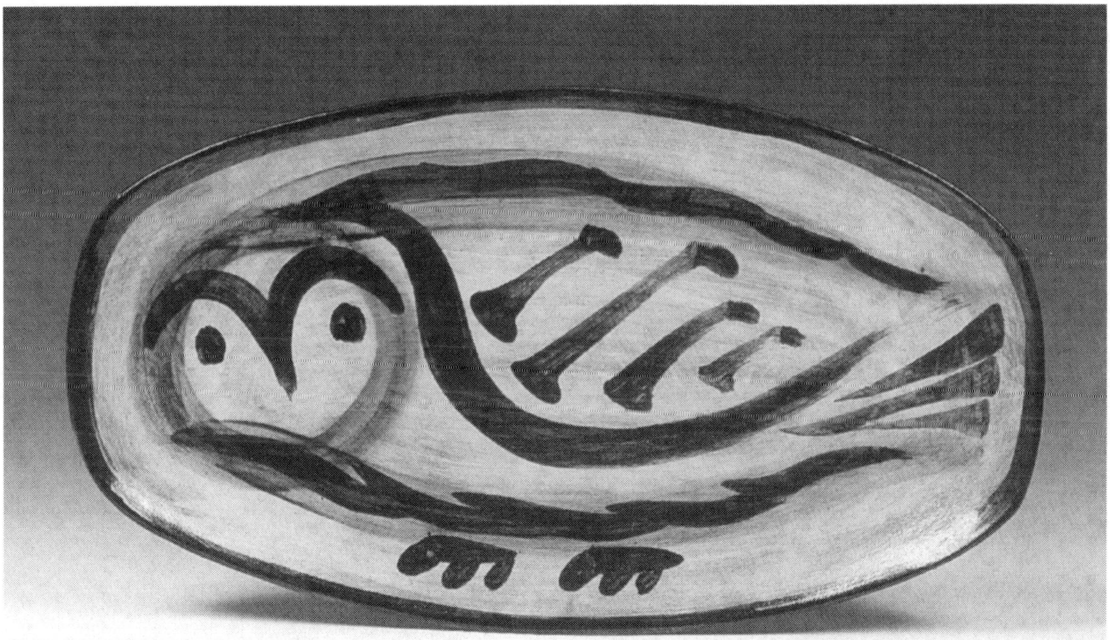

101. Bernard Forrester. Earthenware platter with owl motif. c. 1953. Length 46.2cm. Dartington Hall Trust Collection.

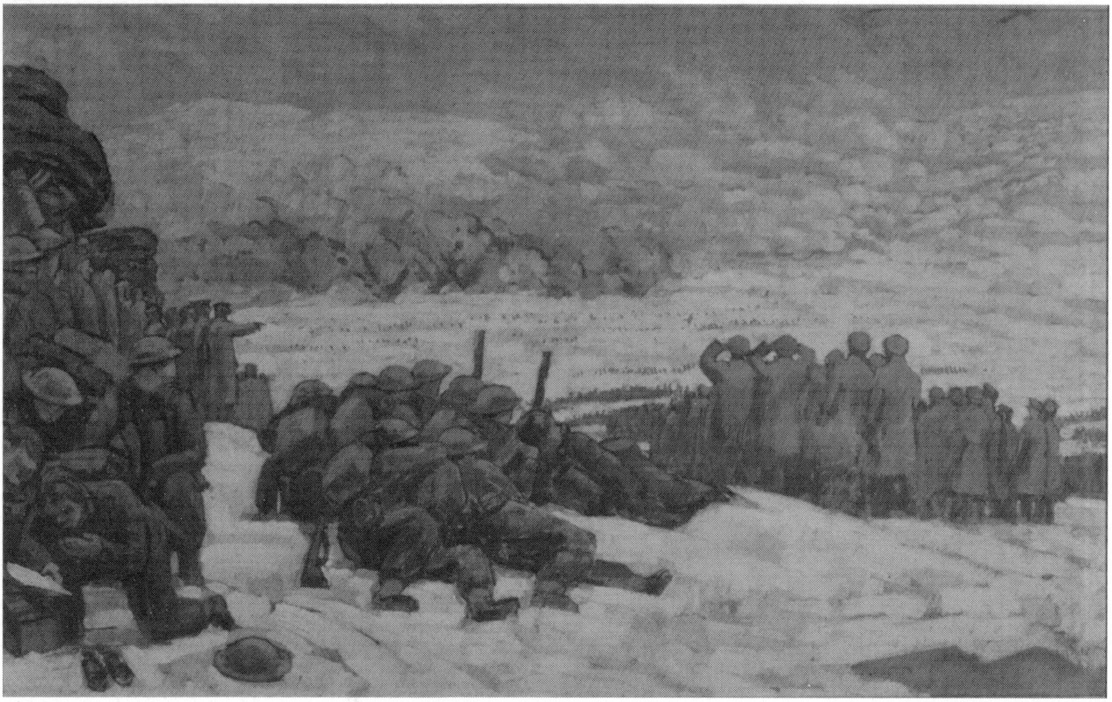

102. Henry Lamb. *Military Exercise, Devonshire*. c. 1940. Oil on board. 45 x 75.3cm. Royal Albert Memorial Museum, Exeter.

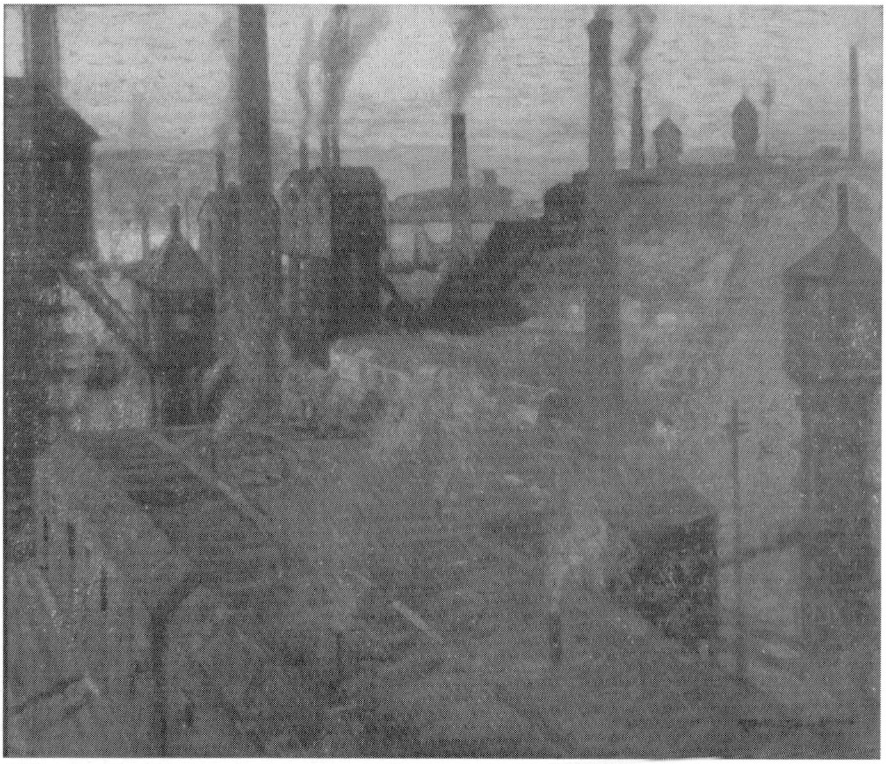

103. R. Borlase Smart. *Chemical Works, Cattedown.* 1924. Oil on canvas. 92 x 106.8cm. Plymouth City Museum and Art Gallery.

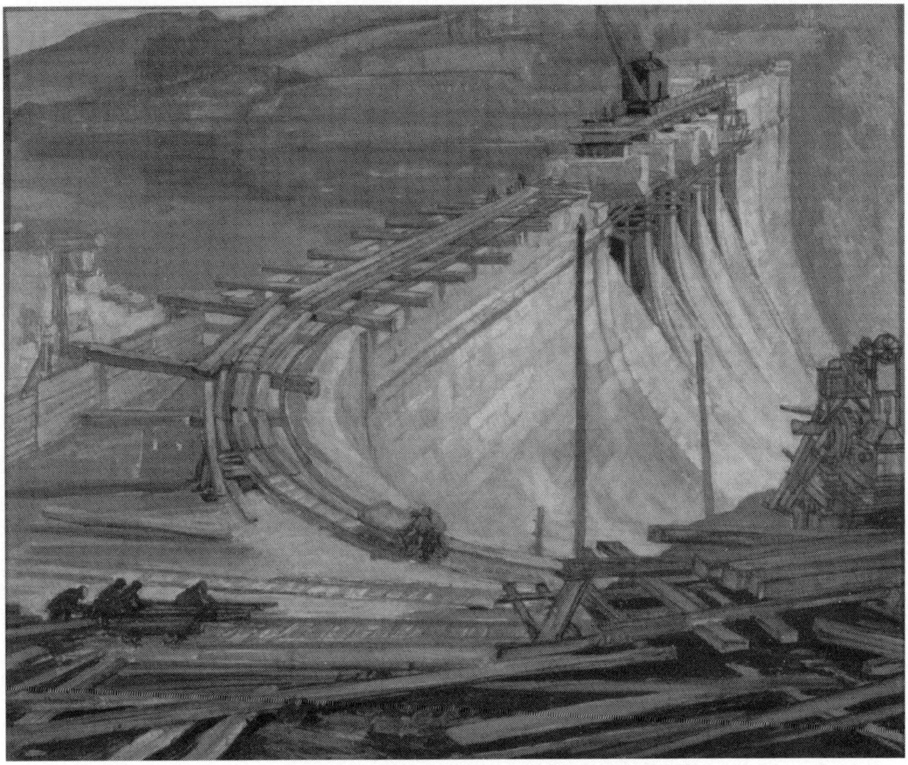

104. R. Borlase Smart. *Burrator Dam (Burrator Resevoir under construction).* c. 1928. Oil on board. 52.5 x 62.4cm. Plymouth City Museum and Art Gallery.

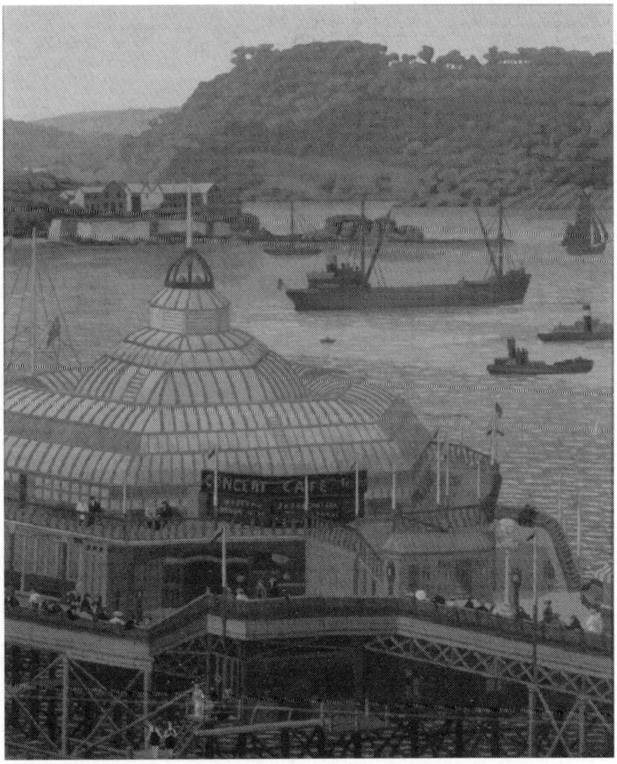

105. Charles Ginner. *Plymouth Pier from The Hoe.* 1923. Oil on canvas. 76 x 61cm. Plymouth City Museum and Art Gallery.

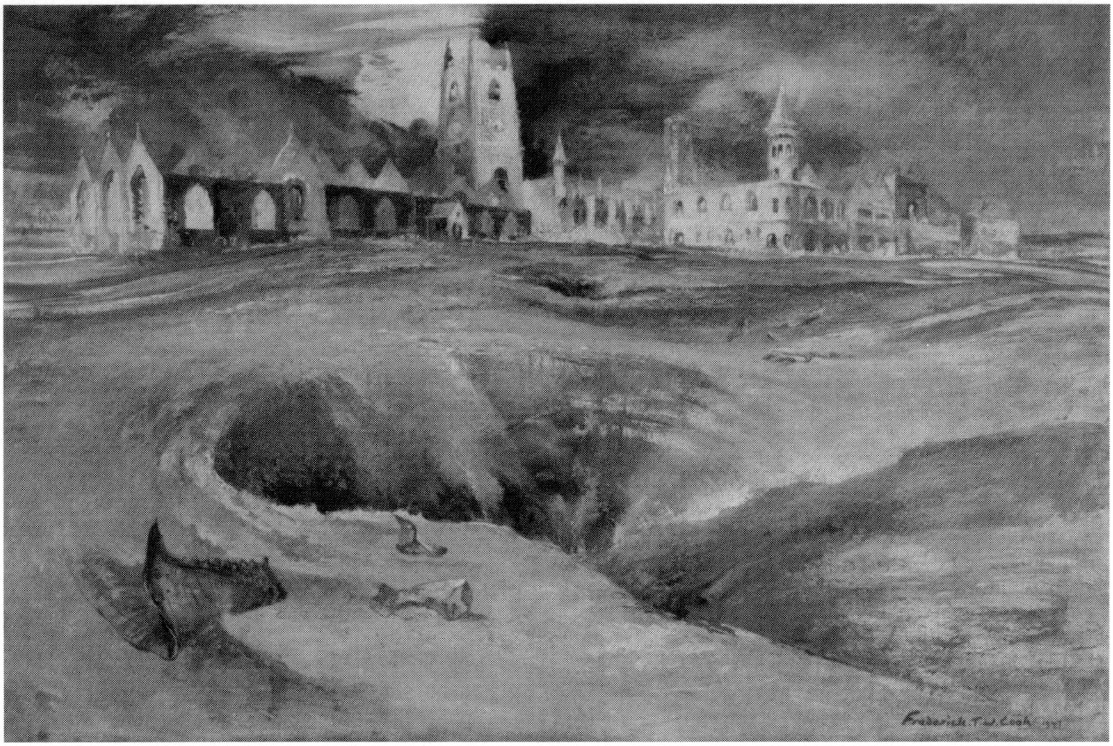

106. Frederick T. W. Cook. *Aftermath of Blitz - Saint Andrew's Church and Guildhall, Plymouth.* 1947. Oil on canvas. 50.8 x 76cm. Plymouth City Museum and Art Gallery.

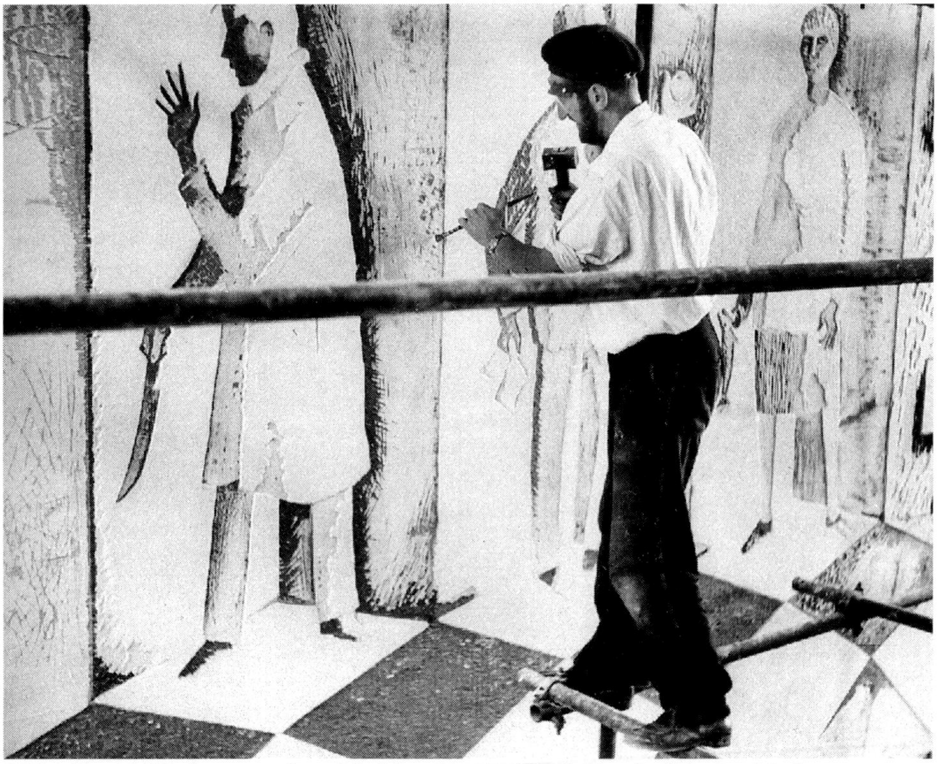

107. David Weeks at work on his Mural in the South Porch, Pannier Market, Plymouth. c. 1955. Photo: Devon Record Office, Plymouth.

Selected Biographies

ABERCROMBIE, Sir Patrick (1879-1957)
Architect and town planner. Born Ashton-upon-Mersey. Educated at Uppingham School. Articled to Charles Heathcote, Manchester and (Sir) Arnold Thornely, Liverpool. Assistant Lecturer in architecture and drawing, University of Liverpool 1907-09. Research Fellow in town planning and civic design, University of Liverpool from 1909. Professor of Civic Design, University of Liverpool 1915-35. Partner in Lockwood, Abercrombie & Saxon Architects, Chester 1920. President of Town Planning Institute 1925. FRIBA 1925. Founder member, hon. sec. and chairman CPRE. Professor of Town Planning, University College, London from 1935. Vice-president RIBA 193739. Member of Barlow Commission 1937-45. Knighted 1945. Royal Gold Medal for Architecture 1946. Gold Medal of AIA 1949. President of UIA 1951-56. *From DNB 1951-1960.*

ADAMS, HOLDEN & PEARSON
Architects of London. Harry Percy **Adams** (1865-1930): Educated Epsom College. Articled to Brightwen Binyon, Ipswich. Office of Stephen Salter, London 1888. RIBA Drawings Prize 1888. Royal Academy Schools and South Kensington Schools from 1890. Donaldson Medal and Godwin Bursary 1897. Adam's son, Percy Webster Adams, became partner in 1925. Charles Henry **Holden** (1875-1960): Born Bolton. Apprenticed to Everard W. Leeson, Manchester 1892-96. Evening classes Municipal School of Art, Manchester 1893-94 and Technical School 1894-96. First Prize *The Building News* Designing Club 1895-96. Certificate of Merit RIBA Soane Medallion 1897. Assistant to C.R. Ashbee, London 1897-99. Assistant to Percy Adams, London 1899. Partnership 1907. Royal Gold Medal for Architecture 1936. Hon. Doctorate University of Manchester 1936. Hon. Doctorate University of London 1946. Lionel G. **Pearson** (1879-1953): Educated Municipal School of Art, Manchester. Assistant to Woodhouse and Willoughby, William Flockhart and E.S. Prior. Office of Percy Adams 1903. Partnership 1913.

CACHEMAILLE DAY, Nugent Francis (1896 -1976)
Architect. Office of Louis de Soissons (*qv*), Welwyn Garden City and H.S. Goodhart-Rendel 1925-28. Partnership with Felix Lander (1897-1960) 1928-35 and Herbert A. Welch 1930-35 as Welch, Cachemaille Day and Lander. Private practice, London from 1935.

CHITTY, Anthony Merlott (1907-76)
Architect. Born Eton. Educated Trinity College, Cambridge and Architectural Association, London. Architectural Association Essay Prize 1930. Member of Tecton 1932-36. Office of Wallis Gilbert & Partners, London. Practice with Robert Hening (*qv*) from 1937. President of Architectural Association 1950-51. Chairman Board of Architectural Education 1952-54. Member of Secretary of State for the Colonies Advisory Committee on

Colonial Colleges of Art, Science & Technology 1955-62. Member Governing Council, Kumasi College, Ghana 1956-59. Architect and planner to new universities at Nairobi and Lusaka 1965-70.

CRABTREE, William (1905-1991)
Architect and town planner. Educated Doncaster Grammar School. Office of T.H.Johnson, Doncaster 1924-6. Liverpool University School of Architecture 1926-29. Office of Helmle & Corbett, New York 1928. RIBA Tite Prize 1928. Office of Joseph Emberton 1929 as perspectivist. Research architect for John Lewis Partnership 1930-39. Design of Peter Jones Department Store, London 1933-35 (with Slater & Moberley and Prof. C.H. Reilly). Planner for City of Southampton 1944-45. Co-ordinating architect for City of Plymouth 1945-51. Designs for New Towns of Crawley, Hatfield and Harlow. Partnership with W.T.Jarosz, London.

DAVISON, Thomas
Architect. Articled to Charles A. Bury of Scarborough. Studied architecture at RA Schools and Architectural Association. Ashpitel Prize 1887. Assistant in various London offices including Samuel Knight from 1887. Private practice, London from about 1905. Resigned from RIBA 1921.

DAWSON, Matthew (1874-1943)
Architect. Trained at Atelier Laloux, Paris. Soane Medallion 1901. Associate of RIBA 1907. Lecturer in architecture at Camberwell School of Arts & Crafts 1907-12 and at Cambridge University. Architect with London County Council. Private practice, London before 1914. Member of panel Improvement of Housing Schemes for the Borough Council of Hammersmith from 1919. FRIBA 1921. Senior lecturer at Bartlett School of Architecture, London University 1929-39.

DE SOISSONS, Louis Emmanuel Jean Guy de Savoie-Carignan (1890-1962)
Architect and town planner. Born Montreal, Canada. Educated privately and Ecole des Beaux Arts, Paris. Atelier of Pascal Nenot Recoura et Duquesne. Articled to J.H. Eastwood. Tite Prize 1912. RIBA Henry Jarvis student 1913. Office of Edwin Lutyens (*qv*). RASC and liaison duties with Italian Army 1914-18. OBE 1918. Partnership with P.D. Hepworth and G. Grey Wornum. Chief planner to Welwyn Garden City from 1920. FRIBA, MTPI and SADG 1923. Vice-principal of Architectural Association 1929-33. ARA 1942. RIBA Distinction in Town Planning 1945. RA 1953. Member of Royal Fine Art Commission 1949-61. CVO 1956. Treasurer RA from 1959. *From DNB 1961-70.*

DORN, Marion (1899-1964)
Textile and carpet designer. Born San Francisco. Educated Stanford University BA Education (Graphic Art) 1916. Resident in England from early 1920s. Exhibition with E. McKnight Kauffer at Arthur Tooth & Sons 1929. Designer to Warner & Sons Ltd., Donald Brothers Ltd., Old Bleach Linen Co. Ltd. and Edinburgh Weavers throughout 1930s. Founded Marion Dorn Ltd., London 1934. Re-established in New York from 1940. Studio in Tangier 1960s.

ETCHELLS, Frederick (1886-1973)
Architect and painter. Studied art at Royal College of Art and in Paris. Associated with Omega workshop with Roger Fry and member of Vorticist group with Wyndham Lewis. Private architectural practice, London from 1920. Translator of Le Corbusier's *Vers une architecture* (Towards a New Architecture, 1927) and *Urbanisme*

(The City of Tomorrow, 1929). Author with Dean D.W.O. Addleshaw of *Architectural Setting of Anglican Worship*, 1948.

FAREY, Cyril (1888-1954)
Architect and perspectivist. Educated Tonbridge School. Studied Architectural Association and RA Schools 1905-09. Travelling scholarship. Assistant to Ernest Newton. Studied Italy 1910-13. RA Gold Medal for Architecture 1911. Tite Prize and Studentship 1913. Private practice from 1913. Soane Medallion and 1914. Mentioned in Home Service Dispatches, Captain 1914-18. Gold Medal and Stott Travelling Scholarship in Architecture 1921. Winner of open competition for Raffles University College in Singapore with Graham Dawbarn 1924, built 1925-30. FRIBA.

FEIBUSCH, Hans (b.1898)
Painter, muralist and sculptor. Born Frankfurt-am-Main. German army 1916-1918. Studied medicine and then painting in Munich, studio of Stanilas Struckgold 1918. *Meisterschuler* studies in Berlin under Karl Hofer 1920. Studied in Italy and Paris in studios of Othon Friesz and André Lhote 1921-24. Member of Frankfurt Artists' Association 1925-33. Exhibitions in Frankfurt, Berlin and Dusseldorf. German Grand State Prize for Painters 1930. Emigrated to London 1933, British citizen 1938. Exhibitions at Lefevre Gallery, London and Royal Academy. German Order of Merit 1967 and Grand Cross of Merit 1989. *From David Coke, Hans Feibusch - The Heat of Vision. London: Lund Humphries, 1995.*

GREENSLADE, Sydney Kyffin (1866-1955)
Architect. Articled to Edward Ashworth, Exeter 1884. Office of Frederick Boreham 1887-88, James Jerman of Exeter 1889 and William Gillbee Scott 1890. RIBA Pugin student 1891. Grissell Gold Medal 1897. Godwin Bursary 1900. Assistant to W.D. Caroe, T.E. Colcutt and Henry Florence. Private practice Exeter and London from 1900, partnership with J.H. Eastwood 1900 and T.H. Lyon 1901. First prize in competitions for South African War Memorial Library, Eton 1904 (with L.K. Hall) and National Library of Wales, Aberystwyth 1909. Collaborated with E. Vincent Harris *(qv)* from 1920s to 1950s.

HARRILD, Fred (1883-1969)
Architect. Educated at Harrow School and Exeter College, Oxford. Architectural Association School of Architecture 1906-08. Articled to Edwin Lutyens 1908-11. Private practice, London from 1911. Army Service Corps M.T. 1914-18. Partnership with Thomas William Latham 1920-23. Office in Totnes, Devon 1920-32 (latterly with Herbert Rea) and London 1932-63. FRIBA 1926. Member of St. Paul's Cathedral Watch 1939-41. Commissioned in Royal Engineers, Garrison engineer, Essex 1941-45. *Information from Diana Ward and Peter Harrild.*

HARRIS, Emanuel Vincent (1876-1971)
Architect. Born Devonport. Educated Kingsbridge Grammar School. Articled to James Harvey of Plymouth 1893-97. Assistant to Leonard Stokes and Sir William Emerson. Studied RA Schools, ARIBA 1900. Architects' Department of London County Council to 1907. Private practice from 1908, latterly as Vincent Harris & Moodie. RA 1942 (ARA 1936), FRIBA. Treasurer of the Royal Academy, retired 1954. Royal Gold Medal for Architecture 1951.

HARVEY, John D.M. (1895-1978)
Architect and perspectivist. Educated in Canada and St. Paul's School, London. Studied at Bartlett School of Architecture, London University. Donaldson Medal 1918. Architectural illustrator for Lutyens, Maufe, Tait and Harris.

HENING, Robert (1906-1997)
Architect. Born Wallasey. Educated Wallasey Grammar School. Articled to Edmund Ware, Liverpool. Studied University College, London. Assistant to Oswald Milne (*qv*) 1930 and resident architect to Dartington Hall with William Lescaze (*qv*) and William Weir (*qv*). Partnership with Anthony Chitty (*qv*) from 1937. Royal Engineers c.1940-45. MBE. *Information from Alan Powers.*

HILL, Oliver (1887-1968)
Architect. Educated Uppingham School. Pupil to William Flockhart, London 1907. Evening classes at Architectural Association. Private practice, London 1910. London Scottish Regiment 1914-18. Supervising architect British Industrial Art Exhibition, Dorland Hall 1931-32. Member of the Council for Art and Industry 1933-38. British Pavilion, Paris International Exhibition 1937. Architect to the Cotswold Tradition for the Festival of Britain 1951. MBE 1952.

HOLFORD, Sir William Graham (Lord) (1907-75)
Architect and town planner. Born Johannesburg, South Africa. Educated at Diocesan College, Cape Town and Liverpool University School of Architecture from 1925-30. American Scholar of the Society of Arts and Sciences, New York and office of Voorhees, Gmelin & Walker 1929. Rome Scholar in Architecture 1930. Florence Bursar of RIBA 1935. Senior lecturer Liverpool School of Architecture 1936. Technical Advisor, Ministry of Town and Country Planning 1944. Professor of Town Planning, University College, London 1948-70. Knighted 1953. President RIBA 1960-62. Royal Gold Medal for Architecture 1963.

LESCAZE, William Edmond (1896-1969)
Architect. Born Geneva. Ecole des Beaux Arts, Geneva 1914-15. Technische Hochschule, Zurich under Karl Moser 1915-19. Office of Henri Sauvage, Paris 1919-20. Office of Hubbell & Benes, Cleveland, Ohio 1921-22 and office of Walter R. MacCormack, Cleveland 1922. Emigrated to US 1923. Private practice, New York City 1923-29. Partnership with George Howe, Philadelphia 1929-34. William Lescaze & Associates, New York from 1934.

LUCAS, ROBERTS & BROWN
Architects of Exeter. Archibald J. **Lucas** LRIBA (d.1945). Charles William **Roberts** (1905-77): Articled to Rawlinson & Hargreaves, accountants of Burnley. Articled to Richard Jaques, architect of Nelson, Lancashire c.1922. Partner with Archibald Lucas, Exeter 1935. Royal Engineers c.1939-45. Partnership with Dennis **Brown** FRICS (caretaker manager of practice 1939-45) 1946. Exhibited at Paris Salon 1950s. *Information from Michael Willis.*

LUTYENS, Sir Edwin (1869-1944)
Architect. Studied architecture at South Kensington Schools 1885-87. Pupil with Ernest George & Peto 1887-89. Private practice, London from 1889. Architect to New Delhi 1912-31. ARA 1913. Knighted 1918. RA 1920. Royal Gold Medal for Architecture 1921. AIA Gold Medal 1924. KCIE 1930. President RA 1938. OM 1942.

McMORRAN, Donald Hanks (1904-65)
Architect. Educated Harrow County Grammar School. Pupil of H. Farquharson 1921. RIBA Pugin Student 1925. Assistant to E. Vincent Harris (*qv*) 1927-35. Private practice, London from 1935 as Farquharson & McMorran and McMorran & Whitby. FRIBA 1943. London Architecture Medals 1946 and 1952. Hon.Sec. Board of Architectural Education 1952-54. ARA 1955. Chairman RIBA Practice Committee 1955-58. Master of Art Workers Guild 1956. FSA 1956. Member Faculty of Architecture British School at Rome. RA 1962.

MILNE, Oswald P. (1881-1968)
Architect. Educated Bedford School. Articled to Sir Arthur Blomfield. Office of Edwin Lutyens, 1902-05. Private practice, London from 1905. Major RASC (dispatches) 1914-18. Hampstead Borough Council as Councillor and Alderman 1937-53. Mayor 1947-49. JP County of London (Hampstead) 1941.

O'RORKE, Edward Brian (1901-74)
Architect and interior designer. Born New Zealand. Educated at Wellington College, Berks. and Jesus College, Cambridge and Architectural Association School of Architecture. Dawnay Scholar and RIBA Bronze Medalist 1926. RDI, 1939 (Member of Faculty 1961-63). ARA 1947. RA 1956.

POTTER & HARE
Architects of Salisbury. Partnership of Robert **Potter** (b.1909) and Richard **Hare** (1924-1989). Potter trained under W.H. Randoll Blacking. Won competition for St. Leonard's, Redfield 1937. Partnership with Blacking 1945-54 and Richard Hare from 1954, specialising in churches.

SAUNDERS, George Gerald Girling (1899-1984)
Architect. Born Bedford. Educated at Blundell's School, Tiverton. Articled to Tiverton Borough Surveyor under J. Siddall. RASC 1917-19. Completed articles in office of Capt. Jos. P. Dixon, Tiverton. Chief Assistant then partner, Dixon & Saunders Architects & Surveyors, Tiverton 1933-41. RIBA 1933. Garrison Engineer, Falmouth 1941-45. Private practice, Exeter 1945. Partnership with G.J. Ireland 1960. Retired 1970. *Information from Peter Wickham.*

SHARP, Thomas (1901-78)
Town planner. Educated Council schools. Worked in local government offices 1917-37. Lecturer then Reader in Town & Country Planning, University of Durham 1937-45. Senior Research Officer, Ministry of Town & Country Planning 1941-43. Private practice as town planner from 1945. President TPI 1945-46. President ILA 1949-51. Member of Council of RIBA 1958-60.

TAIT, Thomas Smith (1882-1954)
Architect and town planner. Born Paisley. Apprenticed to James Donald, Paisley 1896. Joined John James Burnet, Glasgow 1902. Educated at Paisley Technical College and RA School. ARIBA 1913. Assistant to Don Barbour, New York 1914. Assistant with Trehearne & Norman, London. Drawing office of Woolwich Arsenal 1915. Rejoined Sir John Burnet as design partner, London 1918. FRIBA 1926. Partner in Sir John Burnet Tait & Lorne 1929. Appointed as advisor on housing to Secretary of State for Scotland 1934. Architect to Empire Exhibition, Glasgow 1938. Appointed Chief Architect to National Camps Corporation 1939.

Director of Standardisation, Ministry of Housing 1940-41. Partner in Sir John Burnet, Tait & Partners, London 1946-54. Co-ordinating architects' panel, City of Plymouth 1951-52.

WALLS & PEARN
Architects of Plymouth. Herbert Forrest **Walls** (c.1915-78): Partner in Walls Gallannough Nicholls & Barton, Bridgwater 1945 and Gallannough Nicholls & Walls, Plymouth c.1949. Paul **Pearn** (1921-1992): Devonshire Regiment, Mentioned in Dispatches c.1940-45. Liverpool University School of Architecture c.1946-50. President Devon & Cornwall Society of Architects. Advisory Panel to Plymouth School of Architecture. Advisor to Dept. of Environment on churches. *Information from K.S. Bingham.*

WALTERS, Frederick Arthur (1849-1931)
Architect. Educated RA Schools from 1871. Articled to father, Frederick Page Walters. Assistant to George Goldie and Charles Edwin Child. ARIBA 1882. Private practice, London from c.1880 specialising in churches, abbeys and convents. Practice continued by his son, Edward J. Walters (1880-1947) and S.C. Kerr Bate.

WEEKS, David Anthony (1927-96)
Painter and sculptor. Born Bristol. Educated at Plymouth College of Art 1946-49 (NDD 1948) and Royal College of Art 1949-53 (ARCA 1952). Editor of ARK Magazine 1953. Studio at Cookham, Berkshire 1953-57. Scott Memorial, Ford Church, Devonport 1956. Studio at Plymouth 1957 and Chudleigh from 1959. Exhibitions at RBA Galleries, London and at Dartington and Plymouth Museum & Art Gallery. Lecturer History of Art at Reading University, South Devon College of Art & Technology, HM Prison Dartmoor and Swarthmore Settlement, Plymouth. Works at Guildhall and Pannier Market, Plymouth, Exeter City Hall, Totnes Town Hall, Buckfast Abbey etc. *Information from Diana Weeks.*

WEIR, William (1865-1950)
Architect and craftsman. Born Edinburgh. Pupil to Archibald MacPherson, Edinburgh 1881 and Leonard Stokes, London 1883-89. Assistant to Philip Webb, London 1889-97. Private practice, London and elsewhere from 1897 and Letchworth in 1926. Assistant to J.T. Micklethwaite, London. Committee member of Society for the Protection of Ancient Buildings from 1902. LRIBA 1911. Member of the Art Workers' Guild c.1917.

WOOD, William Walter (1896-1990)
Architect. Born Arnold, Notts. Educated at Nottingham High School, Nottingham University and the Architectural Association, London. Articled to Frederick Ball, Nottingham and atelier of Frederick Billerey, London. Assistant Professor of Architecture and Seminar Lecturer in Architectural Design, Royal School of Engineering, Cairo 1926-28. Head of Department of Architecture, Plymouth Central School of Arts & Crafts 1929-32. Head of Department of Building at Plymouth and Devonport Technical Colleges 1931-32. Principal of Mid-Essex Technical College and School of Art, Chelmsford 1932-40. Founder and principal, Delhi Polytechnic, Delhi 1940-46. Private practice in Johannesburg, South Africa 1970s.

Index

CAPITALS indicate Biography entry

A
ABERCROMBIE, Sir Patrick 9, 30, 31
ADAMS, HOLDEN & PEARSON 27
Applehayes, Clayhidon 3
Art potteries 79
Aubin, Melville 24

B
Ballets Jooss 62, 63
Barron and Larcher 57
Beddington, Jack 60
Beech & Curnow Cooke 33
Beer, E. Victor 33
Belcher & Joass 21
Belcher, John 16
Berger, Otti 58
Bergersen, Gerd 58, 59
Best and Lloyd 64
Betjeman, John 7, 8
Bevan, Robert 3
Blinn, Alice 48, 49
Booth, David 63
Braden, Norah 57
Brakespeare 25
Brannam, C. H. 79
Breuer, Marcel 61
Browne, Maurice 70
Bullivant, Roger 26
Burnet, Sir John 31
Burnett, Percy 33

C
CACHEMAILLE DAY, N.F. 28
Cardew, Michael 57, 59
Carrington, Noel 60
Challice, R.M. 24
Chekhov, Michael 11
Chermayeff, Serge 64
CHITTY, A.M. 23, 26, 34
Christie, Agatha 8
Clarke, Geoffrey 29
Collins, Cecil 11, 67, 68
Comper, Ninian 29
Coper, Hans 89, 91
Council for the Preservation of Rural England 10, 30, 51
Coventry, F.H. 32
Cox, Peter 69
CRABTREE, W. 31, 32
Curry, W.B. 22, 23, 49, 62

D
Dartington Conference of the Crafts 89
DAVISON, Thomas 16, 25
DAWSON, Matthew 25
DE SOISSONS, Louis 20, 28, 29, 49-55
De Trey, Marianne 85-89
Delano & Aldrich 20
Devon Guild of Craftsmen 70
DORN, Marion 20, 27, 64
Doyle, Arthur Conan 4
D'Oyly Carte, Rupert 20
Drewe, Julius 17
Dudok, W.M. 31

E
Ede, Jim 65
Elmhirst, Dorothy and Leonard 11, 20, 22, 23, 26, 43 71 *passim,* 81-5, 89, 91
ETCHELLS, Frederick 29

F
Faber, Oscar 25
FAREY, Cyril 20
Farrand, Beatrix 24, 47, 53, 61, 66
FEIBUSCH, Hans 29
Fewster, L.H. 33
Fincham, Albert 48
Finmar 57
Fischer, Raymond 22
Fitzpatrick, Toby 58
Forrester, Bernard 83, 84

Fox-Strangways, Sylvia 'Jane' 57, 58, 65, 82
French, Alec 31, 33
Fry, Maxwell 30, 33

G
Gardner, Rex 46, 47, 49, 58, 59, 60, 70
Garrett, Major Harvey A. 17
Gertler, Mark 3
Gill, Eric 57
Gimson, Ernest 18
Ginner, Charles 3, 4
Glasgow, Miss 69
Goldsmith, Felix 26
Gore, Spencer 3
Gracht, Van der, Ides 47
Grant, Duncan 65
Green, W. Curtis, Son & Lloyd 33
GREENSLADE, Sydney 27, 33
Grenfell Baines Group 56
Gropius, Walter 23, 24, 51, 60, 61, 62, 63, 66
Grose, William 22

H
Hague, Hiram (see Winterbotham, Hiram)
Haile, Sam 85-88
Ham, W.F.R. 24
Hamada, Shoji 81, 85
Hare, Richard 29
HARRILD, Fred 18, 19
HARRIS, Emanuel Vincent 27, 34
Harrison, Harold Bertram 3
HARVEY, John 31
Heals 57, 63
Heckroth, Hein 59, 63-65, 68, 70
HENING, Robert 23, 24, 26, 63, 64
Henry, Sir Tanner 46
Heron, Patrick 86, 87, 90
HILL, Oliver 19, 20
Holden, Charles 27
HOLFORD, Sir William 28, 34
Holst, Imogen 69
Howe, George 22
Huxley, Julian 69

J
Jekyll, Gertrude 19
Jellicoe, Geoffrey 54
Joel, Betty 57
Jones, David 57
Jooss, Kurt 11, 23, 49, 62, 63, 69, 70
Joseph, Messrs. 31

L
Laban, Rudolf 11
Ladmore, P.W. 25, 26
Leach, Bernard and David 11, 57, 59, 67, 68, 80-91 *passim*
Le Corbusier 22, 23, 26, 30
LESCAZE, William 22-24, 48-49, 51-53, 55, 61-63
Lethaby, William 18
Lewis & Hickey 33
Lindsey, Kenneth 55, 56
Little Gallery 57
LUCAS, ROBERTS & BROWN 29, 33
LUTYENS, Sir Edwin 17-21, 23, 28, 31, 34

M
Mairet, Ethel 57, 58
Mallet-Stevens, Robert 22, 23
Martin, Christopher 62, 66, 68, 69
Martin, W. Keble 29
Marx, Enid 57, 58
Maufe, Edward 28
McMORRAN, Donald 34
Medley, Robert 29
Melville, Robert 89
Mendelsohn, Erich 32
Mesens, E.L.T. 68
MILNE, Oswald 18, 20, 23, 46, 48, 49, 51, 55
Moholy-Nagy, Laszlo 61

Monnington, W.T. 28
Moore, Henry 65, 69
Morris, William 18, 21, 90

N
Nash, Paul 1, 2, 12, 26
Nettlefold, Archibald 25
New Handworkers Gallery, The 57
Nicholson, Ben 65, 66

O
Oakes, C. St.C. 33
O'RORKE, Edward (Brian) 27
Oud, J.J.P. 61

P
Peacock, Elizabeth 47, 57, 58, 66, 67
Pel and Summers 64
Penrose, Roland 68
Pepler, Marian 64
Petter and Nissen 22
Phillpotts, Eden 5, 6, 12
Piper, John 29
Pissarro, Lucien 4
Pite, Beresford 16
Pleydell-Bouverie, Katherine 57
POTTER & HARE 29
Prior, Edward 18
Pritchard, Jack 63

R
Rayner, Major Ralph 27
Reed, W.J. 31
Reynolds, Stephen 5, 6, 12
Ricardo, Halsey 18
Rie, Lucie 89, 91
Roberts, William 3
Rohe, Mies van der 61, 67
Rose, Miss 60
Ross, Nancy 60
Russell, Gordon 57, 63

S
Sackville-West, Vita 19
SAUNDERS, Gerald 24, 26
Seal, A.J. of Bournemouth 25
Sedding, J.D. 18
SHARP, Thomas 32, 33, 52
Shaw, Norman 16-18
Sherren, B.C. 32
Sickert, Walter 4
Sieff, Israel 55
Slater, William 60, 61, 84
Soukop, Willi 68
Spencer, Stanley 3
Staite-Murray, William 57, 81, 85, 86
Staverton Builders 24, 49, 52, 57, 59, 60-64
Stirling, H.J.W. 32
Stokes, Leonard 18, 21
Straight, Whitney 26
Studio pottery 79
Summers, Gerald 57, 63

T
Tagore, Rabindranath 11, 81
TAIT, Thomas 31
Tanner, Sir Henry 46
Tapper, Walter 21
Thompson, Flora 6, 7
Thompson, W. Harding 10
Thomson, Stewart Lloyd 25
Thonet 57
Thornely & Rooke 16
Tipping, Avray 46
Tobey, Mark 11, 65, 67, 82
Tozer, Bill 24
Tubbs, Ralph 30, 32, 33

U
Underdown, Alwyn 25

V
Voysey, C.F.A. 18, 19

W
WALLS & PEARN 32
WALTERS, Frederick 16
Ware, Charles E. 33
Watcombe Pottery 80
Watkins, W.H. 26
Watson, J. Paton 30
Waugh, Evelyn 7
Webb, Aston 16, 27, 33
Webb, Philip 21
Weedon, Harry 26
WEEKS, David 32
WEIR, William 21, 23, 29, 46, 47
Wibberley, J. 24
Wilks and Cohen 59
Williams, Raymond 11, 12
Williams-Ellis, Clough 9, 10
Williamson, Henry 5, 6, 12
Winterbotham, Hiram 58, 59, 64
Wood, Christopher 65
WOOD, William 22, 24
Wragg, Arthur 7
Wright, Henry 24, 61

Y
Yanagi, Soetsu 81